Learning from
Neurodivergent Leaders

LEARNING FROM NEURODIVERGENT LEADERS

How to Start, Survive and Thrive in Leadership

Dr Nancy Doyle

Foreword by Professor Almuth McDowall

Jessica Kingsley Publishers
London and Philadelphia

First published in Great Britain in 2025 by Jessica Kingsley Publishers
An imprint of John Murray Press

2

Copyright © Dr Nancy Doyle 2025
Foreword copyright © Professor Almuth McDowall 2025

A CIP catalogue record for this title is available from the British Library and the Library of Congress.

ISBN 978 1 80501 142 2
eISBN 978 1 80501 143 9

Printed and bound in the United States by Integrated Books International

Jessica Kingsley Publishers' policy is to use papers that are natural, renewable and recyclable products and made from wood grown in sustainable forests. The logging and manufacturing processes are expected to conform to the environmental regulations of the country of origin.

Jessica Kingsley Publishers
Carmelite House
50 Victoria Embankment
London EC4Y 0DZ

www.jkp.com

John Murray Press
Part of Hodder & Stoughton Limited
An Hachette UK Company

The authorised representative in the EEA is Hachette Ireland,
8 Castlecourt Centre, Dublin 15, D15 XTP3, Ireland (email: info@hbgi.ie)

Contents

Foreword

Professor Almuth McDowall

My first encounter of Nancy was in 2008, when I was leading a workshop on a technique called 'feedforward' with my late colleague Lynne Millward for the British Psychological Society. Nancy came and chatted to us in the break. It was immediately clear how we shared values congruent with empowering others to live their best possible lives. We talked about the importance of language and framing and starting off from a position of curiosity and non-judgement. And talk we did. Because a conversation with Nancy can be a bit like Formula One cars (which she loves!) challenging each other on the race track. Often her car will win the race. Because she's ambitious. Because she combines capability and an infectious way of being that pulls others with her, yet never loses sight of the importance or plight of others. I had the pleasure of mentoring Nancy's doctoral journey. It was a mentorship of equals as I learned as much about research, psychology and life as I endeavoured to pass on to Nancy. Well, she certainly did learn because she passed her examination without corrections. This is rare in doctoral examinations, as asking people to make corrections that satisfy the examiner, rather than enhance contribution to our field of study, has become a rite of passage.

Nancy inspired me to research and work in neurodiversity. We have remained firm friends and collaborators ever since, and lead our research centre at Birkbeck with sincerity and passion. It's not always easy. We both overcommit. We both get task focused when the going gets tough. Like Nancy, I find it hard to stand still, to remain static, and want to contribute to making our respective environments a better place. We get as frustrated as each other with reams of academic red tape, when there is a quicker and better way of doing things. But we inspire each other to continuously up our game. We hold each other to account. I always have a safe space with Nancy. We have honest and direct conversations which I relish. We debate, we giggle and we share our human experience. Working in any diversity field – the neurodiversity field is no different – means that we get judged – a lot. Being leaders in our respective contexts means that we are visible for what we do, and Nancy far more so because of her social media profile. And Nancy is a highly successful entrepreneur – who walks her talk and leads a social enterprise – as well as a brilliant researcher. But all privilege is relative.

It's so easy to judge leadership, because we all strive for simple expla-nations. Judgement of women remains harsh – if only I could collect a reward for every time someone tells me, 'Oh Almuth, you can't say that.' My German upbringing means that I value candour because we tend to be more direct in general, and after many decades living in the UK I still struggle with people saying 'Oh that was great' when their meaning is entirely different. We've both experienced encounters of: 'Oh I am glad that I am being managed / led by a woman.' There's an implicit expectation that we will be mothering and nurturing, yet leadership can require tough decisions to be made.

Leadership is about humanity. Leadership is a paradox, as Nancy signposts in her Introduction. We want our leaders to be strong as well as vulnerable. Leaders can't lead without a mandate, yet people don't always want to be led. We want our leaders to do what is right, and not what is easy, but berate mistakes. We yearn for strong examples of neurodivergent leader-ship, yet may expect our own preferences and needs to be accommodated at every turn. Such tensions can invoke strong reactions.

The other thing to understand about paradoxes is that they shift and change in front of our eyes. Dr Wendy Smith and Professor Marianne Lewis make the point about leadership skills for managing paradoxes[1] that leaders need to be open and accepting rather than stepping aside from any tensions. They put four skills at the heart of shifting paradox navigation, which Nancy embodies in abundance:

- The first is **cognitive complexity**. I invite you to engage with how Nancy has reflected on her own journey in becoming a leader, recognizing the good (the chance opportunities to enact leadership), the bad (school wasn't great, right?) and the ugly (Nancy's struggles with her mental health).

- The second skill is **confidence**, which Nancy demonstrates throughout the book, but particularly in the middle section of the book about enacting leadership, and how leadership can be ambitious yet also carries risks of 'doing' rather than 'being'.

- The third skill is **conflict management**. For this I signpost you to Section 3 on sustainable leadership. Overwhelm and drama happen in every organization, but are more likely in a cognitively diverse organization. Lucky for us, Nancy brings us tangible solutions.

- The fourth and final skill for navigating shifting paradoxes is **communication**. This book speaks to all of us, and through reflection on Nancy's experience, and her collaborators' experiences, invites us to consider our leadership in a relatable and authentic way.

Nancy, I look forward to experiencing many more paradoxes with you.

Introduction

What is leadership?

The world is in a paradigm shift: the old rules of industrialization, patriarchy and white colonial power structures are being openly debated with wide visibility and participation online. This conversation permeates macro systems of law, politics, culture and media, but also the workplace, education, communities and families. We may find that we are living through a fundamental redistribution of power and access to knowledge, although the end result is as yet undecided and many of the old ways persist. The mainstream view that leadership positions are earned through hard work (meritocracy) has been undermined by discrimination, poor leadership and corruption through the ages. Laws have changed to encourage diversity in leadership, and corruption is increasingly brought into the light by mass and social media. There has been an increase in diverse leaders, people whose demographics / backgrounds have heretofore restricted them from accessing positions of influence. We are now gaining in number, representation and seniority – the first female, the first person with a disability, the first person from the global ethnic majority to do x, y or z. Could this be the beginning of real change, or is it just another idealistic generation thinking that we are making a difference? Is the backlash of authoritarianism a last hurrah, or a sign that we're failing?

Many diverse leaders have sought to change the system from within. We now find ourselves questioning the structures of power that brought us to our careers and provided permission to lead while simultaneously maintaining the dynamics of hierarchy we once challenged. I experience this as a paradox in my own career into leadership – I expressly sought to be part of the system of psychology in order to challenge psychological practice, yet with every additional power I acquired, I experienced a greater sense of my limits. My dependency on my peers has grown, much more so than any independence from the psychology mainstream. I still challenge, hard, from the inside on committees and working groups, but my identity is one of membership. The process of becoming part of any system, of holding a leadership role within a system, required a personal journey in excess of what I had imagined when I started, or indeed for which I was prepared. Perhaps I have become part of the system I once abhorred, or perhaps it has changed; the reality is likely to be somewhere in the middle.

The broader conversations we are engaged in as a society around wealth distribution, basic income, equality and equity, and democracy versus autocracy all play out in the mental models we hold about being a good leader, or having a good boss. We live in a time where our cultural narratives presuppose bosses are often mean and self-serving, that those in leadership roles are inherently undeserving. Conversely, my immediate peer group of leaders seek consensus more than we seek to command and control. We pursue our approach as a welcome change, but it sometimes leads us to self-sabotage as we become overcritical of our decisions, fearful of causing offence and stunted in our ability to make necessary transformational changes. We worry about fulfilling the 'mean boss' stereotype and tie ourselves in knots to counter it, which can be apparent to those we lead. We wind up prioritizing being 'nice' over addressing harm and injustice. This can undermine the respect we need in order to be effective. We share our vulnerabilities, which may be preferable to pretending to be the perfect leader, but can be used to weaken our logic by those who feel cynical, defensive or aggressive.

Tiptoeing on such dynamics is emotional labour and requires a strength of character that I certainly did not possess when I first began to lead. I was idealistic and naive. The incongruency between my positive intentions and their sometimes-harmful impacts caused me cognitive dissonance and turmoil. In the middle of macro-historical flux, diverse leaders like me across the globe are attempting to create new structures and systems of organizing and leading that are (1) inclusive, (2) will support the technological age and (3) help us address the existential challenges of climate change, inequality, disease and war. We are also trying to reconcile our own experiences of marginalization versus empowerment.

Through academic practice and networking I was recently introduced to the African philosophy of Ubuntu[1] (translated from Ndebele, a South African language, as 'I am because we are'), which reasons that leadership is inextricably linked to the well-being of the group that the leader represents, and that the success of others leads to success for all because we are all connected. The Ubuntu concept reminded me of the extent to which my leadership knowledge is bound to our culture, and how limited it was by my education and background. The idea that leadership is intrinsically connected to membership is not new, or limited to Ubuntu, but there we are wrestling with how to make participative structures work in politics, modern workplaces, online communities and local groups, ignoring the many examples that exist outside our immediate environment.

We are in process, and the nature and meaning of leadership shifts in step with our cultural paradigm. The net result of being in flux is that contemporary leaders in white, Anglo-European-dominated, neuronormative cultures have insufficient relevant guidance of alternative options in management schools and leadership books. We're making it up as we go along because we need different advice to the dominant demographic. My book is an attempt to relay my learning, my mistakes in trying to lead while also processing trauma and exclusion, and attempting to develop structures within a Western economy that help us move towards more collectivist, egalitarian values. I share my considered reflections, and some from my peers, on the paradox of leadership, of having power but being unable to act without empowering others, of needing to make sure everything is done without doing everything myself.

Why me?

I am a neurodivergent* leader, in a majority neurodivergent company, working with other neurodivergent people to facilitate them to fulfil their

---

* I acknowledge that our language as a community is still evolving, having broken from the constraints of the medical mainstream. I have considered alternative descriptions such as 'neurodiverse', 'distinct', 'atypical', etc., etc., and decided on 'neurodivergent' as the most popular term at the time of writing. I find 'neurodivergent' accurate, as a psychologist and as someone with lived experience, although I acknowledge that some find it 'othering'. The term is widely accredited

potential. My company isn't neurotypical with a few unusual thinkers; it is unusual thinkers with a few generalists. I realize this is an unusual position. Many of us come to our work with trauma histories; we are intersectionally diverse with higher-than-average representation from the LGBTQ+ community and the global ethnic majority. In this role I have seen first and second hand how neurodivergence intersects with gender, gender identity, race, ethnicity, class, sexuality, age and physical disability. As a coach, support worker, assessor, diagnostician and case worker I have supported disabled and neurodivergent people in supported housing, in prisons, in unemployment and all the way through entry level, transitional and leadership careers. In these many contexts I have experienced and witnessed deep psychological transformations, from marginalization to empowerment, in sometimes tiny, incremental steps and at other times in large gravity-defying leaps. In the evolution of confidence and competence, I have witnessed and experienced a whiplash effect between vulnerability and dominance, sometimes on the same day. Such ricochets are destabilizing to us and to those around us. Our childhood experiences of ostracism and being 'different' hold us in a state of deficit even as we become mature adults, an emotional inner child who is too easy to activate and too hard to pacify. We may miss the social integration of peers in our youth where we learn it is natural to fall out and make up, so we remain fearful of conflict, or mistake disagreement for abuse.

For me, leadership has been a journey of healing, of self-compassion and diligent self-enquiry. For those I have facilitated, typically the same. People who are struggling rarely improve via more self-imposed shame. I write this book not because I know how to lead and want to share with you my deep knowledge of brilliant leadership, but because I have healed enough of my demons to enjoy leading – there are more good days than bad. I have some warnings to share, some learning that might accompany you on your own personal journey and bring you solace and sympathy. I am still healing, I am still learning, and every time I think I have solidified a breakthrough, a change in context, relationships or health can still pull me back to vulnerability in a second. Those of you already in leadership roles

---

to the autistic advocate Kassiane Asasumasu, defined as meaning someone whose neurocognitive functioning is distinct from the dominant societal norms.

will recognize the sense of obligation that occurs when you are trying to lead while simultaneously processing strong emotions.

My personal journey with leadership began with my first school report stating, 'Nancy is a very sociable child, but tends to be a bit bossy.' The trope of 'bossy' is rarely applied to men. Research has shown that women receive this feedback in performance appraisal before they get anywhere near leadership, and men do not.[2] I had this feedback aged four – a long history of being told to pipe down as opposed to having a natural sense of leadership nurtured. My journey includes organizing a strike of the school choir aged 11 and playing lead roles in drama productions as a child. I was chastised for the strike and praised for the acting, but both were leadership. Were my years as a compulsive truant also leadership? The point at which I refused to 'play the game' of mainstream education and put my neurodivergent, emotional and sensory needs ahead of social expectations and to hell with the consequences? Yet, in among the turmoil, I was standing up for myself, in the way that I now stand up for others.

I was diagnosed with anorexia, then bulimia, anxiety, depression and ultimately school phobia (now termed 'school refusal' – see what they did there?). To be clear, this was a serious period of mental distress, and in the first draft of this book I avoided these details because I am self-conscious about finding the right balance between victimhood and being glib. It is not often that I talk about these years and I have forgotten most of the detail; I am left with disjointed images, memories in a random order and a sense of sadness for my teenage self. It often feels like I am talking about somebody else. I spent time in a psychiatric hospital, I self-harmed and tried to unalive myself – a sadly common tale for the undiagnosed neurodivergent teenager. I don't want to dwell on this, because this is not a book about how awful my teenage years were, but suffice to say that my journey to leadership has been long. I don't have many friends still in my life from this era; I had few at the time. Occasionally when I bump into someone I knew between the ages of 13 and 22 they are surprised to see me alive, let alone thriving. Indeed, some of my friends from this time are no longer with us, and many have had harrowing journeys. I also acknowledge that in this history is white privilege, that I was pitied and pathologized but not punished or criminalized, as I might have been if I had Black or

Brown skin, and that I did not experience bullying or discrimination for my sexuality or gender identity.

From today's educated view I can see that I ran out of steam for masking, that I have a pathological demand-avoidant profile, and further, that I couldn't subjugate myself to conform anymore to the social expectations of my gender. It felt like a violent rupture from my family (and for my family), but with hindsight it was also the beginning of my authentic self. I left home at 16 with fury and angst, thus subjecting myself to several years of precarious living and personal risk, but with finally enough control over my day to establish my identity. When I synthesize the rebel, the neurodivergent experience, the social expectations of my gender, my mixed-class background, my race, sexuality and various traumatic events, I see that it is these painful years that started my journey to the hard-won professional status I now hold. They are also the emotional pool from which I draw the empathy for my disabled and neurodivergent clients.

Vivienne Isebor, founder of community group ADHD Babes, explains her own experience of developing leadership, even when this meant risk and challenging convention:

> As a Black woman who is neurodivergent, I have had a complex and rich experience of leadership. Upon reflection I realize there were multiple points in my life where I was displaying leadership but did not class it as such. I remember in secondary school organizing petitions against situations I felt were unfair, such as forcing girls to wear skirts or the lack of Black History in our teaching plans every October. It looked like organizing a leavers prom with a group of friends because the school claimed not to have a budget for it that year. It looked like creating a new society at university to celebrate Black History and culture where I felt this was lacking. It looked like advocating for patients on the mental health ward I worked at to have leave or to purchase a new air hockey table. It looked like challenging false narratives presented by lecturers at university around Black mental health statistics and naming racism out loud, even if it made people uncomfortable. Now, it looks like running an organization that supports Black Women and non-binary people with ADHD in a way that is equity and community-led.

Vivienne's experience of being an ADHDer is intrinsically connected with the racism she faced as a Black woman. The risks she took to speak up during her school days are compounded. Did she challenge and prevail as a leader because she is an ADHDer, or despite being an ADHDer? Many of my neurodivergent peers, who you will hear from in this book, have acted on instinct because we couldn't live with injustice, despite the risk and cost to us personally. This has been called 'justice sensitivity' and we are labelled as impulsive or insensitive to social rules for what could more generously be termed 'moral courage'. Yet while our voices have echoed and created the space for leadership roles to emerge, the risks and barriers we have experienced are not equal. My stories are interspersed with those whose journeys differ from mine. I was able to stand on a platform of being a white person in a white-dominated culture with university-educated parents in order to take risks to move my gendered, neurodivergent self into a position of relative power from where I started. I have unusual insight, as I have explained, but my insight alone is limited, and we need learning from multiple perspectives within the neurodiversity community to illustrate the many convoluted paths possible. My colleagues have different platforms and different barriers. When you start out from any of society's margins, a career journey is not straightforward; it takes many twists and turns from which we can learn.

'Go where there is no path'

My grandad took me for a drink one day when I was 18. I was unemployed and living on benefits in various bedsits, having flamed out of a competitive pre-drama school programme at sixth form college. I had pitched far above my confidence levels and was terrified by success following an audition and being cast in a leading role. I was drinking too much and self-medicating, chain-smoking and floundering as a child living with an adult's responsibilities. I was processing deep trauma and trying to establish a sense of purpose in a world that could not accommodate my 'bombastic personality' (aka undiagnosed female ADHD) and could not hold me safe in education. My grandad advised me according to Emerson (he loved classic quotations): 'Nancy, you must not follow the trodden path; you must go where there is no path and leave a trail.' Right you are, grandad, I thought, thanks for the gin and tonic, smile and nod. I had no idea what he meant really, but 30 years later I do! He encouraged me to stop trying to get an education and to get a job. He advised me that I would learn more by working and could study when I was ready. Bear in mind that this is a man who grew up in the pre-war East End and took accountancy exams while away fighting in the Second World War in South Asia – not exactly a trodden path himself. He was right, of course – work was my salvation, and having 'permission' to take my steps in the order that suited me rather than the traditional school to university progress was exactly what I needed to hear. It is much more common now to work first than it was in the 1990s, which is a huge benefit to young people, many of whom need time to heal and establish a sense of self before committing to a course of study.

The reason for writing this book is to leave a trail for other neurodivergent leaders. We do not follow the trodden path. As with education, our career trajectories are often different from classic, neurotypical careers. We rarely ascend the organizational pyramid in a series of well-timed promotions through middle management. We might find ourselves leaders in corporations, but we are commonly entrepreneurs, activists, artists, healers, musicians, actors and sportspeople, and find our leadership emerges through finding our talent. This can take us some time; we need to shed the weight of mainstream school expectations to be a jack of all trades and find our tribe. And there is a lack of guidance about how to manage leadership when you have a potted history of irregular levels of success and failure.

My dear colleague Paul Stevenson, whom I met while filming a documentary with the BBC in 2015, shares my passion for using our challenges to build connections and provide support for others:

> Reflecting on my journey as a neurodivergent leader, I never imagined myself in such a role. How could I, when I wasn't even aware of my own neurodivergence? I always saw myself as a team player, navigating through life without truly understanding the unique wiring of my brain. It wasn't until the baton of self-awareness was passed to me that my true journey began.
>
> Growing up, I faced the formidable challenges of neurodivergence – Tourette's Syndrome, ADHD, autism – without a diagnosis, in a time

when society understood very little about these conditions. My life felt like a perpetual lesson in the school of hard knocks, constantly trying to fit into a world that didn't quite understand me.

But with my diagnosis came a pivotal moment, igniting a quest for self-education and understanding. Learning about my neurodivergence, unravelling the mysteries of my ADHD and connecting with others who shared similar experiences became my mission. A positive assessment illuminated my strengths, and coupled with my innate resilience, it fuelled my determination to step forward and raise my voice.

Through this ongoing journey, I've not only embraced my neurodiversity but also found empowerment in sharing my story. It's a journey of profound self-discovery, acceptance and, ultimately, using my voice to advocate for understanding and inclusivity. Each step I take and each word I speak is a testament to the power of embracing one's true self and championing the rights of all neurodivergent individuals.

Paul has come from rock bottom mental distress to a successful leadership career as a Tourette's Syndrome advocate and influential voice. He is invited on to boards and commissions to represent his community. Like me, and possibly also you, he cannot quite believe sometimes how he got here.

I am going to share what worked for me, for my peers, but also what hasn't worked, and the stories of how close we have come to derailing our careers (so far ☺). Leadership is not for the faint-hearted. From the outside, leadership looks like power, money, flexibility and choice. While that can be true, there is also a dark side. Leadership is also obligation, accountability and apologizing for things that weren't your fault but were, ultimately, your responsibility. Entrepreneurship is its own very special kind of obligation: you can't resign when you own the company. As owner, the legal and moral buck will always stop with you no matter who else is in charge. My metaphor for many of my transitional years running Genius Within is being trapped on a treadmill that is set 2 kilometres an hour faster than I can run, and having no control over the 'stop' button.

I no longer observe this experience as unique; rather, it is a common burden accompanying all forms of leadership. For example, being an advocate and community leader means placing your central identity at the core of your workload, which can leave you feeling defenceless and raw. It makes it harder to switch off at the weekend and separate your work from your sense of self. Being a corporate leader means constant compromise according to the whims of the board and shareholders. Being a public / civil service leader involves continual direction switching according to the political winds, and having to toe the neutral line. Being a public leader means sacrificing privacy in exchange for publicity. Many do not appreciate the burden of this before they start, and only later regret their choice. My collaborators will say more about their experiences in different leadership contexts. The costs may seem like a fair exchange, and in a lot of ways they are, but it helps to know a bit about what you are letting yourself in for before you commit. As we will share, it helps to practise self-compassion on the days where the burdens exceed the privilege.

Neurodivergence often comes with physical disabilities that emerge later in life – complications from Ehlers-Danlos Syndrome, chronic fatigue, epilepsy, digestive distress and complex autoimmune disorders like Mast Cell Activation Syndrome (MCAS). The latter took me by surprise; along with perimenopause, it disrupted every area of my life and reduced my capacity by half with zero warning. Leading with a physical disability has been a shock, just when I thought I had it nailed. Once you have committed to leadership, changes in circumstance such as the health issues listed above (but also perimenopause and menopause, bereavement, divorce and financial catastrophes) could take you by surprise and make a fair exchange feel like an inescapable burden. However, my intention is that for those of you who are inspired and / or already committed to a leadership journey as a neurodivergent person, this book will give you some assistance in managing the load, decisions, support and culture you have around you, and to ultimately create a sustainable legacy by passing on your acquired wisdom to the next generation. My warnings about changes in circumstances are to provide context on the importance of making your leadership work sustainable. If you lead by doing more than everyone else and running yourself into the ground, unplanned change will be a crisis, not a challenge. Leadership isn't about doing everything, but it is about making sure everything gets done. Sustainable leadership is an ethos I have been working towards for years, and I share insights about this with you in Sections 2 and 3.

How to read this book

There is no need to read this book in order. Go where you are interested and work backwards or forwards; dip in and out as you see fit and depending on where you are in your leadership journey. You might be starting out, aspiring. You may have arrived as a leader and be hanging on by the skin of your teeth! You might have nailed it but are wondering how to create sustainability of diverse leadership around you. Or you might be ready to pass on the baton to those around you. Pick the section that matches where you are if that feels like a better place to start. The first section is the most dense and was a pain to write, to be honest. But I am fully indoctrinated into academic tradition now and cannot start without defining my terms! So exploring what we think leadership is, and its characteristics, had to go first – although feel free to skip it and come back to it.

My writing is both autobiographical and academic, wherein leadership is something I have subjectively experienced and more objectively studied. My subjective experience includes the mentoring I have received from peers, colleagues, friends and family, but also the mentoring I have provided to the same. My scholarship is Occupational and Organizational Psychology, a social science with a heavy emphasis on theoretical frameworks and rigorous data collection, feeding into MBA and Human Resources Management curricula. I have tried to reconcile these multiple perspectives by writing at the levels of self, other and system, in three sections: (1) arriving as a leader, (2) surviving as a leader and (3) thriving as a leader.

In each section there is a chapter with summary vignettes of academic knowledge concerning leadership, a chapter of my lived experience as a neurodivergent, female leader, personal anecdotes and a chapter summarizing the advice. Each section finishes with some self-coaching questions for those of you who like guided reflection space, called 'Doing the Work'. Please note that all pages marked with ★ can be downloaded at http://library.jkp.com/redeem using the code CRSETQD

My style is inspired by autoethnography, which is a relatively recent qualitative research method in which the researcher 'draws on personal experience to extend understanding about a social phenomenon'.[3] Autoethnography is a route to legitimizing subjectivity as evidence and deconstructing the educational privilege barriers that prevent knowledge transfer from and between people with lived experience. It allows space to acknowledge that people with lived experience 'see things [others] will never see', as Dr Chantelle Lewis and Professor Jason Arday wrote in their autoethnographic reflections on the intersection between race and neurodivergence.[4] Although autoethnography is framed within an academic context, this book is not written for leadership scholars, but for those attempting leadership in practice. My hope is that the reflections, in context, will validate some of your own experiences of paradoxical empowerment and disempowerment, of simultaneous dependence and independence, and provide some food for thought on the kinds of practices that may help us develop the infrastructure to support contemporary beliefs about leadership. I have written the book I needed earlier in my own journey.

I have tried to write in a style that will be accessible for the non-academic reader, but I also provide appropriate references to satisfy those who like to delve further into the research. Research-based knowledge helps us understand the assumptions embedded within leadership training and narratives, but also challenges us to debunk historical assumptions. This book is not intended to be an academic review – there are already plenty of those in existence, and the leadership literature would be better reviewed by an academic who has specialized in this area of research. I am aware that there are many more ideas and concepts from which to draw, such as decision making and risk management theory, but I have shared the theories that have provided insight for me personally as a leader. My aim is to keep the book simple enough to be understood by a wider audience, and to not get distracted trying to educate readers on the full range of organizational science theories and narratives. But for those of you who find this interesting, may I be so bold as to recommend a postgraduate degree in Organizational Science or Occupational Psychology?

The personal stories are an attempt to show the 'one step forwards, two steps back' nature of career progression. I am aware that, from the outside, if you came across my work lately, or that of my contributing peers, it might look like our careers were easy. They were not. I write and share our personal stories for encouragement and relatability, so that those who are aspiring and struggling might take heart and carry on. I also hope to help you learn vicariously about a few pitfalls to avoid. I have failed many times in attempting to lead with integrity, authenticity and competence. I am writing this book to help you avoid some of our mistakes, as they have been intrinsically linked with the neurodivergent profile, trauma histories, culture, gender and our experiences therein of marginalization.

When I was starting out, I fell for the idea that it was 'just me' and 'everyone else seems to be nailing this', but as I have grown, I have, of course, come to realize that so many of us share the experience of being out of our depth, self-conscious and preoccupied with doing the right thing. So many of us lead by projecting confidence and control while holding wounded inner child experiences, anxiety and fear of failure. And as a neurodivergent, overthinking and anxiety is part of the package. Does that mean we should avoid the emotional responsibilities of leadership? I have come full circle on my critique of this – I actually think a level of self-consciousness and deep personal reflection is essential and never want to be in a place where I don't question myself. All that overthinking can be productive if channelled. I think neurodivergent people make great leaders, particularly the many contributors whose voices I am sharing. The balance is in ensuring that reflexivity does not limit our ability to act or to thrive. We need to become comfortable with being uncomfortable, recognize our patterns, and be able to separate our triggers from what is a genuine critique or problem that needs fixing.

The 'Advice' chapters might occasionally seem a bit blunt, but I am really thinking about the 'unwritten rules'. Neurodivergent people tend to struggle with unwritten rules. We are usually trying very hard to do the right thing, what is expected of us, but when there are some unvoiced expectations, it can cause us to freeze and become unsure. This is often considered a weakness in our profile, but we can channel it into a strength by refusing to overlook what others would dismiss as 'details'. In my career I have found the details a source of insight and personal growth. If, like me and many neurodivergents, you benefit from clear unambiguous instructions, the 'Advice' chapters are from me, to you, with love. I have tried to pedantically unpick for you the things I have spent hours agonizing over in coaching and counselling, to summarize what I think some of these unwritten rules look like. You don't need to follow them – you must chart your own path and uncover yet more – but they might give you a head start.

Since starting my own business in 2010 I have had the absolute pleasure of mentoring a team of neurodivergent leaders and being peer mentored in return. My experience has shown me that so many of us have to take a psychological journey to overcome internalized shame in order to lead with confidence. So much of that shame comes from neurodivergent ostracism – and indeed, other forms of exclusion – that I have chosen to write what I have learned along the way in case it will support others. My journey is far from unique and my hope is that these stories will provide you with clarity and catharsis before too much goes wrong for you personally or for the organizations you lead.

I have invited contributions from colleagues and peers in the field. Some run advocacy groups, some are senior managers in large corporations. They represent different races, gender identities and sexualities, classes and backgrounds. The sections and chapters include their words, unedited and unrefined, to provide additional relatability and insight. By including my, and my colleagues', lived experience as stakeholders, combined with management science and practice, I'm taking a broad approach to the evidence on which the advice is based. I have included real names of managers, colleagues, coaches and mentors where I have permission, and where I do not, I have adjusted the examples to anonymous representative composite stories.

Marcia Brissett-Bailey and Jannett Morgan, founders of the Black Leaders and Excellence in Neurodiversity network, share their motivation for contributing:

> Learning from Neurodivergent Leaders brings much-needed attention to an underexplored and too often unrecognized dimension of leadership. Our small contribution to this book is to bring a critical lens from the perspective of race, ethnicity and culture. The scope of our lived realities is as wide as it is deep, therefore not limited to a 'single identity' narrative. That said, while the impact of the racialized career context on aspiring and established leaders from Black and global majority backgrounds is no longer in dispute (at least by organizations serious about equity and inclusive leadership), the intersection of racism and ableism is something leaders within the neurodiversity movement (let alone wider society) have been slow to grapple with in a meaningful way.

The space we have here cannot possibly do justice to the complex, painful, transformative work those of us who work at this intersection are doing on a daily basis, work we are compelled to do for as long as is needed. We invite you as readers to use our notes to reflect deeply on the work you need to do to ensure neurodivergent leaders of all backgrounds have equitable opportunities and outcomes.

In each section, under 'Doing the Work', I have made space for you to process, reflect and consider your own journey, and to join Marcia and Jannett in inviting you to aim for equitable opportunities and outcomes in your own sphere of influence. Please note that these sections marked with ★ can be downloaded.

Who is this book for?

For the purpose of this book, I am taking a broad and inclusive approach to defining leadership. This includes the obvious examples of senior executives and leadership roles in communities, charities and religious and community groups. However, in the neurodiversity world, we currently have a self-organizing community in which leaders emerge through their influence in social media, in the arts and media, journalism and through championing and ambassadorial work. I am talking to a readership that I assume is neurodivergent (i.e., ADHD, autistic, bipolar, dyscalculic, dyslexic, dyspraxic, a ticcer* or any other unusual neurotype or combination thereof). I am writing for current and aspiring leaders. In my mind, when I write, I am talking directly to the members of my own company and community, the neurodivergent emerging leaders who agonize over their performance, their relationships, and who are earnestly trying to do the right thing. I am talking to my younger self.

That said, I think (hope) this book will apply to all minoritized leaders. Many insights come from being female, rather than an ADHDer. Many of my light-bulb learning moments have come from reading Black feminist literature and being in the company of leaders marginalized by race, ethnicity, class, sexuality, transgender, other disabilities or age. As such, this

---

* Someone with Tourette's Syndrome or a tic disorder.

book is intended to be relevant to all leaders and aspiring leaders who have not followed the trodden path. We all share a similar experience in that the majority of leadership guidance available in Western literature is designed for the well-resourced, white, cisgendered, abled, heterosexual male – the group that still makes up the majority of influential leaders in society. A lot of the traditional leadership advice is about countering the dominant group's blind spots. The unwritten rules of leadership are not made manifest, which is why so many of us are confused and conflicted in our journeys. We are advised to listen, to care, to be honest. And so we should. But many of us already start with these styles as overplayed hands. We need to also be advised to be firm about boundaries, assert ourselves and trust our judgements.

The current cohort of leaders may be recently diagnosed – Gen X and Millennials had much lower access to diagnoses (particularly if we were female, poor and / or from the global ethnic majority). Many of us experience a whiplash when we are diagnosed that draws us away from our previous compliance and agreeableness into a place of defensiveness, anger and regret. If you are leading while recently diagnosed as neurodivergent, I hope this book will help you unpack the nuances between the characteristics you developed as 'masking' and the natural skills of leadership to hold better boundaries but retain your generous nature.

My own diagnosis aged 38 brought a change in my temperament and a vindication of characteristics I had been trying to dampen. I ceased to find my chattiness, excitability and directness troubling and started to see the benefit. It was cathartic, but I had to relearn the right balance appropriate to my role, and this will have been confusing to my colleagues. My diagnosis of MCAS (with accompanying chronic fatigue) was much more problematic and I became more militant about my disability rights, more demanding of support, and had little emotional energy to socially filter the impact this had on others around me. I was fortunate in this phase to have existing relationships that stood the test of this transition, although not all survived, and I have grieved the loss of significant relationships.

I hope that this book will help you challenge yourself and encourage you towards a more sustainable leadership journey than mine and some of my peers.

BECOMING A LEADER

In this opening section I will review some key academic literature around leadership and critique the extent to which the extant literature reflects the experience of neurodivergent or otherwise marginalized leaders. Much of the work on leadership is around the traits of great leaders, which is a mirror to the existing structures of power. I will also discuss models of community and systems leadership, which acknowledge interdependence and the agency of organizational members, not only leaders. I will share my own early career story, as a representation of the sideways, forwards and backwards nature of neurodivergent careers. I may have started my career with strong and clear values, but I certainly had no strategy for planning a pathway. What emerged can only be rationalized in retrospect; it felt chaotic and perilous at the time.

CHAPTER 1

Leadership Theories

All leadership theories have insights from which we can learn, and problems that limit their explanatory power. Theories that focus on the type of person who can lead are known as great man or heroic leadership theories. Examples of leader-focused theories are transformational, charismatic, coaching and emotionally intelligent leadership; some are more relationship-orientated and / or task-focused.[1] Relationship theories include leader–member exchange (LMX), servant leadership and authentic leadership. Examples of task-focused theories include transactional, contractual and management-orientated theories (see Professors Gary Yukl and William Gardner's book *Leadership in Organizations*[2] for a good review if you find this interesting and want to learn more). In this chapter, I will discuss the idea of leadership attributes, and I will outline some of the popular and historically dominant theories so that we can deconstruct them from a neurodivergent perspective. The goal here is not to tell you what to do, but to outline the assumptions within the stacked deck so we can explore how to navigate our unusual path.

Minoritized leaders

In the 1970s, the first female industrial psychologist in the USA, and one of my academic heroes, Dr Virginia Schein, conducted her seminal thesis called 'Think manager, think male'.[3] She drew up a list of personality characteristics, such as 'decisive' or 'empathetic', and asked a large group of people to tick those that they thought were 'typically male' and 'typically female' characteristics, and then, finally, those they thought were 'typically managerial'. Yes, you guessed it, there was a strong correlation between the 'typically male' and 'typically managerial' characteristics and a non-significant correlation between 'typically female' and 'typically managerial' characteristics. Since the 1970s, Dr Schein has repeated this study across the world, in different sectors, cultures, age groups and more. She has found that some female participants are lately more likely to see a connection between traditionally female and managerial characteristics, but male participants are not shifting in their view.[4] Further, the idea that some characteristics are inherently 'male' or 'female' seems to persist, even though the evidence for this being innate is very shaky, with our childhood experiences shaping our brain according to highly gendered treatment from (even well-meaning) parents, relatives, schools, makers of toys and clothes, etc.[5]

Dr Adrienne Colella and her colleagues conducted research into disability stereotypes and found that managers will make up their mind about a candidate's suitability based on the disability's stereotype rather than the actual skills of the person in front of them.[6] Dr Colella also found that disability stereotypes affected the LMX relationship.[7] This means that even the same behaviours and traits, exhibited by different people, are being perceived very differently and will therefore have different impacts. The trait and behaviour theories of leadership are so tightly bound around our sociological, medical and historical contexts that it is impossible to approach these objectively from the margins. As neurodivergent leaders, we may well be collegiate in our intention, and in our community, but be perceived as insensitive, inarticulate, overly cautious or reckless by the neurotypical world, depending on the mismatch to the norm. And research shows that our behaviour will be interpreted through the lens of our labels – dyspraxic, non-binary, lesbian, Jewish, too young, too old.

Leadership styles

Charismatic leadership was popular in the late 20th century, and we still see its effects today when citizens vote for leaders they like over those more competent for the role. Charismatic leadership[8] traits include 'sensitivity to the needs of members' and 'taking personal risks for the good of the organization'. Debunking from a neurodivergent lens specifically, sensitivity has difficulties in expression. First, the stereotype of some neurodivergents (specifically attention deficit hyperactivity disorder, or ADHD, and autistic) is that we are insensitive and lacking in empathy. This is problematic (see Dr Damian Milton's work on 'double empathy'[9]) because empathy is being judged by behaviour rather than intention, and behaviour is culturally defined. In fact, lots of us are very insightful and altruistic, but we might not verbalize sympathy in the way society expects. Neurodivergents often translate empathy into ideas for solving practical problems for our community or colleagues, and busy ourselves with resolving the issue rather than having 'there, there' type conversations. However, one of the unwritten rules is that not everyone who is upset wants their problem solved! Sometimes people just want to air their frustrations and have sympathy. Which means well-intentioned actions can seem insensitive, even when they are not. Even in this micro-interaction example, we can see the opportunity for cultural clashing – neuronormative social expectations versus neurodivergent behaviour. Both have made assumptions about what empathy looks, sounds and feels like; both could have the same motivation and get very different reactions.

Taking risks for the organization can be debunked from all corners of marginalization; risk taking depends on what you have to lose. It's a lot easier to take confident risks if you are in a demographic that will provide a soft landing – gender, class, (dis)ability, race. For someone with marginalized characteristics, even taking a leadership role can be a personal risk; the exposure to judgement and potential failure can be a leap of faith. I found myself in the unexpected position of defending Margaret Thatcher's role as a feminist leader, simply by virtue of her taking on the role of prime minister of the UK in 1979. My younger conversants were judging her lack of action on women's issues at the time. My defence included explaining to them that in the UK women only won the right to their own bank accounts in 1975 and could still be legally refused service in a pub until 1982! The level of personal risk to which Margaret Thatcher exposed herself simply by attempting leadership cannot be easily understood by women growing up today, but her story shows the added burden of marginalized leaders by the sheer volume of critiques levied at her demeanour compared to her competence. We, as breakthrough leaders, not only have to do our job but we also have to be seen as 'helping' others like us, and are chastised if we are not effective at this task, as my younger conversants articulated. The first cohorts bear a heavy burden for their social demographic and this is, in and of itself, a personal risk. What looks like a 'risk' is dependent on the eyes of the perceiver; it is easy to judge from the outside and hard to quantify from the inside.

In my career, which spans from the late 1990s and early 21st century, the most popular leader-centric advice has come from the relationship-based paradigm (LMX), which predicts that leaders who build strong relationships will thrive – in particular, servant leadership[10] and authentic leadership.[11] But these, too, have their criticism from the position of minorities.* Servant leadership is defined as leading from a position of service to the organiza- tion and its members. The servant leader, it is said, strives to sacrifice their own goals for the greater good; to deliver support and encouragement; to platform and amplify the works of their colleagues. Servant leadership has a deep connection to the religious narratives that have been embedded in many cultures throughout the major world religions, including Christianity, Islam, Judaism and Buddhism. It feels 'right' to recommend servant lead- ership in a context where we have lived at the whim of powerful, selfish, greedy autocrats in large corporations and in political systems. From the position of an organizational or community member, we would want our leaders to be serving our joint purpose, not smugly serving themselves.

However, there is some evidence that, for minoritized leaders, such an approach simply leads to being a servant rather than leading from a position of grace. Dr Helena Liu's study[12] of 'Jeff', an Asian leader of a white male Australian sales team, shows how servant leadership can be enacted and is indeed valued by colleagues. The paper describes, through the interview evidence of his direct reports, how 'Jeff' supports, listens and goes out of his way to make the team's lives easier. However, the study also shows that when the leader's stereotype (Asian heritage, living in Australia) is not 'of power', those same behaviours are used to undermine and take advantage. 'Jeff' is seen as sweet, kind, helpful and intelligent but lacking in drive or

---

*   I struggle with the word 'minorities' because there are more Black, Brown and Indigenous people in the world than white, and women are slightly more than 50 per cent of the population. However, it is true that within the cohort of leadership roles, both women and people of colour are minorities. We are minoritized, rather than minorities. In the case of neurodivergence, we are minorities in the species, but not necessarily in the team. Please accept this explanation as my understanding of the nuance.

ambition. His team don't respect him. Jeff is literally serving the team, not leading the team as a role model. The paper is called 'Just the servant'.

Members' implicit beliefs about good leadership will frame and colour the lens through which they interpret a leader's behaviour.[13] If your organizational culture expects leaders to be bold, dynamic and visionary, deviation from this could be detrimental. This is particularly so when you are working against your identity stereotype. Reflecting back to the data from 'Think manager, think male', we can infer that implicit theories of leadership in Western economies still depend on characteristics such as decisiveness, boldness and ambition. Dr Liu's example considers someone of Asian heritage in a predominantly white space, and how his fidelity to the servant leadership paradigm undermined his effectiveness as a leader. The same will follow for women leaders in male spaces, neurodivergent leaders in neuronormative spaces, and so on, according to hierarchies of power in the leader's cultural context. When I share this story, I don't mean we should 'act white', or 'like men', or 'mask our neurodivergent traits' to be accepted as leaders – I would certainly not advocate for playing to stereotypes of any demographic or neurotype. I share these examples to explain the difficulty we have leading from the margins. I hope to validate your experiences of difficulty and give some names to the very real hurdles you must navigate.

Deviation from the implicit expectations of how leaders should behave can be detrimental, but so can compliance. Dr Faith Wambura Ngunjiri and Dr Kathy-Ann C. Hernandez challenged a related concept, 'authentic leadership', in their 2017 autoethnographic study[14] of being Black and Mixed Heritage female leaders in a white space. Again, on the face of it, authentic leadership sounds great, right? Who wouldn't want that? Leaders who own their experience, their emotions, who speak and act with transparency and high levels of self-knowledge, must surely do a better job than those who do not. However, the authentic leadership paradigm does not make space for the needs of minority leaders, who may need to mask their true emotions, or code-switch to fit in. Drs Ngunjiri and Hernandez describe examples of feedback from white students who alleged they were 'too young for their responsibilities' or 'mispronouncing words' or 'writing well, for someone from the Caribbean'. These are microaggressions that require emotional labour on the part of the recipient. Both authenticity AND the patriarchal leadership styles would be detrimental to these women of colour in their response. Imagine if they had authentically, boldly and decisively called out the students for the racist presuppositions in their feedback. The scholars rightly point out that they felt they must further suppress their authentic selves in these scenarios to avoid becoming embroiled in conflict with their students and colleagues, who would likely take offence if they verbalized their sense of insult. Masking was the most straightforward way to retain their leadership influence, although I note that in writing a paper about it, they have found a way to highlight injustice anonymously and in such a way that we can learn from it. Touché, doctors! A skilled navigation of authenticity, but note the additional labour required to make it so, as is often the case for minoritized researchers writing about being marginalized.

Dr Elliott Spaeth, who is doubly marginalized by Tourette's and being transgender, describes the fortitude he needs to maintain course while grappling with internalized ableism and shame:

> The thing about being a neurodivergent leader is that the way society treats you means that you have to actively go against what your brain and body are telling you is unsafe to do. You have to experience people misunderstanding you all the time, and judging you based on those incorrect assumptions, and I used to just believe them, which wasn't a good place to be. I didn't know that their ideas of 'good' or 'professional' were just their opinions, not objective truths.

> Being a neurodivergent leader means that I now understand that those judgements come from baked-in inequities within society, and that I'm not inherently wrong, but I have to encounter hurtful, misguided mindsets every day and decide – do I stand up for myself and for people like me, knowing that this, too, will be perceived as 'bad behaviour'? Do I throw myself into that lion's den? Or do I stay quiet, feeling the poison seep into my soul? Either way, leading in this area is in itself a defiance of a culture that positions people like me as inherently unsuitable for leadership.

Ability

That leaders should be competent seems, on the face of it, demonstrably obvious. But the story is way more complex because (1) we are distracted by likability and (2) cognitive ability itself is a multifaceted construct, not reliably measured, and subject to social bias in interpretation. From a neurodivergent and marginalized leadership perspective, the very idea is loaded. Now that is a rabbit hole for a different book (see *Neurodiversity in Higher Education* edited by Dr David Pollack,[15] *The Power of Neurodiversity* by Dr Thomas Armstrong,[16] *IQ: A Smart History of a Failed Idea* by Stephen Murdoch[17] and *Empire of Normality* by Dr Robert Chapman[18] for an interesting tangent), but, to summarize, the very concept of cognitive ability, intelligence and deficits has been challenged from the perspective of neurodiversity, race, gender, ethnicity and disability.

The most famous intelligence test (Intelligence Quotient, IQ) is the Wechsler Adult Intelligence Scale,[19] which actually fails to measure creativity, for example, and has very limited scope for measuring memory and attention. In addition, many of the items in the verbal comprehension subtest are culture-bound and advantage those who are educated in a certain style.[20] From the neurodiversity perspective, part of diagnosis often includes an intelligence test in which the assessor is looking to identify specific areas of weakness (such as working memory or processing speed) and contrasts these with areas of strength (such as verbal or visuo-spatial reasoning). Where these contrasts are substantial we have a 'spiky profile',[21] the hallmark of neurodivergence and the pattern that unites all of us: the dyspraxics, ticcers, ADHDers, autists, dyslexics, dysgraphics and dyscalculics. We all share this experience of wide disparities between the things we do well and our challenges. While our struggles have undoubtedly stymied our leadership potential during the industrial, bureaucratic era, when leaders needed to be heroic in terms of their well-rounded abilities, within a system's thinking, or community-orientated leadership model, we might be able to thrive. The neurodiversity movement joins criticism of the idea of a single, overall intelligence level and draws our attention to different types of intelligence, not all of which are adequately captured by current testing.

Theories of multiple abilities abound in psychology and anthropology.[22] One I particularly like is Dr Helen Taylor's theory of complementary cognition,[23] which proposes that humans have naturally diversified in terms of intelligence profiles as part of our survival as a species. She argues that it is necessary to have a blend of specialists and generalists for human communities to work at their best. Her work explores human evolution and, using archaeological evidence, she points out that it made adaptive evolutionary sense for communities of humans to include some people who are unusually specialist at detail processing, or hypervigilance, or mechanical reasoning, or verbal skills. By diversifying, we maximize our resources and adopt an efficient deployment of ability across complex activities such as hunting, travelling, making camp and devising tools. Our natural state of leadership may include a team of blended, complementary specialists who can confer and rotate the decision making and accountability according to the needs of the group at any one time. This sort of situational leadership would require the right team rather than a handful of very flexible, generalist geniuses.

Even without the lens of neurodiversity, intelligence and success are not a straightforward relationship. Research has found that societally valued success for those with the top levels of intelligence (as far as we measure it) is typically worse than for those who are slightly above average.[24] Furthermore, studies suggest that the way we rate the intelligence of our leaders is not necessarily aligned with how intelligent they actually are. The power of believing in our leaders is stronger than having genuinely competent leaders in terms of organizational success.[25] Indeed, the power of believing in our own competence may also be stronger than our actual competence, an aspect that again favours those who come from the dominant group of class, gender, neurotype, race, etc.

Dr Justin Kruger and Dr David Dunning conducted a famous study in 1999[26] called 'Unskilled and unaware of it: How difficulties in recognizing one's own incompetence lead to inflated self-assessments'. They conducted an experiment with students where they asked them to estimate their ability on a test, and then gave them the test. The students guessed that they would score in the top half of the class, which was a wild overestimation for those who did not score highly but an underestimation for those who scored in the top 25 per cent. This experiment is one of the most highly replicable in psychology (although the authors have been criticized for some of their statistical methods). It explains why so many terrible leaders don't stand aside when they are clearly failing, and why so many talented leaders suffer from crippling self-doubt. Of course, the neurodivergent leader has both high potential and areas of significant challenge within the same ability profile. We are reminded of our challenges throughout education, work and even in the diagnosis process, which makes it more likely for us to experience our success as a paradox.

My colleague and business partner Jacqui Wallis explains how this affected her in her early career:

> Although I was diagnosed with dyslexia when I was in the second year of university, I didn't recognize myself in my diagnosis – it was written (as were all diagnoses at the time) from a medical model of deficit.
>
> Once I had my diagnosis, however, the university put in some adjustments, which transformed my academic output and things dramatically changed – from scraping by to achieving high 2:1s and even a 1st in my Shakespeare paper.
>
> So being neurodivergent wasn't really a negative at university and I quickly found my niche in advertising. In my early career, there was a lot of chatting on the phone, and at that time, not a lot of emailing. I did really well, because that type of job suited my neurotype. I got promoted and found myself very quickly in a position of leadership.
>
> I found that leadership was hard for me – there was more writing, reports, written presentations, and much more reading. Those were the things I found more cognitively draining, but I was still brilliant at talking, presenting and winning clients (essential in any job in advertising). I worked very hard to keep excelling – even at those more difficult tasks – and that meant I had to work many more hours than my colleagues. When they introduced motion detecting lights on our floor, I would often be found waving my arms in the air to reactivate the lights after they had turned off – long after the only other person had left the office.
>
> When I look back now and reflect on why I was successful, it was a combination of naturally excelling in certain areas, and then chronically overworking in the areas which I found more difficult.

The areas where I excelled were:

- Creative thinking – identifying unique solutions to challenges.
- Strategy – finding and naming strategies for my clients and communicating them.
- Presenting (talking) to clients.
- Finding solutions to complex issues.
- I could work out the finances of the deal easily.

But equally I had struggles:

- My writing was prone to mistakes – both spelling and meaning.
- The pace of work was fast and it was hard to keep reading and re-reading emails for errors. Emails had to drafted, saved and checked – often taking an hour or more to finalize before sending.
- I became increasingly anxious at having to stand up and present, if that presenting included writing words or capturing ideas on a whiteboard or flip chart.
- It took me longer to read any preparation materials – and longer to process the information contained in the document.
- Overworking took its toll on my emotional regulation – I started to have more periods of poor mental health.

When I reflect on my career during this period, I can see a person on a high trajectory of promotion and what looked, on the outside, like a very successful career. And don't get me wrong, I thoroughly enjoyed most of it. Advertising provided me with a great deal of career satisfaction, a fantastic number of opportunities to visit places and experience things I might never have otherwise been exposed to. We visited Beijing the year before the Olympics, I went skiing in wonderful locations, I got taken to visit the set of *Star Wars* in Morocco. It felt very glamorous and like I was successful on those days.

But there were missed opportunities. I told no one I was neurodivergent. I hid any struggles, masked through chronic overwork, and as a result I sacrificed myself, my mental health, and as I got older, I sacrificed my family, missing out on key events (I was late to my own engagement party), missed my children's early milestones, and missed plays and parents' evening.

I experienced anxiety and self-doubt over why things were difficult. I held myself to a higher account than I held anyone else. I became paranoid that I would be 'found out' as I got more senior. In particular, I was incredibly fearful of anyone finding out I was dyslexic, or that I might find some of my work difficult. I was worried I would be overlooked. As a woman, in advertising, at that time, there were not many at the very top table. I felt like the odds were not stacked in my favour from a gender perspective – why would I add to the odds by admitting to having a different neurotype as well?

Personality

Cognitive ability plays a role in leadership but, as we have seen, doesn't explain all of the impact. Connected to charismatic, likable leadership style is personality, which is also socially constructed and subject to biased interpretation. An amusing cartoon by Australian Judy Horacek depicted the following interchange between two people in an office: 'What is the difference between assertiveness and aggression?' asks one. 'Your gender,' responds the other. Your personality is judged according to the standards expected of your gender, race, class or neurotype, and when we deviate from the norm we are often more harshly judged than others would be for the same behaviour,[27] as Professor Almuth McDowall noted in her Foreword. Personality is therefore an intangible concept, a series of approximations we make about the nature of our fellow human beings based on their outward behaviour, cross-referenced with our moral codes, which are themselves subject to the culture and historical period in which we live. That said, psychologists have found five personality characteristics (known as the 'Big Five'[28]) which tend to be reasonably reliably measured across cultures, eras and genders, albeit with a margin of error. These are the spectrums of extraversion / introversion, neuroticism / stability, openness to experience / closed-mindedness, conscientiousness / carelessness, and agreeableness / disagreeableness. They describe and predict our behaviour from self and other reported observations.

There are many studies relating Big Five traits to leadership effectiveness.[29] The research shows that the correlation between measured intelligence and organizational performance is lower than the correlation of leadership personality factors such as openness to experience, extraversion and neuroticism.[30] Like intelligence, personality is a loaded term for neurodivergent people. What has been termed introverted or 'socially avoidant' for autistic people is increasingly thought to be a feature of a neurobiological hypersensitive perception that makes everyday interaction overstimulating.[31] What ADHDers experience as extraversion can be driven by a dopamine deficiency that makes us sensory seeking.[32] Anxiety becomes part of a neurotic personality when you have been excluded for reasons you cannot control.[33] A well-intentioned leap to solve a problem can be deemed insensitive and may look like disagreeableness, which is then compared to an age, gendered or racial expectation. From a neurodivergent perspective, the idea of a great personality for leadership is deeply flawed and a source of self-admonishment. We are advised to lead authentically, but our authentic style may clash with the expectations of our demography, or the style of leadership required for our context. Leading therefore requires us to understand ourselves, our contexts, and to work on where these rub – not because we are wrong, but because we need to rationalize and problem solve from a position of groundedness. I have seen great leaders with the 'wrong' personality achieve amazing things, but self-awareness has given them the power to buffer themselves where needed.

In leadership personality research there is a body of literature known as the 'dark triad' – Machiavellianism, narcissism and psychopathy – which is used to explain how some leaders fail, falter and harm. Machiavellianism refers to the leader who will engage in political machinations, manipulation and deceit to advance their agenda. Narcissism refers to a level of self-focus and self-aggrandisement that precludes acting in the best interests of colleagues or the organization. It can be overt (the braggadocious, preening big 'I Am') or covert (attracts attention by virtue of expressing how put upon or needy they are, rather than how great they are). Psychopathy means that the individual experiences little empathy or guilt, and indeed may seek to harm others for their own pleasure or amusement. Dark triad traits have been found, historically, to be higher in leaders than in the general population.[34]

I want to note that this body of research is distinct from the psychiatric conditions (e.g., narcissistic personality disorder) where people often have deep trauma histories and are engaged in therapy and self-development. There is a move to include personality disorders within the neurodivergent umbrella, which I am fully behind. Dark triad traits are on a spectrum, rather than a binary yes / no scale, and most of us will err towards one or more of them at different points of our lives, in different contexts. Like many neurological variations, they occur naturally within our species. They are, essentially, self-protective measures, and we can heal within them, work with them and around them. Personality disorder diagnoses do not automatically lead to toxic dangerous behaviour any more than an ADHDer is automatically an addict or a dyspraxic a risky driver. However, like any specialist, unusual thinker, our neurotypes come with increased risks, and, therefore, if we are in a position of influence, we owe it to those depending on us to explore and mitigate. Dark triad traits affect neurodivergent and neurotypical leaders alike, at different times, in different contexts. To dismiss and 'other' them is counter to the spirit of the neurodiversity paradigm.

Such caveats aside, research evidence suggests that excessive coercive or controlling traits are known to derail leadership careers. Unsupported and unchecked, such traits can damage the organization or community.[35] At best, this causes a handful of direct reports to have a bad time. At worst it leads to blame cultures and organizational failures, which cause crises in safety and public health. However, terms like 'narcissism' get thrown around more than is warranted, and there is a tendency to assign them to others when we are in conflict. I have seen incredibly mature and stable women be critiqued as psychopathic when they made tough decisions, and immature and nervous leaders accused of Machiavellianism when they didn't communicate all the facts on time, which was assumed to be deliberate withholding of information. I have been personally accused of narcissism when I started redrawing personal boundaries over my time and ownership. I, and these other women, spent more time worrying that we were coercive toxic leaders than actually being toxic coercive leaders.

I have a great resource in this journey, my colleague Fiona Barrett, who worked in the probation service with violent offenders and domestic violence victims for 15 years and has more experience of working with the worst coercive, controlling behaviour than most. She has helped our leadership team take accusations seriously, but not personally. With her support and good coaching, I can reflect on times where the accusations were fair calls to action, and when they were projections of others' fears. My most narcissistic and psychopathic periods chime with the times I felt most out of my depth and vulnerable. The dark triad, stigmatized as it is, can be an area for self-reflexivity and enquiry with a qualified coach, counsellor or ally, and helps us manage the need for self-protection without becoming too self-centred or dismissive of others. Working to counter the impact of our internal anguish on those around us is more fruitful than denying our dark sides and waging the accusation against others. Isn't it true that the traits we deplore in others are most often related to the traits we fear in ourselves?

Dan Harris, founder of Neurodiversity in Business and senior IT consultant, explains his realization that his internalized anxiety would affect others:

> Reaching the point in my career where I was leading others was a huge moment for me. It was a mix of pride and a bit of panic. That moment of pride came with a realization that I had no clue what to do next. I'm still working it out, but learning to embrace what it means to be a neurodivergent leader is helping me find my way.
>
> Impostor syndrome is tough early on, but as a leader, it feels even riskier. Part of the panic was understanding that my team's success depended on me, and I could either lift them up or bring them down. Up until then, I was motivated by proving I could do it, proving to my colleagues and to myself, and showing that doing things differently didn't hold me back. I knew those feelings wouldn't cut it anymore, so I had to figure out a new approach.
>
> I've realized I get a lot of those panic moments. Once I stopped judging myself by normative unfair standards and started seeing my reaction not as something to hide but something to work with, things began to change. Every challenge starts with a moment of doubt, but it also forces me to plan and set goals. This has become a key part of how I tackle new things. I've learned it's something many neurodivergent

people do, and it's previously helped me succeed as a tech professional, an auditor, and now hopefully as a good leader.

I know I'll always be figuring things out. This journey of understanding my neurodivergence, my leadership style and myself is ongoing. But it's given me a roadmap for facing new challenges. Being a neurodivergent leader means recognizing that potential can manifest in unexpected ways. Sometimes it's anxiety or feeling like an impostor, which is tough. But showing compassion and helping everyone reframe their challenges into opportunities is how I combat my own doubts and help my team thrive.

My neurodivergence led me to these insights. It wasn't easy, but I can't imagine where I'd be if I hadn't faced these challenges head on. I don't have superpowers; I've just found a way through difficulties that many people face. And now, advocating for this approach with others, especially for our neurodivergent colleagues, has become a source of purpose in my career. It's about turning those challenges into a path for success, for me and for everyone I lead.

Dan says 'I know I'll always be figuring things out'. He and I agree that the best guard for being a positive leadership force is ongoing personal development, working on your patterns, reflecting on the impact you have, and considering where you need to develop, reach out, apologize and invest in relationship recovery. Superpowers or strengths in our spiky profile can't always make up for when we have erred. Acknowledging our feelings and considering the influence we have on those around us are the first steps.

LMX and emotional intelligence

Relational theories of leadership take the traits of the leader to a different level and suggest that the success of leaders depends on the extent to which their competence and personality facilitate positive relationships between them and members, thus inspiring the member to act productively and positively for the whole. To remind, this is known as leader–member exchange, or LMX.[36] High-quality LMX has been associated with positive outcomes for organizations such as improved task performance, job satisfaction and lower staff turnover.[37] Emotional intelligence[38] refers to the ability to notice, name, understand and navigate one's own emotions and those of others. Psychologist Dr Daniel Goleman asserts that emotional intelligence is more important for leadership than cognitive ability or what we traditionally consider to be 'intelligence'.[39] Developing emotional intelligence leads to greater social competence and therefore creates the conditions for a positive leader–member exchange,[40] as well as leading to social and cultural intelligence,[41] which improves the diversity of contexts in which a leader can successfully steer an organization to success.

LMX and emotional intelligence are again loaded constructs for the neurodivergent leader. I confess to feeling defensive even as I name them, and notice my body tense at the memory of times I have failed to regulate my emotions, recognize the emotional state of others and therefore damaged the quality of the relationship between myself and a colleague. Talking about emotional intelligence feels like admitting failure; I immediately become self-conscious because I did not acquire this ability naturally, and still falter. Some neurodivergent profiles limit the development of emotional intelligence, experiencing 'alexithymia',[42] where emotions are hard to recognize and name. Some neurodivergent profiles are clinically defined by a perceived lack of social reciprocity. However, received wisdom on emotional intelligence is that we can learn it, practise it and get better at it through diligent self-reflection and coaching.[43] Using this lens, aspiring leaders can focus on developing and naming emotions, regulating emotions and considering their antecedents and impacts. We start with recognizing our own emotions, as eloquently described by Dr Goleman, and then we graduate to observing the emotions of others.

Much of this book is designed to guide you in developing self-awareness of your emotional experience, to unpack some of the motivators behind strong emotions and develop scaffolding for resolving emotional difficulties. However, I caveat that emotions are not in and of themselves bad. Emotional intelligence isn't about suppressing emotions; it is about understanding them, working through them, learning from them and ensuring that our emotions do not unfairly impact others around us. Strong emotions can come from being minoritized in and of itself, neurodivergent brain chemistry aside, and a necessary pathway for me has been to understand

and contextualize this into resilience, rather than letting it damage my self-esteem. A study published in the *Harvard Business Review* called 'Beating the odds'[44] examined the characteristics of 67 African-American female leaders to understand the mechanisms by which they had succeeded in breaking through systemic barriers to success, and found a strong common denominator: emotional intelligence and resilience. This piece was intended to revere the women's fortitude, but it denies the undue burden placed on Black women to require such strength and their right, as fellow humans, to also be sensitive and require reciprocal care. A question for the remainder of this book is how we can simultaneously conjure the strength we need to rise above society's expectations of us, but remain able to express vulnerability and inspire care or consideration when needed.

Pretending to be the 'perfect leader'

Considering ability, style and personality as the determinants of good leadership falls within the cultural idea of a heroic singular figure who is visibly in charge and responsible for others. The literature explores what kind of person the hero should be, how they should act and what they should do. As I have explained, the problem with great man theories for the neurodivergent leader is the extent to which 'traits' and 'behaviours' are socially contrived, meaning that they are biased by whatever we consider to be 'normal' at the time. And 'normal', in leadership, is still statistically the white, cishet, abled male. When heroic leadership styles are the preferred game in town, there is a temptation to try and make ourselves into the perfect leader.

There are many coaching programmes and workshops you can attend to help develop authentic and servant leadership skills, to improve your ability to listen, to handle conflict and more. However, for those of us coming from the margins, this involves additional layers of masking our authentic selves and code-switching between our 'true' and 'expected' behaviour. Responding sensitively to difficult feedback from your team will involve a layer of emotional labour for all leaders, but this takes on an additional level of effort when the feedback includes slurs about your identity. Masking, camouflaging and code-switching[45] for marginalized leaders is typically defined as self-policing how you dress, wear your hair, the food you eat, the vocabulary you use and the stories you tell. It involves a higher level of cognitive processing than if your codes automatically fit your context. You need to mentally filter and cross-reference your words and actions for a match and to prevent mismatches falling through the filter. At its worst, masking involves suppression of intense emotions as a response to insults or pejorative comments about your disability, race, class, gender, as per Drs Ngunjiri and Hernandez's research.

Women are routinely expected to laugh off comments about their appearance or sexuality, even when these distract from the content of their work and serve to diminish their influence.[46] Muslim and Jewish people are often expected to answer questions about the actions of terrorists or political leaders who come from different countries, where they may never have lived, just because they share an ethnicity or religion, whereas white people are rarely expected to answer for the actions of white male mass shooters or legally questionable military invasions.[47] These distractions are emotionally destabilizing in a meeting where you need to get your point across or make decisions about a problem or strategy. They make us feel unsafe, and it is hard to lead authentically and generously when we feel unsafe.

For neurodivergents, masking commonly includes hiding your literacy difficulties with hours of additional reading time outside work hours, suppression of tics or sensory stimulation, and avoiding tasks that involve motor control or finding directions. As neurodivergent people we are trained to suppress our sensory experiences of overwhelm, having often experienced years of being told we are too sensitive or that we are being pedantic. We learn to limit our enthusiasm for fear of intimidating or annoying others, and hide our spelling mistakes or difficulties in processing ambiguous instructions. We have to manage our reactions to hearing people express that our disabling levels of difficulty are 'like that for all of us'. As a neurodivergent leader, I have been told 'We all struggle with memory sometimes', but this is not the point. We do not all struggle to the same extent; such an assertion is like saying to a wheelchair user that 'We all struggle to walk sometimes'. Comments such as 'In my day, we were just told to get on with it,' 'It's rude when people don't try to spell properly in emails', 'You're too sensitive', 'Please look at me when I am talking to you'* – these stack up

---

* I once supported an autistic friend in an HR disciplinary meeting where the head of HR had literally told her to make eye contact to show she was listening!

and chip away at our sense of self. We start to feel that we have made it all up, that we are struggling because we are incompetent or incapable, not because we are having a different internal experience that requires a different appreciation. Mismatches between our intentions and the impact we have on others is a common neurodivergent conflict, which I have experienced many times in my leadership career.

On one occasion, when acting authentically to offer training to some staff who needed to improve their financial acumen in order to manage their workload, I was told I was 'acting like a man'. Interestingly, the men in the room did not have this impression and thanked me for taking a supportive approach to help them develop the skill they needed rather than chastise them for not having it already. What was happening for the women? My inference is that their shame in not already being good at finance was triggered, and that they had expected me, as a woman, to predict and plan for that with them individually, rather than talk about it openly in a group meeting. As a woman who doesn't struggle with maths and finance, I have strayed from my gender stereotype. As an ADHDer, I went directly to a solution rather than spending time in the sympathy space, which even further strays from my gender stereotype. In these situations of leadership, I can promise you that no one would have benefited from my authentic response! The situation required me to mask, at least long enough to unpack what was happening for the group.

Much neurodivergent community advice is directed to unmasking and living as our authentic selves, but again, this has a race, gender, class and sexuality caveat. For many Black and Brown people living in white spaces, the ability to mask your neurodivergent overwhelm is literally lifesaving when in police custody or emergency medical care.[48] De-masking and being authentic in leadership is a privilege. If you feel safe enough to do so, you are likely to match the demographics of your wider organization or community or be part of a truly inclusive community. You may, like me, express yourself authentically and be chastised. Coach and speaker Brené Brown controversially said that the opposite of belonging isn't always exclusion; it can also be the feeling that you need to put effort into fitting in.[49] Fitting in means you must assess your surroundings and work out which aspects of yourself you need to change in order to be included, whereas belonging is associated with being included for who you are.

While leading, we are in a spotlight. If we are leading in a culture that does not value diversity, leading will require additional masking, and this is the fundamental problem with the authentic leadership paradigm. When these are the layers of additional cognitive and emotional labour expended from the margins, the authentic leadership paradigm seems patronizing and insensitive. Further, masking isn't just about avoiding saying or doing things that clash with the dominant culture; it is also about having the sense that if you are less than perfect you will experience a harsher penalty for imperfection than your peers. We have seen this time and time again – the female, Black, disabled leader who is held to a higher standard than their peers, or given more challenging roles with the expectation that they will fail. This is the fatal flaw in the attempt to be the perfect leader for marginalized groups; we probably won't succeed, and the sense of tension required for being perfect all the time is absolutely exhausting. It plays to our trauma responses, and not the fulfilment of our potential as leaders.

Post-heroic leadership

Economists Professor Benjamin Jones and Professor Benjamin Olken conducted a natural experiment to see if leadership quality was essential to the welfare of the greater whole.[50] They analysed the relationship between leadership changes and economic growth / recession from more than 50 nations during the 20th century, noting the drops and rises in gross domestic product (GDP) and the extent to which they followed leadership transitions. They found a strong correlation between changes in leadership and the economic fortunes of the nations. So, leaders matter. They also found that this relationship was strongest in autocracies, where institutions are dependent on the leaders' whims and have very little agency (ability to act) of their own volition. The relationship was weakest in democracies, where the institutions are more independent and empowered to act. In other words, a strong community under / around the leader was able to buffer a change at the top / middle, for better and worse. So it makes sense for us to consider the relationships and wider system as well as the characteristics of the leader themselves. Philosopher Hannah Arendt offers this critique of great man approaches to leadership:

History is full of examples of the impotence of the strong and superior man who does not know how to enlist the help, the co-acting of his fellow men. His failure is frequently blamed upon the fatal inferiority of the many and the resentment every outstanding person inspires in those who are mediocre.[51]

This shows us how essential the act of followership is to the success of the leader. How followers can undermine a leader when they are disengaged, but equally, how little responsibility for this some leaders accept. Management philosophers have tried to move our thinking beyond heroes and address the complexity of the leadership phenomenon by reconnecting leadership to followership, purpose and activity, understanding it as part of complex adaptive systems rather than a single factor. Dr Jessica Dinh and her colleagues proposed that leadership serves the function of 'direction, alignment and commitment'[52] within the organization, prioritizing the organizational function rather than the style or quality of the leader who delivers. Dr Joseph Raelin[53] described leadership as a practice in which the community / members are agent actors in co-creating the leadership role, rather than subordinate recipients of whichever structures are enforced from above. These developments provide a road map for a more inclusive, ethical leadership narrative.

Ethical leadership

The relational leadership theories of the 20th and 21st centuries gave rise to a sense of and need for moral, or ethical, leadership. Ethical leadership builds on the traits of leaders who must, of course, be transparent, honest, conscientious, agreeable, low in coercive controlling traits, etc., but also outlines a more pragmatic engagement with their members than simply caring for their well-being. Dr Michael Brown and Dr Linda Treviño suggest that 'Ethical leaders also frequently communicate with their followers about ethics, set clear ethical standards and use rewards and punishments to see that those standards are followed. Finally, ethical leaders do not just talk a good game—they practice what they preach and are proactive role models for ethical conduct.'[54] They practise 'moral management', enacting ethics for the whole team.

Ethical leadership is attractive to neurodivergent leaders. We are known for our commitment to justice and altruism, to the extent that this is sometimes pejoratively characterized in psychiatric research as 'justice sensitivity'[55] or 'pathological altruism',[56] meaning that we can pursue our sense of justice to our own detriment even when it is annoying or damaging to those around us. Pathological altruism at its worst has been used to explain the abusive actions of religious fundamentalists and violent offenders, when the moral reasoning is deeply flawed and based on erroneous or single-sourced, biased knowledge. On an everyday level, it can appear as self-righteousness (head to social media for a live example). Yet for many neurodivergent people, altruism and justice sensitivity manifest as confusion and ostracism when we are chastised for 'doing the right thing', such as whistleblowing or raising concerns about a risk. We need to acknowledge our justice sensitivity and find the tricky balance between activism and disruption. This was a problem for me after my MCAS diagnosis in my period of long-term chronic fatigue. Before I received treatment, I became very militant about my disability rights, and I am sure that I caused unnecessary upset fighting the wrong people for the right support in a system that had no flexibility or resources. Just because something is right doesn't mean it is feasible, and as neurodivergents with justice sensitivity, we often have a hard time accepting pragmatic compromise. Yet it can also lead to careers in social justice, the law, diversity and inclusion and many of the paths expressed by my collaborators in this book.

Drs Brown and Treviño use the term 'moral reasoning' and suggest that the extent to which this inspires ethical actions throughout the business ('moral management') is moderated by our 'locus on control' (i.e., whether you believe actions are located within your gift, or externally driven). An internalized locus of control is not an easy state to achieve when you have been minoritized or marginalized. Many of us feel out of control and dependent on feedback from others to validate our decisions. As well as having a lot of coaching to support my personal development, I have found a good alternative has been to develop shared leadership accountability, where I shared ownership and decision making in my company between the leadership team, such that we can support and maintain ethical leadership decisions by committee. Sharing the reasoning and seeking multiple sources of information on which to base moral judgements protects against the dark side of moral grandstanding and harmful take-downs; we need to remain open-minded and curious about alternative views in order to prevent flawed conclusions. And further, we need to remain open to changing course when our conclusions turn out to be flawed despite our best efforts. I recognize this in myself as a trait that can be both instructive and destructive, which is, again, the reason for surrounding myself with alternative perspectives and multiple sources of evidence.

Shared leadership

Shared leadership theories began to emerge in the late 20th century and are broadly influenced by systems thinking and systems dynamics. Systems thinking requires us to consider the power and influence of dynamics on multiple levels rather than the top-down hierarchical pyramid. It is naturally embedded in community-orientated leadership paradigms and is increasingly affected by how companies are organized according to flatter, matrix-style leadership rather than the hierarchical single lines of 'divisions' and 'departments'. Shared leadership tends to operate in knowledge-based industries, where there is high team cohesion and humility on the part of leaders, who gravitate towards ethical, authentic leadership.[57]

A practical example is agile management within the technology industry. Techies have developed a project management and decision-making protocol that is less reliant on single hero leaders and more on autonomous, self-organizing teams. There are a number of books you can read from a practitioner or academic perspective.[58] Essentially, agile involves continual process innovation and reflection in micro loops of evaluation, rather than transformational changes or pivots. The latter are classed as a waterfall approach, where a plan is articulated at the top and then flows down through the organization. Waterfall approaches rely on the skill of those at the top devising and articulating the plan. Agile leaders will devolve decision-making responsibility to experts in the team and focus on a role of facilitator, ensuring that wisdom and observations aren't lost in communication, such as regular 'scrum' meetings. They are operating from the servant leadership paradigm. Agile processes are particularly useful in neurodiverse teams where people with deep expertise who have not sought leadership roles may bring their wisdom to the whole group, and they also prioritize expediency and avoiding long, laborious meetings.

Agile principles hold within them a thread of one of the leading systems thinking authors, Professor Chris Argyris, whose concept of double loop learning[59] recommends that we don't stop when we have solved a problem; instead, we examine how the problem arose and additionally change the conditions that created the problem. For example, with my managers who had missed some key financial information, I was attempting a double loop. As well as explaining the mistake to them and fixing the problem (single loop learning), I offered them training in financial management so that they wouldn't miss this information in the future (preventative double loop). Continuous improvement is a process, but it is also a value; it moves us along from the idea of the perfect leader and into the realm of a journey, progress, shared mission. Systems thinking in organizations takes our attention to organizational culture and change, to performance management, organizational citizenship and engagement, and the idea of the organization itself as the entity, which has learning potential: the whole being greater than the sum of its parts (see Professor Peter Senge's *The Fifth Discipline*[60] for a good place to start). These topics are traditionally taught within Management Science and Organizational Psychology; they provide a great balance to the hero leader paradigm, and may be far more interesting reading for a neurodivergent leader.

Shared leadership is not without biases, however. An agile scrum meeting, for example, prior to the pandemic, was typically conducted with team members standing up in a circle, without consideration of the implicit bias created by gender height differentials, wheelchair users, and the confidence to speak in group meetings. Shared decision-making processes might be disrupted by a charismatic team member who disagrees and creates dissent, or taken over by a member with an interest in leading but without the competence to do so.[61] Further, as is my experience with moral reasoning, a shared leadership approach takes longer and might be disrupted by crisis. Social psychology research suggests that when humans are in a time of change, uncertainty or volatility, we are more susceptible to deferring to a strong leader[62] who will do the thinking for us; certainly this is the case for those of us with implicit beliefs about strong leaders. In the early weeks of the pandemic and in response to some internal crises, I have found it necessary to depart from shared leadership styles and make quick decisions and changes to secure the business's survival. This can be comforting to those who are frightened, but it can also be experienced as an incongruence in values and destabilizing, and has sometimes led to rupture.

Two women I greatly admire, Marcia Brissett-Bailey and Jannett Morgan, share leadership of the Black Leaders and Excellence in Neurodiversity network, and work in tandem to bring recognition to the intersectional experience of their community. Their joint venture embodies the strengths of shared, authentic leadership in which they have created the safe space they need to unmask and lead their network by example:

MARCIA BRISSETT-BAILEY

I grew up on a large council estate in the East End of London with my parents who were both of Jamaican heritage. The diverse community where we lived felt like family. From very early on, I understood inequalities, injustices and marginalization as I was living it. A world which said that the colour of your skin made you not good enough. How could that be so? Why did I have to work twice as hard to achieve half as much?

I am grateful for my journey as it has made me who I am: I do not come from a place of lack. However, I have had to heal from my personal intergenerational trauma, and the community trauma that my ancestors experienced, in order to thrive at home, at work and in wider society.

I have worked for the last 30 years as an educator in the early years foundation, primary, further and higher education, youth and community sectors. The majority of my career has been in further education as a careers educator and special educational needs and disabilities (SEND) lead, both providing pre-entry information advice guidance and supporting careers development and management across the sixth form college. I also worked for a London local authority empowering parents and young people with SEND, and I continue to advocate for social justice through mentoring and providing guidance and information as an educator, speaker, author and consultant.

I am neurodivergent, as are many of my immediate family members. Being able to state this with pride and without apology has been a long journey. Now a dyslexia and neurodiversity champion, I use my influence to provide a space and a voice for those who have been denied the freedom to be who they are, people who are an afterthought in the neurodiversity conversation. Through my work, including most recently my book *Black, Brilliant and Dyslexic*, which provides a unique insight into the diverse lived experiences of 25 neurodivergent people, my aim is to provide critical insights on neurodiversity, intersectionality, race, culture and leadership.

JANNETT MORGAN

Growing up as a Black girl in a working-class, multiracial town, I was acutely aware of the racism all around me. Unfortunately, it was a time when few people had the words to fully express what they had to endure, or simply didn't bother to complain because **that's just the way it was**. The internal racism was real!

I learned very quickly that being a 'bright' child who could navigate the UK education system would offer me some protection from the endless messages telling me I was and would never be as able / worthy / beautiful as my white peers. As a parent, by the time I accidentally figured out that one of my sons was dyspraxic, I'd already seen how his navigation through life as a Black neurodivergent male was far more complicated and challenging than my neurotypical journey. Thus began a lifelong curiosity and the complex relationship between how we learn and the systems of power that shape, reward and punish us for who we are. As such, I have spent the last 30 years helping people lead in spaces that weren't designed with them in mind. At the core of this work is the decentring of the Eurocentric paradigms that dominate leadership theory and practice.

MARCIA AND JANNETT

One of us is 'neurotypical', the other 'neurodivergent'. While in this and many other ways our lives couldn't be more different, our shared desire to see better support for neurodivergent people of African heritage – mainly in the UK – who experience the double bind of racism and ableism (not to mention misogynoir directed towards Black women) brought us together.

Looking outside our cultural narratives

Unpicking cultural clashes in leadership expectations[63] can take us outside ourselves to increase insight. What could an agile leader learn by becoming or conversing with a wheelchair user? How have I, as a white woman, developed more respectful listening skills by following the leadership of Jannett and Marcia? Cross-cultural leadership competence is increasingly relevant in our hyperconnected world with global corporations whose turnovers exceed the GDP of some nations and global problems that require collaboration. Neurodiversity is an international, species-level phenomenon. Neurodivergent people exist in all cultures, races and ethnicities; marginalization by gender, gender status, race, sexuality, disability, age and class exists across the world. Divergent leaders have an opportunity in this new landscape due to our insights as outsiders on the inside. We have learned to speak multiple codes of communication and to rise above the 'norm' to see the 'norm' for what it is. Yet, just as the dominant culture in which I have practised and studied leadership has driven my experience of 'otherness', going outside my own culture allows me to see that there are patterns that I have accepted as true, from which I have benefited even as they cause 'otherness' for my colleagues, peers and friends.

The Ubuntu philosophy is seen across many African communities, expressed in different languages by slightly different axioms that all lead to a straightforward ethos:[64]

The left hand washes the right hand, and the opposite is true.

I am because we are.

Ubuntu is new to me, something I am beginning to see creeping into the white, Anglo-spheric academic literature, but it is, of course, well known to colleagues such as Marcia and Jannett. It resonates with the values I hold around inclusion, but makes an important philosophical distinction to the heroic leadership paradigm, and even the agile / systems thinking paradigm. Ubuntu inspires us to centre the interdependencies of organizational members, of communities, of society; it adds a relational nuance that is missing from the mechanistic descriptions of the agile process. In Ubuntu, leaders are undoubtedly of the servant leadership genre, but the roles of members are also agentic and defined. It is not for the servant leader to take the role of 'mummy' (as opposed to leaders as 'daddy' in a patriarchal system) because the role of followers is not 'child'. Within Ubuntu, each member understands that, without their role, the whole could not function (the left hand and the right hand). This means that the leader sacrifices their individuality to focus on the whole, but the members recognize that this is a sacrifice and act to protect the leader from demands that are not within their remit. This is a far cry from the experience of 'Jeff', but also from Drs Ngunjiri and Hernandez, who were required to subjugate their own needs without an exchange of favour from their students who challenged them and needed corralling to complete basic work. Servant leadership does not serve minority leaders in a culture where patriarchy has trained followers to be passive and undervalued. Servant leadership does work well in a culture when everyone pulls together and understands their essential role, no matter the level of responsibility.

If you are curious and fancy digging into this further, I also signpost you to the work of Indigenous leaders in solving our global climate crisis. For example, Dr Melanie Goodchild is an Anishinaabe woman of the moose clan, identifying as she / her and the founder of the Turtle Island Institute and Waterloo Institute for Social Innovation & Resilience. In her paper 'Relational systems thinking: That's how change is going to come, from our Earth Mother',[65] she writes in two columns, the left a narrative from Indigenous leaders and the right a narrative from systems thinking researchers (interestingly, one being Peter Senge). Her presented text and framing challenged me to recognize the limits of my culture for addressing transcultural global issues, and to acknowledge the overplayed role of rational thought in organizations to the exclusion of spiritual connections to our ecology, humanity and ancestry. It helps me to move past choosing between binary options and embed the sense of multiple realities and truths co-existing: the 'both, and' approach, rather than the 'either, or'.

Genuinely I don't think I understand the models of relational systems thinking and Ubuntu yet, but I feel a visceral pull towards the lack of familiarity, almost as though I am developing new neural connections just by reading, listening and trying to absorb. As I have learned through my own cognitive dissonance, being comfortable with the validity of multiple truths is a precursor to acceptance and inclusion. I am inspired to ask whether, as outsider leaders, we could be pivotal in fostering tolerance and cross-cultural cooperation if we work through these contradictions in our own practice. It's so easy to fall into in-group, out-group, self-righteous patterns, and requires a concerted effort to hold a position of positive regard for all. The two-column thinking approach piques my interest.

Summary

So, what have we learned during my summary march through some academic management science and occupational psychology literature? My overriding sense is how anchored we are to the limits of our culture, and how much there is to be gained from critical reasoning and exploring outside traditional spaces. I am grounded in a sense that leaders matter, that we have power and influence that must be wielded thoughtfully to avoid harm and precipitate success. Leaders from the margins have hurdles and barriers to overcome in order to lead with authenticity and ethics, even when this is our purpose. We have a tightrope to walk in terms of being aware of the judgements people will make about us before we even open our mouths or send an email, and knowing how far we can play to a stereotype for the win, or counter it to prevent discrimination. Our journeys require self-discovery, knowledge and compassion, if we are to lead with love.

We are living and leading through a period of transformational human evolution in our work, education, society and relationship with the planet. The need for ethical leadership is clear to us all, yet one study[66] found that only 8 per cent of CEOs consistently demonstrated moral behaviour, and nearly half did not display moral behaviour at all. As we move further into the post-industrial age, we increasingly aspire to disrupt the norm of top-down, hierarchical hero leaders and move into a more systemic, shared system of making decisions, distributing risk and accountability. The influence of neurodivergent leaders, with our so-called justice sensitivity, is a potential contribution to these conversations.

CHAPTER 2

Becoming a Leader

Following my grandad telling me to 'go where there is no path and leave a trail' and to get a job, I actually took his advice (shock). My first full-time job was in social and personal care for adults with learning disabilities and physical disabilities and older people. This is grounding and humbling work; you learn attendance and time discipline because the impact of not turning up or doing your best has an immediate and detrimental effect on those who rely on you for bathing, eating and being physically safe. It is poorly paid and hard physical work, but I found that I enjoyed the connections that I made with the people in my care. I found creative ways to improve their dignity and comfort, and found joy in their joy.

My first management role was aged 22, when I was studying for my Bachelor's degree in Psychology. I was making money outside lectures by working in an out-of-hours helpline for a social care company in London. I had a lot of experience with night-time and early morning calls, to deliver personal care and social connection. I knew what the carers were facing if there was an emergency, a death or a failed attempt to gain entry, and my ADHD brain works brilliantly in a crisis. In 1999 I came back from a long summer break and burnout sabbatical, and was very surprised to be promoted to manager of the Out of Hours team. I was very excited, to be honest. Having failed so hard at school to fit in and to manage full-time attendance, disability inclusion work had enabled me to claw back a sense of purpose. Excitement for work won't be true for many neurodivergent aspiring leaders, I am sure, but something will be – perhaps the arts, or music, or advocacy. What's important is the sense of catching a wave, the wind behind your sails, momentum and progress, and for me, work was the first time I felt that passion. I learned a lot in these early years of corporate management. Of course, there was no way I was going to manage to stay in corporate land forever, but I learned a few hard lessons about what it means to be in charge. I was keen to make my new role work, and the feedback I got from my bosses signposts the essential behaviours you need to get started as a leader.

'Nancy, you are the only manager who brings me solutions, not just problems'

I never passed the buck up the management chain. Out of Hours was my little fiefdom and it was up to me to make it work. When we were struggling to handle the call volume because the company had merged and taken on three new regions, I spent a working weekend doing a time and motion study showing how many calls were coming from the old regions and now the new regions, to show that our workload had increased by 50 per cent. I then worked out a new rota system to plug the busy periods so that our vulnerable lone residents were safe and had a guarantee of someone answering their call if they were in a crisis. I took all these bits of paper to my boss with a proposed solution to the issue.

Solution-focused, creative thinking is often a neurodivergent strength – lots of us have this for different reasons. It could be our ability to see the details, or our ability to see patterns, or the bigger picture, or our hypervigilance. Creativity comes from many position points, the key being that they are unusual positions to take. My creativity usually comes from being annoyed with something! And this is a key part of my leadership journey – being annoyed enough to change something. You know the old Serenity Prayer: 'God grant me the serenity to accept the things I cannot change, the courage to change the things I can and the wisdom to know the difference.' High on courage, low on serenity and still working on the wisdom. I started studying psychology because all the psychologists I had seen as a troubled teen annoyed me. And the psychologists who worked with my disabled clients in social care annoyed me. I eventually got cross enough to think, 'Right, that's it, I am going to study psychology so that I can argue with you lot.'

So, in my twenties, while I was studying and working full time, I busied myself finding problems that I could solve, and these turned into my career. I didn't have a plan further than to learn psychology so I could make it better for people like me. But along the way, I found it easy to get promoted into management roles from simple entry-level employment because I loved fixing problems. Every senior manager loves a junior who thinks for themselves, someone they can send away to fix something who will come back with a workable plan, someone they don't have to do all the thinking for. Leaning into your neurodivergent strengths as a creative problem solver is a great opener to management and leadership; it will set you apart. I still do this today, and what's more, I have actively promoted people who solve their own problems and find it exciting to do so. I see this as a huge green flag of leadership potential. The only caveat is, of course, how you communicate your plan.

'Nancy, you can't show them that!'

My boss loved the time and motion study and suggested that I take it to the management meeting. I headed off with my pile of papers. 'Not like that! You can't wave a pile of papers with tallies and ticks; you need a summary graph and a set of bullet points on the front page to flash in front of them. They won't process your data that quickly.' She was right, of course. Solution-focused thinking is one of my Genius Withins. I can see risks further ahead than most people, but I can also run through alternatives and think of solutions quickly. A problem that continually plagued me in my early career, and can still rear its head today, is that I go from the risk to the solution so quickly that I leave people spinning. I was fully prepped to walk into that management meeting with a list of demands and a handful of papers with pencil tallies on them. I wasn't going to 'tell the story' that would have brought people with me. I wouldn't have been successful. The management team would have been confused and I would have been annoyed that they couldn't see it. So I had to learn to slow myself down and – yes – do the admin.

Administration can be a deal breaker for many neurodivergent thinkers, and I understand how hard it is – I genuinely need ADHD medication just to get to the post office some days. But earlier in my career, my ambition and the novelty of the work saw me through. I found a way to hyperfocus on presentation skills of written work, writing reports that other people could read, and my hyperfocus actually turned into a strength and a point of pride. This is a common theme for neurodivergent leaders – we find a way to break through the procrastination and the fear of failure when it comes to getting our ideas out there in a palatable, on-time manner. I have become somewhat fixated on this now – I am formatting this writing as I go, using automated heading formats, 1.5 spacing, indented first line of paragraphs. I actually find it easier to have the presentation skills part of the writing because I find it easier to process my own jumbled thoughts when they are laid out well.

This won't come as easily to everyone – I am hyperlexic, and was literate before I started school. But you will have your own version of this. My business partner and CEO of our company, Jacqui Wallis, is dyslexic. And while she can write a banging discussion paper when required (and uses speech-to-text software to do so), her Genius Within is presentations that tell a story with graphics. Having your own style is important, but so is finding some way to meet the brief, even though it might not be your favourite activity. Indeed, it can be liberating for you and your colleagues to find a way through what you might think of as your challenge.

With this example, the rota was driving me up the wall in terms of ADHD time-blindness. So, instead of giving up, I made a huge month map on the floor with flip chart paper and Post-it® notes representing each employee's hours and the new people I wanted to bring in, and placed them all on the map, moving them around until I had something that worked. And then I wrote that up in a simple presentation and took it to my team and showed them the logic. Turns out they had also found thinking through the rota hard, and my visual worked for them, too. We all agreed the timetable, and everyone felt like it was clear and fair for the first time ever. I also managed to turn my sheet of ticks and tallies into charts so that I could bring the management team along for the ride.

'The trouble with you, Nancy, is that you wear your heart on your sleeve'

Oh, this feedback! It is true. I am laughing as I write this because I initially thought it was a compliment! It was not a compliment. It was my boss trying tactfully to tell me that I needed a social filter on what I said. Tact doesn't work with me, hence why I am also not good at it. I would be the world's worst poker player. I find it very hard to disguise my alarm, my concern, my horror, and this rubs off on anyone around me, damaging those who feel vulnerable. I also find it hard to disguise my joy, my admiration, my excitement. This also rubs off, which is a good thing and can be a huge boost for those who were lacking confidence. But for the hypersensitive team, or the bewildered neurotypical team, it feels like inconsistency. I used to get grumpy about this feedback – 'At least everyone knows where they are with me' was my comeback. Sure, but they don't know where they are, Monday compared to Friday!

As a neurodivergent, social communication can be the Achilles' heel of leadership. A classic autistic factual commentary on an error will be perceived as a slight, or insensitive. An urgent, crisis resolution-focused ADHDer will issue commands without sufficient hesitation to give those around them time to join in (I can already hear my inner voice pushing back on this statement – if I'm not giving time, it's because there isn't any time to waste! Grr, the instinct is strong here even when wrong). Dyslexic leaders may spend their time feeling self-conscious about literacy and fighting judgements about how quickly they read – and we DO need to process information quickly for many leadership roles. Ticcers may find that observational tics are reacted to with alarm by direct reports. At what point do neurodivergent leaders need to be accepted for their challenges just as any other person, particularly a person with a potentially disabling condition? We wouldn't chastise a leader who was a wheelchair user for being slow to get to meetings, but we DO chastise autistic leaders for being too direct, ADHDers for not filtering their thoughts, dyslexics for typos and taking the time to read the material...where is the boundary?

In the previous chapter I looked at the various styles of leadership, personality factors and dynamics that can predict leadership success or failure. My conclusion, early in my career, before I was diagnosed with ADHD, was that I had to work at being the perfect leader. Since the early days of my management career, I have had long, immersive personal development coaching and regular supervision to help me unpack these adjectives and learn more about the conditions in which an intended 'decisive' will be framed as 'autocratic'. I have dedicated hours each month to understanding and unpacking the reactions of my neurotypical colleagues and my neurokin who have opposite spiky profiles. I have learned 'metacognition', which is the ability to think about thinking. It is a fundamental skill that you can learn through cognitive behavioural therapy, clean coaching, acceptance and commitment coaching / therapy, mindfulness and more. It gives you the ability to spot your own patterns and scripts that you run, to honestly appraise your own behaviour and that of those around you. I learned to separate my inferences and interpretations from evidence in day-to-day communication.

I was diagnosed with ADHD at the age of 38 by a psychologist and then again at the age of 41 by a psychiatrist. This is very late for someone who had already specialized in neurodiversity for more than a decade by then. Diagnosis was simultaneously cathartic and devastating. I felt vindicated on some levels; finding out that I was different due to my brain chemistry is very different from thinking I was different because I had a maladaptive personality. I began to develop different coping strategies and give myself less admonishment for my challenges. I took medication for the first time and found it transformational, although not sustainable on a daily basis.

After the initial relief came anger. I regretted the decade or more prior to diagnosis where I was on the journey carrying self-chastisement and absorbing criticism with those who interpreted my behaviour as intentionally malevolent or rude. I felt sorry for my younger self, who had failed her A-levels, left home before she was grown, naively placed herself in risky situations out of a desire for social acceptance, only to experience harm. I regretted that developing self-awareness had initially led me to perceiving that coaching and therapy would make me more palatable to people who simply didn't like me. I felt grief for the ambitions I had let go because I didn't think I was good enough, the relationships that had failed because I had lacked the ability to self-advocate before being pushed to the edge. I became more militant about my 'rights' to accommodation and adjustment and less deferent of those who didn't think it was their role to support my needs. This reduced my sense of independence and increased my experience of vulnerability. Having worked tirelessly from my teenage years to build a wall around said vulnerabilities, these started to break down, and at times this was hard to bear.

Of late, I think differently about the years I spent unpacking my sensitivities, learning about what other people were experiencing in response to my communication so that I could understand their alarm. I value the learning I invested in developing reflexivity, self-awareness and finding 'the pattern level' of miscommunication themes so that I could de-sensitize them for myself and others. This was and continues to be hard graft. But looking back, I can now reframe the experience. I learned that I didn't do it because I am neurodivergent and needed to change myself to be a better leader. I did it because every single person in a leadership role will benefit from accurate self-appraisal, the ability to understand their own responses and heightened understanding of the reasons other people respond to them positively or negatively. Do the work. Hopefully spend less time in the self-chastisement phase than I did! Do the work with neurodiversity-affirming practitioners rather than judgemental behaviourists. But do the work! You will not regret it.

'You Just Haven't Earned It Yet, Baby!'

When I look back now at my early roles in management, I wince. It is cringy to remember the mistakes I made with my absent filter, how rude I was to colleagues, how many times I was a huge emotional drain on my bosses, clearing up my social faux pas. But I was also a bonus. I did a lot of work that punched above my weight in terms of strategy and problem solving. I also made a bunch of money for the company and was generally financially very competent. Was I worth the trouble? You'll have to ask them. The title for this section reads 'You Just Haven't Earned It Yet, Baby!', which is the title of a song by The Smiths about searching for recognition as a musician and singer. It's a great song, and I fell for the Kirsty MacColl version. There's a sense in an early career of having to earn your path to success. This is the choice you make with some leadership careers, and I was voracious in my early career, taking on anything that came my way. There are risks to this approach; it is not always wise to take on everything and have few boundaries. But in every career, there is a period in which you have to hone your craft. A marginalized leader rarely assumes a leadership role by virtue of who they are; we often have to work harder than our peers to achieve the same level of success. For me, I needed to feel confident that I had something to offer, and for me, that meant gaining experience and working hard.

I couldn't handle corporate life; the constriction and pantomime of social convention was exhausting once I realized that few other people really understood it either. I remember a time, after being promoted and taking on a branch that was failing, arguing with a finance director. He was suggesting that my budget forecast needed to be improved. He told me that my boss wouldn't be happy with it. I retorted:

> Is it my job to lie to my boss to make her happy and then be in trouble in six months when I haven't delivered? This budget is a reflection of what is possible given that I've just taken over a new area and there's a huge amount of poor practice in filing, record keeping, health and safety. By the time I've unpicked all that we'll be lucky to maintain, let alone grow.

Now, you can imagine how annoying I was to that finance director. I certainly lacked tact and was too direct, but I wasn't wrong. Those conversations were the grind I couldn't do; I couldn't pretend and play politics. But I did think big. I do like expansion and growth – it works for me. I see growth as the natural result of quality – growth by bums on seats is shallow, empty and unfulfilling. Doing something well and picking up a trajectory is exciting and very dopamine enhancing from an ADHDer perspective. So I moved from a 'proper job' at the tender age of 25 and became self-employed. Career wise, I wasn't ready – I didn't have enough kudos or credentials to sell myself on the open consulting market. But because I was able to put in the hours and I (nearly) had my Master's degree in Occupational Psychology, I could just about fudge it. I was very lucky to fall in with a group of coaching and training professionals at the time who taught me the basics of consulting and devising projects with social value. I worked in and around the unemployment support and disability employment industries for about 10 years, delivering one-off projects, or repeat specialist support services.

I never knew exactly where the next piece of work was coming from. It was fraught sometimes, and I would panic about money, panic about not having enough time – feast or famine. Being self-employed and working in small partnership-style consultancies is very liberating on the one hand. You can write your own rules – I used to have planning meetings in pyjamas to maximize sensory comfort, which was a sea change from the power suits of corporate life. I would allow myself to follow the flow of my hyperfocus, working days in a stretch but then having the freedom to take long walks during the business day to recover and recharge. These are the joys of self-employment. The hard part of self-employment is that you are the only backstop. If you don't do it, no one will. And that can be the difference between making rent or being in debt. So it taught me a hard lesson in stepping up and avoiding procrastination, but it also taught me that I work at my best when I can be the own boss of my time and my sensory experience. A note – obviously I put proper clothes on and arrived on time when I was client facing. But the ability to let off the pressure in preparation time was enough of a release valve for me in those early years, particularly after my kids arrived and I could only really focus after they had gone to bed. I was on top of my admin, my email inbox and my invoicing because I had so much latitude between times when I had to be 'on duty' that I could manage. Much more so than when I was a CEO.

I consider these the years in which I honed my craft that would eventually become the fundamentals of my PhD, my love of coaching psychology and how we run Genius Within. I was no longer the boss, I was the underling; I had to carry the bags of more experienced professionals and justify my earnings by being useful, rather than being profitable. I worked for free a lot, to test ideas and generate some testimonials. I used to do the lion's share of the admin, the finance for the more experienced colleagues so that they would tolerate me long enough for me to learn. In some ways, it was a backwards step, but it was a backwards step onto the solid skills of project admin and budgeting that I had learned in corporate life. Sometimes in our careers, backwards steps are essential. Careers are not a one-way rachet, only going in one direction. In fact, there is a good evidence that neurodivergent people take circuitous career routes.[1] Careers can zig-zag across the disruption of parenthood, coming out, perimenopause, immigration, transitioning and health crises. However, despite all the book learning and professional ethics I learned studying psychology, working with actual people is where I earned my place as the psychologist I identify as now.

Between 2002 and 2012 I conducted thousands of coaching and training hours with people who were almost universally neurodivergent and unemployed, precariously employed or career thwarted. I trained coaches, and I wrote training programmes for facilitators, coaches and managers. I managed large consulting projects. I ran career development groups for people who would turn up high on drugs; some were selling drugs and all were desperate to find a sustainable career. Some people came from three generations of unemployment. This work taught me to think on my feet, to ground myself in the harsh reality of problem solving without resources. I conducted disability assessments for the government support service Access to Work and hoped my clients would get a good coach to support them with time management, memory, etc. Eventually I became that coach because I was so worried about the quality of coaching in the disability support market. This problem is what eventually led to me starting Genius Within, but before that was even an idea, I was putting in the hours, the graft of working with people on their own psychological journey. This taught me how to set aside my own journey and focus on others. I learned the importance of supervision and how essential it is in people work (which includes leadership) to have good, reflexive supervision.

In this early stage of psychological practice, I worked with a group of people, training them to support unemployed people. At the end of each day, we spent an hour giving and receiving feedback to / from each other. Every day. Every person. This discipline carried forward during 10 years of my early career with every joint project that I undertook. It was rigorous self-exploration. These are the years in which I knocked off those tactless corners. We had to be genuine and humble, or we failed. In the morning we would share with our groups the learnings we had from the previous day, which included acknowledging our mistakes and our vulnerabilities, to build rapport and insight. I still find it beautiful when I see this level of human connection in action, stripping back the pretence, the hierarchy, the social conditioning and just asking ourselves as a group: 'What do we want to have happen?' We were very successful, by the way. We were part of a team who shifted the employment success rate from 25 per cent to 55 per cent in the space of six months. I used to be asked all the time how we did that and was scorned by sceptics: 'Oh, you must have picked off the low-hanging fruit.' No. We did not. We created the conditions for others to find their own jobs rather than patronizing them by doing it for them. Yes, even those who had never worked before. We shared with them the unwritten rules of job searching (don't apply for jobs on the internet, find the hidden job market), and we counted ourselves, as self-employed, among them. We were authentic and we held the ethos that we wouldn't run a workshop that we didn't personally find useful.

As our mutual trust increased, we were more able to give each other intense personal feedback. This meant we were picking apart social rules. One group member's silence was interpreted as rudeness, but to others it was diligent listening. Another would arrive 10 minutes early every day, which some thought was too keen and would make it harder for the facilitators to prep. Another arrived exactly 33 minutes late every day and reported being 'terrible with time'. We quipped that he was actually very consistent with time, he just needed to get the earlier bus! In my coaching and group work, I have played with so many social communication norms and assumptions, debunked them for myself and others – finding people who think the opposite is how I have gradually shaken off the shackles of the assumptions I inherited from the world according to my gender, race, class, generation and cishet presentation. As much as any coach I paid to work with me, as much as any qualification, these groups and clients are where I earned my expertise as a psychologist and developed metacognitive flexibility. I highly recommend my erstwhile colleague Dr Caitlin Walker's book *From Contempt to Curiosity*[2] as a source of reflection and inspiration on the matter of exposing yourself to diversity in order to learn.

I have seen similar approaches to self-development in anti-racism and racial justice groups, the Pride movement and recovery communities. You don't need to follow my career to develop self-awareness and the leadership skill of communicating across difference, but you do need to do it somewhere. And it doesn't stop. I don't consider myself finished; I consider myself a constant work in progress, with ebb and flow, yin and yang (alright, still mainly yang). I am currently engaged in health coaching to learn how to manage my chronic health condition more effectively, which is unpeeling yet another layer of my ability to hold my boundaries, to say 'no' and prioritize my work. In some ways I developed these unhealthy patterns in my eagerness to thrive and succeed, and now that I have some modicum of externally referenced success, I need to redefine what internal success feels like. I definitely took a hard route and I survived, but it is not for everyone. The metaphor I use often for this concept of 'doing the work' is an artist, musician, athlete or dancer. In the audience we see freedom of movement, power and skill. We don't see the many hours put in at the barre with repeated exercises to develop muscle tone. We don't see the injuries and the setbacks. We don't see the failed auditions and the crying after the criticisms. But you don't get to achieve fluency in dance without practice; you rarely see concert pianists who didn't practise scales until their arms ached.

Ambition is NOT a dirty word

The drive and ambition needed for a leadership career is undermined by misogyny, which we can internalize. My sisters and I once asked my dad if he could sum us up in one word, and he said that my sisters were intelligent and wise and that I was ambitious. I was so offended. But this is because I had absorbed left-wing, English narratives about not 'pretending to be above your station' and women's narratives about being meek and deferent to others, putting others above yourself always. Ambition, to me, was something dirty, something associated with the greed of the 1980s 'yuppy' phenomenon and the antithesis of the values I wanted to embody in the world. However, is that really what ambition means? Luckily, I grew up in the era of Madonna's 'Blonde Ambition' world tour and had a handful of role models who inspired me, like Debbie Harry and Sinéad O'Connor (I have an eclectic music taste).

In 2016, I came across Reese Witherspoon's acceptance speech for her Glamour Women of the Year award, which she earned by setting up her own production company to platform female-driven content in the movie business. If you haven't heard the speech, stop reading this book now and go search for it.* She talks about having the courage to change the things she couldn't accept – the lack of female representation in media. She states that 'We are in a cultural crisis. In every field and every industry, women are underpaid and underrepresented in leadership positions.' Reese encourages all women to think about the problems in their own fields of work and challenge themselves to address them. And then, she drops the mic when she says 'I believe that ambition is not a dirty word. It's just believing in yourself and your abilities. Imagine this. What would happen if we were all brave enough to believe in our own ability? I think the world would change.' This speech can still give me goose bumps, because it lifted the lid on all the shame I carried about success. It is hard to deliver a leadership role well if you are ashamed about success and don't think

---

* See www.youtube.com/watch?v=JKKRBnpDpBY&t=4s

you deserve it. It was a deeply feminist awakening that permitted me to strive for my PhD, to name myself publicly as Dr Doyle and to share the positives. It requires overruling so many external messages that society throws at us and connecting with the successful role models that are 'like us' for the benefit of those who are yet to come and need inspiration.

My final tale from my early career carries my deepest warning of which path NOT to take. Ambition, self-confidence and leadership are weirdly paradoxical. Those of us coming from identities that are minoritized in leadership roles are acutely aware of the demon boss, the white supremacist, patriarchal bully. The overconfident, braggadocious, smug, entitled, underserving leader. Now, many of us take this risk to heart so deeply, we want to be the opposite of that. But the opposite of that is not the deferent, martyred, servant leader. Servant leadership might be a useful thing to teach the neuronormative, abled patriarchy, but it is not the lesson for us. We have already overplayed that hand, by virtue of our feeling the need to earn our seat at the table. We need a different message. The reason I love Reese's speech so much is because she reframed ambition and confidence for me. Confidence and self-belief don't have to translate into unearned privilege and hierarchy. What if ambition is a healthy appreciation for life, a desire to set realistic goals to achieve what will work best in your field?

So many of the mistakes I made as a leader came from not believing in myself, from not being ambitious enough, from hearing a different opinion and having no internal reference to counter-balance with the value of my own judgement. I was so externally referenced in my sense of worth, so reliant on other people's opinions of me, that I couldn't separate those who were and those who were not acting in their own interests. I allowed myself to be swayed by people who were not acting with integrity because I didn't trust that small feeling in the pit of my stomach that was warning me 'no'. I allowed myself to continue with projects, relationships that ultimately failed because I carried on saying 'yes' when I had the 'no' feeling. I overshared ownership for work I completed alone because I was frightened to not share or to argue my corner. I was socially conditioned to believe that emotions were bad, that they reflected feminine weakness or ADHD pathology. I was trained to ignore my inner voice ('Don't be so sensitive'), like so many neurodivergent people. As such, I was also trained to ignore my moral compass and own decision-making capacity. I gave away too much of my power because I was worried that power was automatically corrupt. I sought to create checks and balances around me in case I became a despot. Checks and balances are good – I am genuinely proud of the governance we have at my company – but I wasn't at risk of being a despot. I was scared of success, ambition, the conceptualization that I had of power. I used to smoke cigarettes to manage my emotions every time we won a new contract. At one point, I was nominated for an award, the Disability Power List 100. It should have been a career highlight, a moment of celebration, but I was too overwhelmed to attend the ceremony. And I wasn't alone.

My colleague Neil Milliken, who has experience of leadership in both small businesses and large multinationals, shares the experience of initially leading through overwork:

> I didn't enjoy school much and found university life at Oxford gruelling, probably only being saved by the fact that there is an oral tradition of discussions with tutors rather than writing.

> I appreciate unconventional leadership and many will say that I practise a style that is not the norm for the kind of organization that I work in: a very large multinational IT company.

> In my earlier career and pre-diagnosis (of dyslexia and later ADHD), like Nancy I made many mistakes, annoyed a lot of people, but also found myself given the trust of leadership because I was somehow able to make things happen.

> I gravitated towards the things that gave me energy, initially music and video, and later technology. I had a Road to Damascus moment with tech when I saw how it helped me compensate for things I struggle with.

> A decade working for a small but rapidly growing assistive technology company gave me the ability to experiment and find a leadership style.

> I default to trust and seek to build teams that have a shared sense of purpose. While some might say I trust too much, I find the energy

wasted not believing in people is much higher than the energy dealing with failures.

That said, overwork, a servant leadership approach to management and disability advocacy, has definitely led to near burnout several times; Nancy wrote that she was too burned out to celebrate being in the top 10 on the Disability Power List – she was not alone. I was also in the top 10 and I didn't have any energy left to celebrate either. We messaged each other to share our overwhelm.

The incident, while seemingly small, had a profound effect on me as I realized that in order to lead I needed to take better care of myself, not be the saviour, and to build functional teams that are closer to the Ubuntu community model mentioned in this book.

In 2023 Nancy and I were both back on the Power List and made a point of celebrating together. This time we had the energy.

While corporate life was not the path for Nancy, I have found my path as an intrapreneur changing massive organizations from the inside and leveraging their scale to create systemic changes that go outside the walls of the organization.

I love variety and problem solving. My strengths have been to find new models of business and convince top management to implement them – when everyone says something cannot be done, I think, challenge accepted.

As I rose through management I was able to access executive support that removed many of the things I found challenging, and was freed up to be creative and challenge the status quo.

Given the executive function issues I have due to my ADHD, an executive assistant is the perfect accommodation. What I wish for and am working to implement is this support to be made available for many more neurodivergent employees, to enable them to break through the management glass ceiling. We should not have to rely on seniority to access such support.

I count myself as one of the lucky few that got the breaks I needed and the support from friends, family and employers to succeed and stay out of trouble.

I hope others reading this book and finding their paths will also reflect on how they can be the role models that give ND [neurodivergent] people embarking on their managerial journey the support and leadership they need to be successful too.

Looking back, my fear of success started because my initial psychological and coaching training was not neurodiversity-affirming. I had become deeply self-conscious after realizing how powerful I seemed to others because of my ADHD energy and quick thinking. These traits were framed as negative behaviours that I would learn to control or suppress, rather than understand and work with. They were also dissonant with my experience: I didn't feel powerful, I felt scared. I had become intimidated by my own potential and worried about the potential to harm, similar to the story articulated by Dan Harris in the previous chapter. But in creating webs of 'checks' around me and giving away my independence, I also inadvertently placed people under too much responsibility for my work. I muddied the waters, the boundaries and the goals. Trusting myself was the biggest, hardest and most fruitful lesson of leadership. The more centred and self-referenced I became, the less despotic I appeared! This is the paradox. In order to listen generously and hold a safe positive space for others, you have to have faith in yourself. The despots aren't typically the bosses with the mature, reflexive self-appreciation of their strengths and challenges; they are the ones masking trauma and self-distrust. You are actually an easier leader to relate to when you are confident in your own abilities. There is, of course, a fine line that you tread either side of every day, but trust me when I say good leadership doesn't come from constantly questioning every decision and needing other people to validate you. Healing work isn't just for you; it's for the good of the community you lead.

I mentioned in the previous chapter a story about when some of my female colleagues commented that I was behaving like a man when I suggested finance training to help them cope with their management roles. I was so upset by this; I saw it only in terms of their view of me and didn't consider what might be going on for them. I got really self-conscious about my communication style and how being ADHD may have interacted with the stereotype of the servant female leader. I flipped between self-reproach for failing to suppress and anger at being asked to confirm. I was entirely focused on me. I then derailed my decision with their anxiety and I didn't arrange the financial training for them. Instead, I hired additional expertise in our finance department to buffer them. Looking back, this was the wrong decision. Those women deserved my faith in them that they would be able to cope with the finance training; they deserved my support in overcoming maths anxiety and learning the language of management finance. They may not have ever been the financial whizzes of the company, but constantly being in a position of not understanding where the money was coming from and how to predict cash flows left them at a constant power disadvantage. The whole event was destabilizing for the team cohesion and some of them left over the coming years as Genius Within grew and the need for financial literacy increased.

The next time the opportunity arose, I tried again. This time, the financial training happened, with a concerted effort from an external consultant providing one-to-one support, in tandem with Helen Charnock, our finance director. My observation is that it raised confidence levels and created the conditions for growth and agency on the part of those managers. They now don't feel in the dark, they don't feel left out of conversations, and they feel able to make decisions independently. They have the language to liaise with their finance colleagues without needing me to intercede and explain things to them. I could have provided that learning for others had I not been so tied up in my own self-consciousness of upsetting others. I needed more ambition, not less. I needed ambition for them as well as for my company.

Along with ambition comes competitive spirit. I have also had to rediscover my love of competition in order to lead. A competitive spirit doesn't have to mean other people fail so that you succeed. You can compete against yourself and learn to love progress, no matter where it comes from. It doesn't have to be a social comparison thing. This is where being a dual national American and Brit comes in handy for me. When I do well in the USA, I get a high five and a 'hell, yeah!' When I do well in the UK, I am more likely to feel like I can't talk about it in case it makes other people feel bad. I was once asked to not run in the mums' race at my children's sports day because some of the other women had warned the school that they wouldn't take part if I was running (I was a runner for many years and used to jog to and from school runs). Again, I took this personally, like I was in the wrong for deliberately making them feel bad by trying hard at something. This is a social convention; it doesn't have to logically follow that other people's abilities signpost our own failings. I ran the race backwards, came second, and laughed it off, but the incident still reverbs. I can see all around me the negative effects of social comparison. There are times when I have been jealous or felt victimized because others are better than me at something, or when others have complained about me because of their own anxieties. This is a topic for me to work on.

I spent several years in a triathlon club and in various cycling and running clubs, with a group of extraordinarily supportive athletes. We would routinely stay at events until the last member had finished. 'Hell, yeahs!' were issued for **any** personal best, whether that was a sub-20-minute 5K or a 45-minute 5K, or the first 5K attempted since injury. Any and all effort was praised, including the restraint of not racing because you had an injury. It was a very supportive environment, in which everyone was ambitious, but this did not detract from each other at all! And to be clear, we had some ironman triathletes and some sub 3-hour marathoners. But their clear talent and commitment wasn't positioned as hierarchy; it was celebrated and inspirational, not gloating or smug.

I learned to turn jealousy into ambition, to channel my competitive spirit into my own goals. If someone had done something that made me envious, I taught myself to interpret this as a signal of where my next challenge should come from. Jealous of the psychologists I was meeting at conferences that had a PhD? Time to do a PhD. Jealous of someone who was doing a really good job of maintaining a work–life balance? Time to learn how to say 'no'. Once I started working on my own goals and feeling the success, I got a lot less jealous, a lot less antsy about what others thought about me. I also started to let go of the need to be a perfect leader. Jealous of how rigorous my colleague Whitney is about her reflective practice? Copy her. Jealous of how well my colleague Meg can listen to a client in distress on the phone and follow through on all their needs? Celebrate her. Peer learning, celebrating others' successes and setting your own stretch goals is a rewarding aspect of leadership that comes as a gift in return for a bunch of hard, self-development work on feeling valued and having an internal reference point for your own worth. You can rise above the jealous and self-consciousness when you engage in healing work and instead turn those emotions into drivers of growth.

I'll leave you with a story from my esteemed peer, Tumi Sotire, who illustrates both the 'one step forward / two steps back' career paths that many of us take, and also the need to focus on our own goals rather than letting social comparison eat us up:

> I was born into a British Nigerian household, where I held the distinction of being the oldest boy and the eldest grandson among all my relatives. Growing up in a cultural context that upheld patriarchy, particularly influenced by Yoruba traditions, some might argue that my familial position destined me for leadership. However, I've come to understand that true leadership transcends age or familial hierarchy.

> My upbringing often involved responsibilities beyond my years, with my parents entrusting me to ensure the house remained tidy in their absence. Despite their intentions, I often fell short – not due to an inability to perform chores, but rather from a lack of confidence to delegate effectively among my siblings. This lack of assertiveness stemmed from my awareness that my brain was wired differently; I grappled with dyspraxia and learning differences affecting both fine and gross motor skills. Moreover, my struggles were compounded by the cruelty of school bullies who branded me with hurtful labels like 'retard' and 'spastic'.

> In the midst of these challenges, I found it difficult to recognize my own worth or envision myself as a leader. My confidence was shattered, and I felt as though I had little to offer the world. Yet despite these feelings of inadequacy, a flicker of hope remained within me. During my early teenage years, I struggled to form meaningful connections and didn't have many friends. However, as time passed, I eventually found companions who accepted me for who I am. Understanding the value of genuine friendships, I made a conscious effort to cultivate traits that would nurture these relationships. I prioritized showing compassion and

understanding, even when faced with adversity or misunderstandings. It was through these experiences that I discovered my exceptional interpersonal skills, a strength that set me apart in a world not always attuned to neurodivergent individuals.

Nurturing this key strength became essential for my survival in a society that often overlooks or misunderstands neurodiversity. I learned that people are more willing to assist and offer advice when they see your genuine care and concern for them. This principle guided me through university and into my twenties, where I invested time and effort into building a personal tribe, a community of individuals whom I could rely on in various aspects of life. Whether it was seeking assistance with academic tasks like formatting my dissertation or receiving support from my wife in editing social media posts, I understood the power of leveraging the skills and competencies of those around me.

Until university, I was unaware of terms like 'extrovert' and 'sanguine' to describe aspects of my personality. In my first year at university, I joined the University of Exeter NOOMA Society, a multicultural Christian group led by a dyslexic student pastor passionate about leadership. Through engaging activities and introspective questionnaires, the society encouraged us to explore our leadership styles and capabilities. This experience was pivotal, shaping my perspectives on leadership and reinforcing the belief that everyone possesses the capacity to lead in their own way.

Leadership cannot exist in isolation; it inherently involves other people. True leadership, in my belief, should stem from a deep love for humanity. As a person of faith, I regard Jesus as the epitome of leadership, emphasizing the importance of loving one's neighbour as oneself. While achieving profits and meeting key performance indicators are significant, genuine leadership must have love as its core element.

In my second year of university, I had the opportunity to apply my leadership philosophy as the president of the university's African Caribbean Society (ACS). This role marked a significant milestone for me, considering my lack of confidence in my teenage years, compounded by hurtful labels like 'spastic' and 'retard'. The transition to being addressed as 'Mr President' by my peers was nothing short of euphoric. At the society's Annual General Meeting (AGM) I delivered a passionate speech outlining my vision for the ACS, concluding with the rallying cry, 'Vote Tumi so that I can bring this vision to you.' However, the real work began after securing the role, as I was tasked with transforming my vision into reality.

Being president of the ACS proved to be the perfect fit for me. Despite my challenges with dyspraxia, I excelled in this role, leveraging my strengths to drive the society forward. I possessed a keen understanding of the big picture, and envisioned not only the society's potential during my tenure, but also the legacy it could leave in the years to come. My leadership style was characterized by a wealth of ideas, coupled with an entrepreneurial flair. With my brain functioning as an 'ideas factory', I constantly sought innovative ways to enhance the society's impact. Moreover, my interpersonal skills made me approachable and enabled me to represent the society effectively. Recognizing my limitations, I assembled a committee whose skill sets complemented mine. Together, we worked seamlessly, with each member contributing their strengths to achieve our goals. Through effective delegation and collaboration, I led a team of eight exceptional leaders to quadruple membership, triple our profits and lay a solid foundation for future success.

Despite the challenges and obstacles along the way, my experience as president of the ACS reaffirmed my belief in the transformative power of leadership driven by love and fuelled by a commitment to service and excellence.

In my fourth year as an undergraduate, I continued to hone my leadership skills as the president of the NOOMA Society. During committee meetings, I found myself generating multiple ideas, often presenting five different concepts for discussion. I realized that fostering an environment where ideas could flow freely was essential, as each idea had the potential to offer unique perspectives and solutions. This approach led to fruitful discussions and ultimately contributed to the success of our initiatives.

These experiences were recognized when I received Exeter's Leaders

Awards, a testament to the impact of my leadership journey. I learned that having a clear vision was paramount, and I didn't need to know every detail of how that vision would manifest. Instead, I focused on my leaning into my strengths, thereby fostering a team culture where competent individuals could collaborate effectively to bring our goals to fruition.

One advantage of leadership is the ability to tailor a team to fit one's skill set perfectly. However, transitioning into the workplace proved challenging. Despite my leadership experience and academic achievements, I struggled to secure roles in programmes like the NHS leadership schemes. Unfortunately, my performance on psychometric tests hindered my success, highlighting the disconnect between my leadership abilities and traditional recruitment processes.

In my current professional role, I lack the opportunity to lead teams or delegate tasks, instead finding myself on the receiving end of directives. To thrive in this environment, I recognize the need to develop strategies to become a better generalist, enhancing my proficiency in tasks that do not naturally align with my strengths. As I navigate these challenges, I am aware of the changing dynamics within my tribe and community. While their support was instrumental in the past, I understand that their capacity to assist may be limited. Moreover, the value placed on independent workers in the workplace further emphasizes the importance of refining my skills as a self-sufficient contributor. Despite feeling like a square peg in a round hole at times, I remain committed to maximizing my potential in my career. Through reflection and assessment, I am exploring ways to adapt and evolve, ensuring that I can make a meaningful impact in my 9–5 role while staying true to my leadership ethos and values.

Many of the individuals I collaborated with during university have gone on to achieve remarkable success in their careers, and I often come across their LinkedIn updates as they ascend the career ladder. While I am genuinely happy to see their achievements, I am reminded of a saying from my mother: 'They do not have two heads.' This serves as a reminder that there is no reason why I should not continue to progress in my career and further develop as a leader. I am inspired by the accomplishments of my peers, but I also recognize that each person's journey is unique. Just because others are excelling in their careers does not mean that I am any less capable or deserving of success. Instead, I view their achievements as a source of motivation and encouragement to strive for excellence in my own endeavours. As I continue to pursue my career goals, I am committed to making a positive impact in my world. Whether it be through my professional accomplishments, leadership endeavours or contributions to my community, I am dedicated to leaving a lasting and meaningful legacy. With determination, perseverance and a strong sense of purpose, I am confident that I can achieve my aspirations and make a difference in the lives of others.

CHAPTER 3

Advice

☑ **DO** expect to experience discrimination.

What? Yes. If you are a neurodivergent leader you are likely to be discriminated against at some point. I have been told I am 'brave for admitting I am ADHD'. I have been in business meetings where someone points out that they remembered me for the short skirt I was wearing last time we had met. I was asked where I 'schooled my children' in a business meeting as a proxy for identifying my class. Expect it, plan for it and get yourself some reflection space to process what will happen. When I was younger, I didn't quite process the impact of all this, and it is only as I now see similar playing out with my colleagues that I truly understand the weight I have carried of these subtle slights and misdirections that undermine credibility. Ableism, ageism, sexism and classism have affected me, and in true neurodivergent style, I found it odd in the moment. I had a weird feeling of something not being right but couldn't pinpoint it until after. Reflect on where you might experience discrimination and subtle slights, and get some support for handling it.

☒ **DON'T** assume that all negative feedback is discrimination.

I was too direct and I did wear my heart on my sleeve, and yes, that is an ADHD trait, but it is also inappropriate for management. Being a neurodivergent thinker doesn't absolve me of the responsibility to manage the relationships I have with others. Working on relationships is relevant for gaining enough credibility to be offered a leadership position but also vital practice for when you are a leader and you have more power over people.

☑ **DO** aspire to be the best version of yourself.

Work on yourself. Don't head into a leadership journey without making space for self-reflection and personal development. This is necessary for all leaders. As I explained, there are serious consequences of toxic leaders and defensive, unchecked coercive and controlling leadership styles. As a leader, you need to be guarding against them, both in yourself and your colleagues. Neurodivergent people are more likely to have experienced ostracism and trauma. Trauma might lead to developing so-called 'dark triad' traits as a protective mechanism, but it might also make you vulnerable to those exhibiting coercive traits. But healing changes our brain, just like trauma, and working on yourself will lead to improvements.

☒ **DON'T** try to be a perfect leader.

A common response to trauma is actually perfectionism.[1] You can waste a lot of cognitive energy trying to heal yourself by being the best, most helpful, most valuable leader. Nonsense. For starters, it doesn't exist. A perfect servant leader is not ideal in a crisis when decisions need to be made swiftly and without negotiation. No one in the Covid-19 crisis wanted to spend time in a democratically organized scrum debating the right responses. They all breathed a huge sigh of relief when the leadership team presented a top-down plan for remote working and reassured them as to how long the money would last in a downturn. So focus on being you and leading in the style that suits you best. Find people to balance you rather than trying to be someone you are not. Masking is exhausting and leads to burnout. An approach like acceptance and commitment therapy or coaching (ACT)[2] can be really helpful here. ACT supports you to think about your values and weigh up decisions against them, observing yourself in the moment rather than judging your success or failures. I found ACT coaching really healing after a prolonged period of trying to change myself to not make mistakes. Similarly, explore appreciative inquiry[3] to help you draw out the positives.

☑ **DO** look outside your current culture for guidance and insight.

It's easy to fall into leadership traps by accepting current convention as 'normal' when it is, in fact, a product of the time and space in which we live. For example, before feminism (and this is still the case in many communities) women were (are) assumed to be biologically unsuitable for leadership due to their alleged neurotic sensibilities and smaller brain mass. Thank goodness the likes of Mary Wollstonecraft and Sojourner Truth didn't accept these limitations! Likewise, we currently operate in a paradigm in which corporate leadership is predicated on personality characteristics such as extraversion, which don't always deliver the goods. What can we learn about leadership from Buddhism? What can religious leaders learn about psychological safety from LGBTQIA2S+ communities? Go outside what you have been taught to challenge your assumptions.

☒ **DON'T** assume you can take shortcuts to access cross-cultural knowledge.

Diversity communities are wary of outsiders for good reasons. You can't just march in. You'll need to signal safety and a certain level of self-education before you approach. I felt very much part of the gay communities in England and New York in the 1990s. But I would still wait to be invited to conversations, because I have not experienced rupture or discrimination because of my sexuality. You can learn through books, videos and online discussions. Bide your time and don't expect other marginalized people to educate you for free. You can get started online in social media forums, reading books and watching documentaries. Listen. Learn.

☑ **DO** take responsibility for your work.

If you have been given a role, own it. Developing a leadership journey means seizing opportunities and being seen as reliable. Now, as a neurodivergent person, you may find that sometimes your health or well-being gets in the way of this, but there is nothing stopping you from owning that and managing expectations by making it clear to others that your situation has changed. I say to young aspiring professionals all the time – no one expects you to be perfect, but we do expect you to communicate. If you're going to miss a deadline, let someone know before they chase you for it so that they have time to reorganize at their end. If you are stuck on a task or having an ethical dilemma about it, say so early so that it can be resolved before it becomes late or urgent. I see so many neurodivergent leaders still needing reminding of this! An unwritten rule is that no one is going to promote you if you dump them in it. Even if you have the best ideas. Reliability and keeping people informed matters. End of.

☒ **DON'T** wait to be asked.

You need to show leadership potential before anyone will place their faith in you. People who wait to be asked don't get asked, simples. This isn't the same as acting outside your remit. You have to think through the actions you'd like to take and present them as options, in case you've missed something essential about the bigger picture that only your boss has knowledge of. This is another unwritten rule, but take it from me, the brilliant person hiding all their genius in the corner and not telling anyone about it will rarely be discovered. Excruciating as this might be at first, you have to put yourself out there. If bravado is not your thing, find a mentor or close colleague you can trust to test your insights and who won't steal them and pass them off as their own (yes this happens).

☑ **DO** present your work and ideas well.

Presentation skills count when you are proving yourself, annoying as that is. Jacqui Wallis, my business partner, has a saying that sometimes direct reports ask us to 'mark their homework'. C or a B+ grade work might get you a qualification in education but it won't win you a contract or be good enough to sell to a client. We need A-grade work in our careers, and if we're handing in B- and C-grade work, it means we're expecting someone else to tidy it up. I have regularly promoted people whose work I don't have to 'mark'. This isn't the same as teaching and developing; I actually love working with people who are doing new things, and showing them where they need to develop their content by marking up their work and sending it back. But in terms of work within your remit, it is a subtle and non-verbal communication that you respect my time when you take care to make your work finished and well presented. Those of us with a propensity to typos and errors need a strategy for our best work – assistive technology, copyeditors, printing it out before checking it – there are lots of ways to improve, and a good coach can help you work out a strategy for you.

☒ **DON'T** beat yourself up about your neurodivergent challenges.

We have a tendency to present what works for us. I am hyperlexic, so I write too much for some people. Jacqui, my colleague, is dyslexic and prefers me to summarize or talk it through, and she makes the most glorious PowerPoints I have ever seen. She has spent hours beating herself up about slow reading and I have spent hours trying to learn the right 'rules' of PowerPoint. But together, we work well! I am better off working on the content and flow and asking for help with the graphics. I can send her a written document and she can turn it into a visual delight. She can send me a rough draft and I can turn it into ordered prose. If you struggle with formatting documents, either choose a presentation format that works for you, take some time to learn or ask for help / delegate. But do remember that it is important! You need to strategize around it rather than assume people will overlook it.

☑ **DO** listen to your emotions and instincts.

Oh, it is so easy to be blown about in the breeze when you lack confidence in your own leadership and decision making. If you struggle with internal referencing in regard to what is good or not, seek wise counsel. Have a few trusted colleagues or family members you can debrief with, or a coach, rather than letting yourself be drawn into situations that won't work. This is where I did the most work in my leadership journey, for sure. An emotion is a signal, a message to our conscious mind to pay attention. It requires reflection, even if you decide the emotion is a trauma response, an overreaction or a symptom of being tired rather than a warning. But don't suppress them; they didn't magically appear from nowhere. Train your attention to notice what is happening around you when you experience strong emotions or instincts. What did you realize, see or hear just before the emotion? Emotions are either an indication that something is wrong / right, or they can lead us to better self-awareness of our patterns and triggers. Both are extremely helpful.

☒ **DON'T** assume that your inferences are true.

When we operate as outsiders, we very often have different social rules from those around us. What we see as insincere may be intended as tactful. What we see as resistant might be intended as patient. Again, this is a time for wise counsel, but also continuing to interact with people who are different from you so that you can learn more about the assumptions you are making. Taking time to debrief and unpack miscommunication is without doubt the most rigorous self-development I have engaged in. Start with the assumption that very few people get up in the morning intending to be mean, abrupt or to cause dissent. Give people the benefit of the doubt. Most of the people you are disagreeing with are not trying to malevolently derail you. They are more likely to be misunderstood, coming from different values, and you might find common ground if you hold them in respect and remain curious about their perspective.

☑ **DO** celebrate the success of the people around you.

Notice what you appreciate, notice what you think is worth celebrating; this will light your way to your goals and help you build allies and collaborators. Most people have anxieties, worries about whether they are good enough, a need for external validation and appreciation. Being a celebrator is a lovely way to start reforming your thinking towards solutions, aspirations and a positive affirmation. I had to consciously develop this trait, but in some circles I am now known for it. It costs nothing and it generates so much joy and positive thinking. You know you can reprogramme your social media algorithms like this, right? If you share likes, appreciative comments and repost what you love rather than what makes you angry, your feeds will start filling up with more things that you love. Social media platforms are all trained on what you engage with. Your brain is not dissimilar.

☒ **DON'T** compare yourself to others.

You have no idea what other people are experiencing on the inside. You have no idea what advantages they have. A friend recently asked me how I managed to get so much done when she was struggling to organize a major project while solo parenting two neurodivergent teenage boys. She was after strategies and tips for planning and managing procrastination. I responded that I had an active partner as a parent and that I sometimes take ADHD drugs to get me started when I get stuck in a procrastination loop. I don't think this is what she was expecting, but it certainly helped her to stop giving herself such a hard time! Social comparison wrecks relationships, ambition and success in my experience; I have had times where it has eaten me up and spurred thoughtless comments and actions.

Focus on what you want and what you can achieve with the resources you have, on what will make you happy rather than what others think of you. I realize this is easier said than done, and it took many decades for me to achieve it, but I wish I had known earlier how much difference letting go of comparisons would make to my mental health.

CHAPTER 4

Doing the Work

Understand the biases people have about you and work with them

In Chapter 1, I outlined the various leadership styles and personality types and how these are culturally bound by our neurotype, but also by our race, gender, age, sexuality, class and more. Use the blank table below to explore your own identity as a leader, what people might assume about you, and how you buck that trend. I'll show you what I mean in the following table:

I am...	People assume...	However, I...
I am an ADHDer	People assume that I will always be extraverted, self-focused and will interrupt people	However, I often recognize people who are in great distress, even when they don't verbalize this directly. I can hear a tone in someone's voice, or a slight halting in their speech that flags this for me, and I know they are not okay. I am sometimes the only person who spots it and acts on it
I present as a cisgendered heterosexual woman	People assume I will be deferent and modest and naturally good at servant or transformational leadership	However, I have learned to put myself first in terms of care for my energy levels and volunteering for roles where I can lead. I have learned that servant leadership requires boundaries and engagement from colleagues
I am a white person raised mainly in the UK	People assume I will adhere to the social niceties of the UK, uptight, blind to the privilege I hold, and find leadership easy because I am part of the dominant race	However, my leadership style is more direct and sincere. My openness is more typical of the New Jersey origins of my family in which politeness is experienced as being uptight. I am working on understanding my privilege and processing the paradox of having done nothing to deserve this head start on leadership confidence while simultaneously not always feeling confident

I am an extravert	People assume that I am confident in social situations	However, I am often very socially anxious, particularly in the presence of groups of other white, middle-class women, because I know they will expect me to be like them and I am not always. I mask this by talking too much, which makes it even worse! I often need two days to decompress from a social event, which I didn't realize until my forties, meaning that I was frequently overwhelmed

I am...	People assume...	However, I...
Neurotype:		
Gender:		
Race / ethnicity:		
Sexuality:		
Age:		
Class:		
Health status:		
Personality type:		
Anything else:		

Emotional intelligence

Consider some emotional intelligence characteristics[1] and notice your responses to them. Can you think of a time that you've done each of these well, and a time when you have struggled?

Emotional awareness. Individuals with this competence:

- Know which emotions they are feeling and why.
- Realize the links between their feelings and what they think, do and say.
- Recognize how their feelings affect their performance.
- Have a guiding awareness of their values and goals.

Accurate self-assessment. Individuals with this competence are:

- Aware of their strengths and weaknesses.
- Reflective, learning from experience.
- Open to candid feedback, new perspectives, continuous learning and self-development.
- Able to show a sense of humour and perspective about themselves.

Self-confidence. Individuals with this competence:

- Present themselves with self-assurance and have presence.
- Can voice views that are unpopular and go out on a limb for what is right.
- Are decisive and able to make sound decisions despite uncertainties and pressures.

Self-control. Individuals with this competence:

- Manage their impulsive feelings and distressing emotions well.
- Stay composed, positive and unflappable, even in trying moments.
- Think clearly and stay focused under pressure.

Trustworthiness. Individuals with this competence:

- Act ethically and are above reproach.
- Build trust through their reliability and authenticity.
- Admit their own mistakes and confront unethical actions in others.
- Take tough, principled stands even if they are unpopular.

Conscientiousness. Individuals with this competence:

- Meet commitments and keep promises.
- Hold themselves accountable for meeting their objectives.
- Are organized and careful in their work.

Adaptability. Individuals with this competence:

- Smoothly handle multiple demands, shifting priorities and rapid change.
- Adapt their responses and tactics to fit fluid circumstances.
- Are flexible in how they see events.

Innovativeness. Individuals with this competence:

- Seek out fresh ideas from a wide variety of sources.
- Entertain original solutions to problems.
- Generate new ideas.
- Take fresh perspectives and risks in their thinking.

What do you notice about when you successfully manage emotional intelligence and when you don't?

. . . .

. . . .

For me, tiredness is critical. When I am tired my ability to recognize and respond to my own emotions is compromised. I am more likely to act impulsively, let things go that I should act upon, act when I should wait, or get in a flap about change. Developing a chronic health condition that leads to serious fatigue has meant I am going back to the beginning of my emotional intelligence journey and relearning new strategies to handle emotions when tired.

Identity and leadership traits

Answer the following questions:

1. Which of your stereotypes give you a leadership advantage in your current context?

    ....

2. Which stereotypes are a disadvantage?

    ....

3. Which stereotypes about you are true?

    ....

4. Can people's assumptions about you derail you, like being thought of as 'trying to be like a man' did for me? What happens?

    ....

    ....

5. Can you think of a time you have been discriminated against in your leadership journey?

    ....

    ....

6. From where did you draw support in this event?

    ....

    ....

    ....

    ....

7. From where can you draw support to unpack your own internalized stereotypes?

    . . . .

    . . . .

    . . . .

    . . . .

8. What are the characteristics and demographics of your inspirational leaders?

    . . . .

    . . . .

Creativity

We have looked at intelligence as a predictor of leadership success, but, for neurodivergent people, intelligence is somewhat loaded, and creativity isn't always measured as part of intelligence assessment. However, it is widely reported that creativity is a strength for neurodivergent people. Creativity can be problem solving, it can be fixing something that has annoyed everyone for ages, it can be suddenly seeing a gap in the market or a flaw in our assumptions. Consider your frame of what you think of as creative work. For example, memes are creative, as are PowerPoints and blogs.

Do you consider yourself creative or able to solve problems?

. . . .

Where does / could your creativity come from? Are you like me, and it starts with being annoyed at something that should be better but isn't? Or do you have a different process?

. . . .

. . . .

When does creativity start for you?

Maybe you need three days of clear space in your diary before you can be creative. Maybe it starts with a conversation. Or taking part in something completely different from normal.

....

....

Write what you know about your own creative process in this box (or outside the box):

```



```

If you are stuck, ask three people who you think of as creative and / or good problem solvers how they do it. Ask for examples. Ask them where they do it. With what tools or equipment. What actions they take. Compare your responses to theirs and then write what might work for you in (or outside) the box.

Self-organization

Being considered reliable and able to deliver is often necessary in the leadership journey. To gain and cope with responsibility, you need a baseline of organizational skills that will inspire trust in your leadership. However, this is often an area in which neurodivergent people really struggle.

Rate yourself out of 5 on the following, where 5 = great and 1 = not great at all:

Managing your time	Meeting deadlines	Prioritizing tasks	Presenting written or graphic work	Remembering all your obligations	Organizing information and resources

For example, I am terrible at managing my time but excellent at meeting deadlines because my fear of letting people down is so high! As a result, I need to work on managing my time because otherwise I will make myself ill.

Consider the following resources that you might have available for you to help with self-organization. If you don't have these resources, perhaps give yourself some credit for how well you are doing and plan some longer-term changes?

Resource	I have this	Could I find this?	Notes
Flexibility on where and when I work to self-organize			
Choice over workload and obligations I take on			
People I can rely on to help me with self-organization by talking it through or delegating			
IT skills			
Assistive technology such as a diary planner, mind maps, memory aids or literacy support			
Self-awareness skills to predict what I am likely to struggle with and plan around it			
State of health that gives me resources to work on things I find hard			

Verbal communication

Leadership often requires public speaking, and managing others typically requires some form of verbal communication skills. Note, however, that I include text-to-speech technology within the realm of verbal. Non-speakers can lead beautifully via their writing – Google Elizabeth Bonker's valedictorian speech for a great example.* I speak louder and faster the more anxious I am. This is really counterproductive because it makes people assume the very opposite (i.e., that I am confident), and, as a female, this makes me stick out like a sore thumb. However, this does not mean I lack communication skills. But context is important! I have practised public speaking through amateur dramatics in my local community and this has helped me to overcome my fears, and I have got much better at this in later years.

1. How does your identity affect your communication?

   ....

   ....

2. In what environments do you communicate at your best?

   ....

   ....

3. About which topics can you communicate really well?

   ....

   ....

4. Which communicators do you admire and why? What do they have in common?

   ....

   ....

---

*   See www.youtube.com/watch?v=8g5aJExZQwg

5. Where can you practise public speaking?

....

....

....

6. Think of a time you handled a conversation really well. What happened?

....

....

....

7. Where can you practise having difficult conversations?

....

....

....

Earning it

What is your metaphor for putting in the work? Are you like the dancer, putting in hours of practice and toning, turning up to multiple auditions and handling rejection? Or do you have a different experience?

Speak to three people whose leadership you admire. They can be a parent, a community member, someone from a religious group instead of a work colleague. Ask them the following questions:

1. Where did you learn how to be such a good leader?

....

2. What do you do to make it work that people don't see?

....

....

3. Do you think you have the balance right between work and rest?

· ·

4. What do you consider your advantages and disadvantages in terms of putting in the work to develop a leadership journey?

My advantages, for example, are being raised in a white family in the UK where no one was addicted to substances or in jail, and where my parents had broken the class barrier with university degrees. Neither of my children or my partner are disabled. Until my forties, I was in excellent health myself and had an extraverted personality, which meant I could at least introduce myself to strangers, even when I was anxious and coming on too strong! I was born in an era that meant I went to university for free and could afford to get on the housing ladder. I have strong literacy and numeracy skills.

My disadvantages are that I now have a health condition that affects my energy levels. I have a trauma background, anxiety and a neurotype that meant I struggled at school even though I am hyperliterate and numerate. I didn't have any financial help after I left home at the age of 16 and worked from 13 as my family were not rich, to the extent that I now know is possible. My gender means I have to attend to presentation and emotional resilience more than my male counterparts, which can make me resentful. My ADHD means that I regularly take on too much and don't have enough time to process.

Now consider your own situation in terms of putting in the work. What are your advantages and disadvantages?

Advantages	Disadvantages

In my list, I have focused on the things I cannot control about my life that give me advantages and disadvantages compared to others. But there are other aspects that enable me to put in the work I can control. For example, I have a strong work ethic and I have stuck to work I am good at, and even when it wasn't well paid, I enjoyed it. I married someone who doesn't ascribe to gender norms either and is an active and equal co-parent. I got a dog for the family to force the need for better work–life balance. I made myself go to the gym / run / eat well even when I wasn't in the mood so that I could be well enough to handle a heavy schedule.

What advantages can you or have you facilitated for yourself that enable you to work on your leadership journey?

Self-awareness development

What is your Genius Within? By that, I mean what are you so good at that it doesn't even feel like an effort?

....

....

What feedback do you get frequently?

....

What feedback would you like to get?

....

....

Where can / do you engage in self-development with other people who can help you learn more about yourself? This could be a religious group, a recovery community, an online advocacy community, a coach, workshops and more.

....

....

What does being your authentic self mean to you?

....

....

....

In which environments are you masking?

....

....

....

In which environments are you able to de-mask?

....

....

....

What do you want to have happen?

....

Ambition

I hope that by now you have Googled Reese Witherspoon's Glamour Women of the Year speech, and reflected on whatever assumptions you may have of her as a pretty white woman with means, and what that signifies for her leadership! Consider her ambition questions that she asks at the end of the speech:

1. What is it in your life that you think you cannot accomplish?

   ....

   ....

2. What is it that people have said you cannot do?

   ....

   ....

3. How would it feel to prove them all wrong?

   ....

   ....

Consider my learning journey of turning jealousy into ambition. What are you jealous of right now in your circle? Who is doing something you would like to emulate?

Write down your goals here:

Who is doing something that you think you could never achieve? What is it?

....

....

What would you like to do instead?

....

....

How can you celebrate this person?

....

....

SURVIVING LEADERSHIP

In this section we will explore how to survive a leadership journey while being neurodivergent. Our well-being is not a given. We have typically come from a childhood where we developed hang-ups as a result of being the proverbial square peg in the round hole at school. And that's at best – it is possible that you have other issues to deal with as well. When I was forming my leadership journey, I was working on some deep personal healing and self-development, but none of it prepared me for the clash of being marginalized and powerful at the same time. The first few years of actually being a leader and running a company were a crucible, which I am not sure I would have maintained if I had had the choice. I was running headlong into my own internalized ableism, sexism, shame and that of those around me. I was naive. I genuinely thought that I could be fair to everyone and that, as a result, everyone would just play nicely and perform at work. I believed I could create a safe space where the lack of corporate insincerity would be as healing for everyone else as it had been for me as a consultant. I was very, very wrong. First, it's a lot harder than it looks. Second, not everyone will respond in the way that you expect. I have therefore dedicated this section to the learning journey of self-care and well-being because, in the end, it was only when I properly learned to trust and care for myself that I began to create the psychological safety around me that others needed as well.

CHAPTER 5

Work and Well-Being

In this chapter I will outline three different theoretical approaches to managing your well-being in a leadership role: balancing your job demands and resources, understanding relationship conflicts and psychological safety. There are many more in the occupational psychology literature, but I have selected these three because they are particularly pertinent to neurodivergent thinkers.

I had the privilege of studying for my Master's in Organizational Psychology with one of the world's leading experts on well-being at work, Professor Rob Briner. He has a fantastic lecture on YouTube that I encourage you to watch because it charts the development of our Western knowledge on workplace well-being through the ages.* It starts with the idea of stress at work, which we first started researching in the 1960s in management science, and is now a leading cause of sickness absence from work.[1]

Before we start unpacking well-being, I want to pause on a reframe of stress for you, as Professor Briner did for me. We've got some kind of weird toxic positivity narrative going in Western society that stress is always bad and that our job is to avoid it. But research shows that the relationship between stress and performance is curvilinear;[2] by this I mean that, as the stress goes up, so does performance. Yes, that's right, performance goes **up** with the stress, not backwards – until we hit a tipping point, and then the performance goes backwards. So the goal isn't to avoid stress; it is to understand where your limits are and to respond appropriately. In his talk, Professor Briner reminds us that usually the things we are most proud of

---

* See www.youtube.com/watch?v=73KQNB4Auvk

were stressful – having children, starting a business, getting a qualification, training for an athletic event, redecorating your house, training your puppy. Undoubtedly many jobs are harrowingly stressful, and that may explain why so many neurodivergent people seek entrepreneurship[3] rather than staying in larger systems where we have no control. However, we are also more likely to wind up jobless[4] or incarcerated[5] than neurotypicals. Managing our well-being is essential in all leadership journeys, and neurodivergent people have different well-being needs from the general population. But this should not be interpreted as seeking some sort of easy life where you coast along. Leadership will always require effort, stress and periods of high demand. The trick is identifying, predicting and remedying your personal tipping points.

Job demands and resources

A popular model of well-being at work is the job demands-resources model (JD-R model), conceptualized and researched by Professor Evangelina Demerouti and her colleague Dr Arnold Bakker.[6] In Chapter 4, 'Doing the Work', I encouraged you to consider your advantages and disadvantages at your identity level. In the JD-R model you reflect more practically on the job you have, the demands it places on you, and the resources you have at your disposal. In this model, the experience of stress occurs when the demands of the work exceed the resources. Control over your job is considered a resource – that is, the more flexibility and choice you have, the lower the stress. Many of us thrive when we can choose where and when we work because we have sensory overwhelm needs and hypersocial situations can be stressful. Some of us can concentrate more effectively or use our assistive technology when we are in quieter, more controlled spaces. That said, I do my best writing work in cafes, on trains and planes and when listening to fast-paced music! But rarely in an open plan office or draughty workshop. I'm going to explain a specific neurodivergent demand that sets us at a disadvantage to our peers.

Sensory sensitivity is often associated with autism but it is not limited to one neurotype. Many neurodivergent people experience acoustic, tactile, visual, olfactory, gustatory, vestibular, proprioceptive and / or interoceptive sensitivity, or indeed lack of sensitivity. We might have difficulty separating input that should get our attention from input we should ignore, such as background sound, bright décor and food smells in public places. In case you are not well-read on neurodivergence yet, or indeed not neurodivergent yourself, let me take a moment to explain this. Neuroscientific studies have shown that there are observable differences in the sensory cortex of neurodivergent people.[7] We aren't making this up. We literally have more (and sometimes less) electrical activity processing our senses, which is experienced as hearing noises as louder, feeling temperature transitions as more extreme, and light, smell or taste as more intense. This is a serious demand in a modern world dominated by electrical noise, overpopulation and city living. You're not being sensitive, you ARE sensitive. I am noise sensitive. I can tell the difference between a song played via digital streaming versus vinyl. Digital noise is thinner, more treble-based and sounds scratchy in my ears. This noise sensitivity can translate into finding social situations draining, and is compounded by living with different social codes, such as how much you like to speak, make physical contact, how direct you are, etc.

Disability adjustments represent the additional resources that should balance the increased demands of being disabled and / or neurodivergent.* As a disability workplace needs assessor, I used to recommend remote working as a disability adjustment, but was often told by employers that it 'wasn't reasonable' and that people needed to come to work. And then, in 2020, the world undertook a global experiment in which jobs could be delivered remotely! In fact, my most-read *Forbes* article ever was at the start of the pandemic, when remote work became instantly reasonable for non-frontline workers across the whole world. For this reason, some neurodivergent people really benefited initially from the pandemic-enforced remote working; but in the long term, this initial relief also brought the risk of increased anxiety[8] and time-blindness.[9] Remote working isn't a panacea resource for all neurodivergent people. In our study of over 500 autistic people's work experiences, my colleagues Professor Almuth McDowall, Uzma Waseem and I found that availability of remote working wasn't effective in improving work experiences, but the sense of being accommodated was. This contrasts with the current thinking around disability accommodations

---

* Neurodivergence isn't automatically a protected disability characteristic. Disability status isn't typically based on a diagnosis, but the extent to which it affects you in normal everyday life.

where we are presented with tick lists of things we should have / provide but without the nuance that this is a conversation, a negotiation of what works best when. People don't want a transaction; they want to feel valued and accommodated. A sense of control is a resource – being bequeathed an adjustment isn't the same as having the agency to negotiate your own supports.

If you haven't explored the full range of possible disability adjustments for neurodivergent workers before you start your leadership journey, it is not too late. Leadership places additional demands on you that you might not have experienced in your early career. In my company Genius Within, we see thousands of clients each year for assessments and coaching, and we find that the first promotion is a typical tipping point for needing help. Imagine being a physiotherapist who spends their time working with people, using their visual and spatial reasoning ability to help patients solve problems around their movement, balance and dexterity. Great! Plays to a neurodivergent strength. Now imagine being promoted to the manager of the team where your job is to sit still and read other physiotherapists' case notes and reports. Suddenly you are using a different part of the brain – the visual and spatial areas are less used, and the literacy processing areas in demand. You might need a completely different set of supports. You can't concentrate on the busy ward now that your role involves reading; you need quiet. Your reading speed is now a large factor in your success. It's a completely different job from a neurocognitive perspective. My colleague Jacqui Wallis had a 30-year leadership career in media advertising before she found assistive technology. I spent 15 years as a qualified psychologist before I hired someone dedicated to supporting me with time management administration. These were resources that we may well have benefited from earlier in our careers, but we absolutely couldn't thrive as leaders without them now. Adjustment resources expand the demands we can handle and reduce stress.

Jacqui explains her learning journey on understanding cycles of stress, burnout and recovery in corporate management, followed by the revelation of adjustments:

> As I understand now, when anyone operates in a high stress state for long periods of time it has to have a negative impact. Every action

has a reaction. By the end of 25 years in advertising at a senior level, I found myself oscillating between peak performance and deterioration. And the periods of poor mental health got longer, as did the recovery periods, and the time back to my peak performance got shorter before I started on a decline again.

The pattern I was running was overwork. When something was hard, I would just work more hours. In my mind, it was only my time I was putting in – no one would know that I took twice as long to do something. I would send it overnight and it would be in their inbox as soon as they arrived at work. Work was my saviour; it was my safe space. I knew if I worked hard enough, or long enough, I would be able to achieve whatever it was that I was aiming for. But that overwork did have a price. And eventually I burnt out.

When I consider my experience as a neurodivergent leader, in hindsight, I know the changes I needed to make. I needed to allow myself the freedom to be brilliant at things I found easy. And to acknowledge the areas that I struggled with. I needed to find the confidence to be able to disclose those things without fear of failure. I needed to be able to work to my natural ebb and flow. Do the hours when I found the work was flowing, and to be allowed to rest when the day seemed hard and I had no energy to give. When I work with my team now, I openly acknowledge that we benefit from amazing strengths we have, but to acknowledge that as neurodivergence leaders we come with areas of equal struggle.

As a leader in Genius Within, we offer many different possibilities for adjustments when someone first starts or discloses – and we have a great deal of insight into which ones might work. Certainly, in my first week, we discussed which ones might work for me. I found some assistive technology that has transformed my email life! Who knew it didn't take an hour to write an email – turns out, not me!

Some adjustments needed agreement of the team, e.g., flexible start and end times, but others were about my ability to try out different strategies that work specifically for me.

I had some in-work coaching from one of our specialist coaches – and through that I had many 'coin drop' moments, where I understood my previous patterns and was able to find strategies that I could immediately put into practice, which are still benefiting me four years on.

During one of my first client meetings at Genius Within, I experienced that very real liberation of that way of working in action. I know I am not a good note taker. I find it hard to listen and make notes simultaneously. This struggle is not something I had previously admitted to. However, in my new role, I did confess, and immediately Nancy shared that she loved taking notes in meetings. She confessed that it helped her process the content of the meeting and to retain focus. Suddenly I was able to work at my best, and my colleague was able to work at her best. The meeting notes were taken, nothing was sacrificed, and the quality of the meeting was excellent (the client told us so), and I felt nothing short of euphoric. I understood – probably for the first time in my life – what it felt like, not just to be accepted, but to be appreciated for what you can do, and what sharing our skills can deliver in terms of performance and output. A good team is unstoppable, and right then we were a fantastic team! In an open, transparent culture where there was no shame and no stigma, there is literally no one stopping you from being your fabulous best!

It is a shame that Jacqui did not have these things in place already – her advertising career could have been more of a pleasure to her. As an assessor and coach working in corporate settings for over 20 years now, I can assure you that these reliefs are possible in all environments. The critical difference wasn't that Jacqui moved role, but that she felt able to disclose and ask for help. As the neurodiversity movement has grown, this is one of the key successes – more people able to come forward to see what might help rather than hiding in fear of being discriminated. There is much less stigma in big business now than in Jacqui's career building days of the 1990s and early 2000s, thank goodness. But it is my observation that there are generational differences. While Generation Z are starting to feel able to request reasonable scaffolding and flexibility, sadly too many middle-aged and older workers go through multiple burnout cycles before finding the relief of disability adjustments.

Burnout

While some stress can be motivating and too much stress can cause frustration, anxiety and discomfort, burnout is the next level. Burnout is characterized by despondency, lack of hope, apathy and emotional detachment. The additional sensory demands and masking experienced by neurodivergent people creates a higher stress level than the general population before we even apply minimal stress, which can lead to additional vulnerability to burnout. Dr Shae Wissell and her colleagues used the JD-R model to explore burnout with 14 dyslexic employees.[10] They found that the additional demands reported included fear of not meeting expectations, fractures to relationships and systemic organizational barriers. Those with experience of burnout described a sense of mental fatigue that comes with having to put more effort into delivering the same level of work as their peers, due to needing to mask sensory overwhelm and literacy-based communication. Dr Dora Raymaker and her colleagues conducted experiments with 19 autistic employees experiencing burnout,[11] and found it to be distinct from typical occupational burnout, primarily due to the lack of understanding they received from their colleagues. Burnout is a significant risk for all neurodivergent adults in the workplace, and a leadership role presents a particular challenge since you will have taken on accountability and responsibility, which is harder to shift to others when you need a break, as there are generally fewer leaders by definition.

Stress researchers have created self-assessment tools to measure levels of burnout, which they define on two axes of disengagement and exhaustion.[12] As well as the additional risks of neurodivergence, some studies have found that diversity and inclusion professionals experience burnout at higher levels than most occupations due to the dual role of having their identity tied up in their work.[13] For many neurodivergent leaders working in the advocacy space, this is compounded by being a sole trader, working without the support of colleagues, an HR department or someone to even pay the bills if you stop working for a while. The emotional labour of working in a social justice context where you are dealing with human rights, discrimination and a prevailing sense of injustice is draining.

One of the reasons I am writing this book is because I am increasingly concerned about the well-being of individuals taking a leadership role in our neurodiversity community without qualified support. In my company we have reflective practice sessions, one-to-one coaching, an employee assistance programme for instant remote counselling and referral to therapists if required. We have a rota for social media engagement at weekends. We have a no email policy out of office hours and use delayed send. But I remember when it was a smaller company and we didn't have those resources. I also remember that the internet wasn't always as fractious as it is now, and that weekend community engagement was a positive, uplifting experience, with fewer spats. If you're seeking to prevent burnout it isn't a 'once and done' plan; you need to shift your resources according to changing demands.

Dr Bernadette Dancy, a health psychologist and coach, who is neurodivergent herself, explains why neurodivergent burnout needs careful consideration:

> ND [neurodivergent] burnout is typically the exacerbation of ND traits or struggles, making it challenging for a ND person to perform daily cognitive and behavioural tasks. It's caused by excessive stress (amount or duration / exposure) and can last for an extended time, often until the stress is removed and the individual has time to recover emotionally and physically. This could take months to years. ND burnout can also happen really quickly, meaning some people burnout weekly – regrouping over a weekend (if by regrouping we mean being completely unable to do much other than sleep or have a duvet day) and reappearing at work on a Monday ready to 'go again' only to repeat the process again and again. This pattern is more likely to happen when someone has a high baseline of stress due to a history of ongoing / chronic stress (which is the case for almost all NDs), which will eventually lead to a bigger burnout / breakdown, which will most likely have physical and psychological symptoms and take a long time to recover from (we're taking months to years).
>
> When it comes to stress exposure there is no getting away from the fact that people experience physiological changes in order to help the individual tolerate / deal with the stress or demand they have been exposed to. This physiological stress response is actually very advanced and effective with chemicals (neurotransmitters and hormones),

increasing when needed and returning to baseline if sufficient recovery time is provided. However, the problems arise when an individual is exposed to chronic stress, meaning their body is perpetually exposed to physiological stress including raised cortisol. NDs have different cortisol responses to neurotypical individuals to begin with, meaning they're more likely to experience a stress response, but added to that, that most tasks and demands expose NDs to stress means that they're more at risk of chronic stress – the precursor to burnout.

I would recommend ND leaders pay more attention to rest and recovery. That they impose intentional periods of decompression and recovery after periods of high demand in order to allow their body and mind to tolerate stress better and the stress response to return to baseline. The amount of decompression / recovery time is specific to the individual and the baseline levels of stress that they started with. It takes practice to be aware of subtle signs and symptoms that stress is building, but once achieved, it is possible to plan ahead and put 'firebreaks' into their lives. A simple strategy might be to choose a work to decompress / recovery ratio. I personally use a 3:1 ratio, with one week of lighter or creative work without meetings or social engagement after three weeks of higher demand work.

I'm personally noticing that strict stress management isn't the elixir when it comes to preventing ND burnout. Yes, while stress IS a big part of burnout and will contribute to ND burnout, I'm starting to wonder if ND burnout can also happen independently of physiological stress. We need research that considers physiological and psychological monitoring of stress to prove this, and not just in ND people; we need this sort of research in stress / burnout across the board. It may be possible that neurotypical people burnout independently of physiological stress too; I just think ND people are more at risk because we're more sensitive to stressors and have a smaller bandwidth for things like sensory stress, social stress.

Here's why I say this. I manage my stress levels very intentionally, with a carefully curated diary and lifestyle that means I get good food, plenty of sleep, zero alcohol, the right type and amount of exercise and I work 5 hours a day. All of this means I have excellent heart rate variability (a measure of nervous system activity, thus physiological stress), but I have noticed I am still vulnerable to burnout. This appears to be more related to expending emotional energy, compassion fatigue, socializing and changes in routine (such as the children's school holidays every six weeks, meaning more parenting / 'parental burnout'). These are stressors to an ND brain, so it makes sense that they would contribute to burnout. BUT my physiological stress is low (as seen by heart rate variability remaining high); what I'm noticing in myself and my ND clients is that ND burnout is caused by (1) chronic stress AND (2) exposure to stressors specific to ND such as cognitive load, empathy, compassion, social engagement. The problem is, these stressors come from us doing things that we might really enjoy and want to do. (As a stress management coach who does a lot of corporate speaking, this is my life!)

Burnout prevention and response

Stress management approaches are sometimes thought of in terms of prevention and cure, or primary, secondary and tertiary.[14] Primary approaches operate on the conditions of work and attending to healthy working styles, such as having the right number of people for the workload, designing jobs where employees have control over their workflow, appropriate breaks, well-trained and effective leaders, good communication and safe, operational equipment. Secondary approaches include working on your personal habits and proactive approach to your well-being, such as taking exercise, engaging in a social network and eating well. Tertiary approaches are how you deal with stress when it comes, such as counselling, mindfulness or yoga and medical or clinical treatment. Too often at work we focus on tertiary stress responses and don't think about how to prevent it in the first place. The right time to get reasonable adjustments in place is before you have too much on to cope. So many times I have found myself in a total overwhelm and too stressed to explain to someone else the help I need!

Finding a sustainable pace to begin with, and responding quickly at the first sign of trouble, requires practice for many neurodivergent leaders. We're so used to subjugating our needs (e.g., sensory) that we often don't notice until it is too late. Sensory differences can make this worse, as can 'alexithymia' (the inability to name or recognize nuanced emotions).[15] I have a sensory difference in being hyposensitive to my feelings – I don't experience pain, for example. When my twins were toddlers, I would regularly realize I was freezing after being in the park for an hour in a t-shirt in January because I simply don't process my internal sensations (called interoception). This translates into my career as getting carried away with a momentum or an idea and following it through with hyperfocus until I realize, too late, that I have overcommitted myself and can only escape by letting others down or beasting myself to complete. As neurodivergent leaders, we should over focus on primary and secondary stress management measures and set up systems for ourselves that boundary self-care. We need a tertiary response on speed dial. Failing to do so as you take on responsibilities of leadership leaves you wide open for a burnout and a total derailment of your leadership career. Health coaches like Dr Dancy advise us to plan demands and resources annually; this is how elite athletes stay tip top.

My work has a natural rhythm, ebb and flow across the months, with conference seasons and busy periods as well as childcare peaks and troughs. By forward thinking and diarizing rest **before** the time crunches, I am more likely to handle them. But I didn't learn this until recently, and many times I have overexposed myself to an unmanageable workload. By the time I started working with Jacqui, I had learned enough to avoid the devastating corporate commando culture that pervades many workplaces, but I was still on a long journey of unpicking my relationship with self-care and investment, feeling worthy enough to deserve rest, etc. As she was being onboarded, working with her as a colleague and peer-to-peer mentor, intending to deprogramme her work addiction, I found a new layer of how embedded my own remained.

Nothing prepared us for what came next, as Jacqui explains:

> I won't lie, it took me some time to adjust to this new workplace culture (still ongoing!), moving from a culture that praised and rewarded overwork to one that wanted my best performance without the sacrifice of my long-term health. I have learned that good work performance could be sustainable.

I also want to talk about acquired neurodivergence and disability, as this has been a very real part of my recent journey. The Business Disability Foundation did some research that said that 83 per cent of all disabilities are acquired, and the average age of acquired disability is 53. We also know that 90 per cent of all disabilities are not visible. (I appreciate that not everyone will consider their neurotype a disability, by the way.)

My world was tipped upside down when, in 2022, I was diagnosed with breast cancer.

This news tumbled me into six months of treatment, during which I worked for some periods, and was off for other periods. When I came back to work, my spiky profile (as identified via our Genius Finder™ tool) had changed. One of my strengths had always been a good memory – I could remember my notes, the colour pen I used to make them, the side of the page, the doodles that ran alongside them. Suddenly, that visual memory ability dropped. Like a stone. It was no longer a strength; it was now a challenge.

In reality, what this meant for me was that I lost most of my short-term memory.

My words failed me – sometimes they still do, especially when I am tired or stressed – and I am more prone to misspelling and mistakes in written work.

BUT the amazing thing was, that now I had this information I was able to put in place strategies for me at work – but also in my life – that helped me manage – and in some part mitigate these new areas of challenge. Luckily for me, most of this cognitive change has been temporary. But my pre-illness memory spike is still not as high as it once was.

In stark contrast to my previous career, however, I tell people. I tell people not because I want to make excuses or have their sympathy, or to get out of delivering some work, but to keep me accountable and on track. To give myself the chance to be my best, even when my health is compromised. I make it okay to be imperfect and to strive to perform at my best in a way that doesn't compromise my overall self.

I am not unique, this happens all the time – people get ill, they have accidents, their cognitive profile changes. Sometimes it is temporary and it changes back; sometimes it doesn't.

I am still a great employee and a supportive colleague; I have a great range of skills and I am still a leader. I just have a couple more challenges I need to work through and make some adjustments.

But with the knowledge comes the power to make those necessary changes.

A new relationship at work, handing over the CEO control of the company I had built from the ground up, during a pandemic, while being in perimenopause and diagnosed with MCAS, and my dear colleague in treatment and recovery from cancer. Her departure from corporate leadership, learning a new industry and culture, then her diagnosis of a life-threatening illness. You would think that our relationship would be strained. In fact, it has deepened along with our relationships with our colleagues. I think a key factor is because we got so much better at supporting each other to rest, and focused on our mutual well-being during these years.

Drama and ego states

I found it interesting in Dr Wissell's paper[16] on dyslexic burnout that one of the three common causes of burnout was fractured relationships for neurodivergent people. It certainly rang true for me, and leads me to discuss one of the academic theories that I have found most useful in understanding how to manage well-being at work, both for me personally and for my team. Transactional analysis was instigated by the very wise Dr Eric Berne many years ago[17] in his seminal work *Games People Play*. Transactional analysis is rooted in the idea of archetypal responses that we defer to in conflict or stress. He introduced us to the ego states of 'parent–child–adult', which have become the foundation of substance misuse psychology (e.g., dependent and co-dependent). Transactional analysis is incredibly helpful for understanding power and power-imbalanced relationships in families and communities, but also careers. As a leader, you will be viewed as powerful, but, as someone with a history of marginalization, you will have experienced powerlessness. Dr Berne describes his colleague Dr Stephen Karpman's conceptualization of the drama triangle, in which there is a persecutor, a rescuer and a victim, as well as a bystander (drama diamond). Dancing between these roles is a great way to understand the pattern of fractured relationships and to find ways to heal them.

The persecutor role is defined by blame, calling out problems in others but not recognizing their own role and accountability. A victim position is experienced as helpless, unable to act and unhappy because of what others are doing to them. The rescuer jumps in to help, but simultaneously disempowers because they take over. A bystander is someone who should be engaged but who is deflecting responsibility. None of these roles make healthy relationships at work. A persecutor assumes they know best and wields their opinion without collaboration – the archetypal mean boss. A rescuer can take the form of a servant leader, someone who engages and listens but who doesn't give others the space to grow. Neither represent good leadership and leave their colleagues feeling disempowered (victim) or disengaged (bystander). A leader who feels unable to act, like a victim, or has disengaged, like a bystander, is also ineffective.

In organizational roles, we typically assume the stereotype of the manager as persecutor. Such managers are the source of much stress at work and they definitely exist! Indeed, a 10-year longitudinal study found having a bad boss meant people were more likely to have heart attacks![18] Now this doesn't have to be a direct correlation; being the sort of person who will put up with a bad boss might also mean you are more likely to put up with other unhealthy states, or that you feel like you have little choice over your finances and are more likely to be living in poverty. But the finding is stark. A Gallup poll famously found that people don't leave companies; they leave managers.[19] But like everything in management and leadership science, there is nuance to this claim. First, a different research arm found that good senior leadership and a healthy company can moderate the response to a manager who is out of their depth.[20] Further, one of the most common complaints about alleged bad managers isn't that they were mean (persecutor), but that they let colleagues get away with not pulling their weight (rescuer / victim / bystander).[21] I hope this explanation helps you realize that there are no 'good' drama roles. I have witnessed many people articulate that the rescuer role is the 'least offensive' when actually it can be highly toxic and totally derail a leader and / or their team or community.

As we discussed in Section 1, some marginalized leaders may trend towards the servant / rescuer style, and can therefore be derailed by martyrdom, rescuing or deference. This has a direct connection to our well-being and the primary responses we have to stress management. Being a leader does not mean being the person who does the most work. It does not mean that you relentlessly pick up all the work your team have failed to do (if they are victims or bystanders) during the week and crashing your weekend to catch up. Again, I have witnessed many leaders make this mistake – often because we were raised without wealth and are uncomfortable with earning more money than others. We equate money with hours worked, and feel we need to justify our pay increases. So consider decoupling pay from time or output: a pay rise on promotion is relevant to the practised speed at which you can undertake complex tasks and the amount of risk you bear in order to hold the accountability and responsibility. A higher salary that doubles your working hours is not a higher salary at all.

By focusing on your boundaries as a leader, you can actually be better at your job and give people the space to develop. I remember once being in a crisis at Genius Within and discussing how to get our geographically dispersed management team together to discuss a response. A colleague pointed out that it was the start of term and that some managers wouldn't want to travel. They had decided for their colleagues that we should exclude them from the discussion to protect their time and resources. Now family-friendly policies are at the core of my company, but making decisions for grown adults is not. I intervened, gave them the choice, and one woman made the decision to travel while the other dialled in via video. Making decisions for people places them unwillingly in a child role and is disempowering. It looks like care and can be hard to spot initially. But those who we treat like adults will rise to the occasion, and it is to the benefit of their career journeys to do so.

Direct communicators are sometimes interpreted as persecutors, even when they mean well. I have definitely experienced this, and indeed persecution is in the eye of the beholder. This is where the relationship between gender roles, neurodivergence, race, etc. becomes complex. Have I ever intended to harm a colleague? No. Have I ever unintentionally harmed a colleague by giving harsh feedback? Yes. And the complexity deepens when we dig into the psychology of those who accuse and blame – they are very often feeling like victims. My typical response to feeling victimized is to be angry, and the second I verbalize anger I am in danger of the persecutor role. We all respond to danger with a variant of flight / fight / freeze / fawn. These map neatly onto bystander, persecutor, victim and rescuer respectively.

My fight response is over-developed, which is great when I am being the social justice warrior, but rubbish when something isn't working out. There is also the rescuer / persecutor flip switch. Sometimes when we rescue those around us, we start to get fed up and realize that we've taken on too much, and then we get cross with them for sending too much our way, even though we offered. The best prevention technique I have learned so far is to be well resourced in the first place and manage my stress. We can unpick these dynamics by taking a step back and engaging our adult brains and talking to each other like adults.

Dr Chantelle Lewis, a sociologist engaged in academia at the University of Oxford, who also does social justice work and is the co-founder of the 'Surviving Society' podcast, describes her journey of overcoming her rescuer patterns in an episode that she generously gave me permission to transcribe:

> And I think over the past seven years we've witnessed some incredibly difficult and challenging times as a society. And I'm a doer. I'm a big doer. I'm also a people pleaser. I'm also someone that probably overworks and I think that I wanted to do something that contributed to these difficult times. I wanted to be part of something that contributed, and I didn't know what. I didn't know what that was for such a long time. You have something within your spirit where you're 'I know I want to make a difference, I know I want to help people, I know I want to create and I care so much about people.' What can I do? And it's a small thing, it's a tiny thing. But if I can help people. If I can contribute to the histories of our people that have created knowledge and education materials that can make life that little bit more liveable on a day-to-day basis just by actually knowing how society works, then that is something that I can do. And that has been a huge driver for me.

It's ['Surviving Society'] really tested me in terms of how I relate to people and how I understand myself in relation to people. The thing that I'm working on is my boundaries with working with people and how boundaries keep us safe. Boundaries create consistency, boundaries are productive, boundaries are loving, working on boundaries with work and life will be the test for me for the rest of my life. I know that. But it's something that I've worked through and I'm working with via what we do and what we have done at Surviving Society. And I don't know if I would have been able to realize that about myself this early in my life had it not been for this show. So yeah, I think that I definitely have issues when it comes to people pleasing. I definitely have got a very big heart, which means I constantly want to do stuff for people. And that's not always a positive thing. People need agency and people need to be able to help themselves. The other side of having a big heart is that I actually can be really controlling. And that's also embedded in things about me that I'm very committed to working on. And I think working with self-awareness and how my actions or how I work and how my personality and character impacts others, what I can do to set an example of how we're all imperfect, but we can all do better, is something that I just don't know if I would have been able to do had it not been for Surviving Society.

The concept of psychological safety

The concept of psychological safety was put forward by Dr Amy Edmondson,[22] and she defines it as 'a shared belief that the team is safe for interpersonal risk taking. For the most part, this belief tends to be tacit, [i.e.,] it is taken for granted and not given direct attention either by individuals or by the team as a whole.' It is an unwritten rule, rather than an explicit agreement. Psychological safety has been found to predict organizational performance and creativity,[23] particularly related to responding to crisis and opportunity. Psychological safety predicates include priority for safety, support, camaraderie, a focus on learning and an egalitarian approach to status and hierarchy with inclusiveness of individual differences.[24] As I am sure you can see, this is the opposite of the drama triangle. It is a phrase I am noticing used in the neurodiversity community of late relating to unmasking, but respect for individual differences is only a precursor of psychological safety.

The descriptions of unmasking in the neurodiversity space are actually more aligned to the experience of finding your in-group than psychological safety. Further, the formation of a new in-group is typically characterized by the opposite of psychological safety – a period where rules are fragile and so strictly adhered to, where the relief of finally finding people who consider you 'like them' is juxtaposed against the fear that you might be cast out. As I have said before, unmasking also has different implications for people who are minoritized by race or ethnicity, sexuality, transgender, and indeed gender – the ability to unmask is reduced. As well as needing to take steps to 'fit in', other minority / minoritized groups hold the pressure of needing to be perfect, of knowing they will be criticized more excessively for minor errors. Taking risks and feeling able to make mistakes is the critical element of psychological safety, and we do not currently have equal risk exposure footings between members within the neurodivergent community. Psychological safety is only manifest when people feel able to make mistakes and talk about their concerns, about risks, without serious rupture of relationships.

An interesting paper by Dr Daniel Costa Pacheco and colleagues in 2015[25] characterized an element of psychological unsafety as silence: 'Intentional withholding of ideas, information or opinions related to the workplace.' They conducted a review of psychological safety papers, noting the influence on employee voice / silence, and summarized the different types of silence that occur:

1. Acquiescent silence, when an employee plans to resign and withdraws.

2. Defensive silence, withholding facts for self-protection, to avoid being penalized.

3. Prosocial silence, withholding confidential information to protect others or the organization.

4. Deviant silence, remaining silent to deliberately make their supervisor or colleague look bad.

5. Diffident silence, composed of insecurities, self-doubt and uncertainty.

Dr Pacheco and colleagues found that the following categories are motivators or inhibitors of employee silence:[26]

1. Individual differences such as personality – levels of conscientiousness, assertiveness, ambition.

2. Job and organizational attitudes and perceptions such as the extent
   of organizational or work group identification, job satisfaction and
   breadth of their role.

3. Emotions, beliefs and schemas such as anger, fear and futility.

4. Supervisor and leader behaviour such as openness, consultation
   and ethical versus abusive leadership.

5. Other contextual factors such as a caring climate, formal mechanisms for sharing 'voice', hierarchical structures and change
   resistance.

Creating psychological safety in a workspace is thus personal and interpersonal. You can also build safety into the systems and processes of your
organizational routines, like the double loop learning approach mentioned
in Section 1. *Antifragile*, by Dr Nassim Nicholas Taleb,[27] explores this concept
using the metaphor of materials in physics. He explains that some materials,
such as metals, become stronger when stressed. The more you apply pressure to them, the tighter the molecules become. In a company, this looks
like a rigorous process for reflection on success and failure, leaning into
mistakes to learn from them. Processes such as quality management (e.g.,
ISO 9001) help to institutionalize learning at the organizational level and
make events safe to discuss and free from blame. In online communities
we need to lean further into content moderation and having stewards to
support conflict through to the solution. But as you can see from the work
on silence, this is not enough on its own. There is a role for community /
organization members as well; their own emotions, pre-existing beliefs and
individual differences will also nurture or disrupt psychological safety. As
a leader you can control the systems and processes of your domain, but
you cannot control the individual reactions of all members.

The most essential learning point from the work on psychological safety, for me, has been to plan for problems. By making the logical and predictable assumption that humans will not always be perfect and will sometimes disagree, we give ourselves permission to not feel devastated when this happens and we deploy our resources to prevention. Rejection sensitivity is a common trait for neurodivergents, and we need scaffolds here. Creating agreements and routines facilitate us to reason our way through a problem while acknowledging our fear responses to the problem. They provide a safe boundary for fear, which makes fear itself less fearful. If you are having a fear response, listen to it. But unpack it and avoid the drama triangle; this will allow you to lead authentically and without damaging your own or others' well-being. Creating structures to manage dissent when you are not experiencing dissent gives you a fighting chance of handling it from the adult ego rather than the parent or child.

Relationship rupture

Sometimes we work with people who are entrenched in a role. They might perceive the absence of being rescued as persecution. In my coaching work, I have found this a theme with clients who are used to being infantilized and helped. This then gets compounded by unhealed rescuers who dive in. I once delivered training to a charity that had coaches working with neurodivergent people. I outlined the drama triangle model for them and they pushed back, 'But it is our job to rescue people; that's what they expect and want.' I argued back: rescuing breeds dependency; they lose power, and you are locked into a co-dependency. Having other people feel dependent on you might feel very validating for **you**; it can be seductive as a form of valuing yourself with external appreciation. However, it is not sustainable, and it will not serve you or them long term.

Staying in adult mode when people around you are trying to engage you in parent / child dynamics requires strength! If you have set up good reflective practice routines, you will need them in these scenarios. I have spent a long time reflecting on interactions and trying to tease out if I was actually being unfair, or whether I was working with someone who would always interpret me as unfair unless I did their work for them or let them off the hook. And, like my anecdote about the managers who didn't want finance training, sometimes both positions are true at the same time. Understanding that two versions of reality have equal value, that there is not one truth (yours versus others), is a necessity in leadership and learning, and has helped me continue to hold others in high regard, even when I fundamentally disagree!

A peer and collaborator, Dr Tiffany Jameson, has been a board member of a large US-based corporation for many years, and also runs her own neurodiversity consultancy to support others. She shares her experience of the personal turmoil that accompanies fracture:

Nothing good comes without challenges. As a neurodivergent person, entrepreneur and manager of a consultancy, the traits associated with my neurodivergence can magnify my efforts in running and leading a business. The beauty of my agile and fast-processing brain, my empathy and my passion are significant contributors of why I am successful. But nothing is fully good or bad.

My neurodivergent traits are inconsistently represented in my day-to-day life but manifest as impulsiveness, minorly manic and, at times, depression. Because of this, I have to invest extensive resources in being self-aware of my moods and put in extra effort when my environment triggers some of the more intrusive traits. As a leader, I don't always have the option to be vulnerable nor let my intrusive traits affect those around me. I have to mask more than most because I am there to support my team. It can be very taxing, and often, these traits come out in some way. We may be leaders, but we are very much humans.

As a leader balancing the beauty and challenges of being neurodivergent, I am compelled to create a workplace that gives my team members the psychological safety to ask for what they need to be their best selves at work. But this does lead to the fine line between being a compassionate leader and still establishing boundaries necessary to run a growing business effectively. I have found it extremely difficult at times to make solid business decisions because of my compassion for my neurodivergent employees and my deep desire to see them succeed and thrive.

My friends and family console me constantly through reminders that

I am not responsible for someone else's happiness. I can only provide support, flexibility and allyship. It is inevitable that the ebbs and flow of our traits can be triggered, either positively or negatively, from our outside lives. And yes, this can seep into the workplace, regardless of our best intentions. My challenge comes from being empathetic and understanding that the outside world can impact someone's ability to work, collaborate and be a productive team member, but having to draw a line at some point at how understanding and flexible I can be while still running a sustainable business.

My consultancy advises businesses to be neuroinclusive. The pain and personal disappointment are magnified when I feel I have failed at this within my organization. It becomes hard to separate someone not fitting the business need from the human being. This is when my empathetic nature becomes my biggest weakness, often triggering my generalized anxiety disorder and depression. The difference with being neurodivergent is the magnification of these reactions and the extreme effort I put into being a calm and focused leader through a mask. This often leads to passing out or the opposite extreme of challenging exercise as the day progresses.

There is so much good that comes from being a neurodivergent manager. I wouldn't change a thing. That still doesn't make it easy.

Ruptured relationships are a source of stress and healing is a source of well-being. For neurodivergent or marginalized leaders this is particularly loaded because we often come with baggage from exclusion and lack internal references for what is right or wrong. Trauma and exclusion make us porous, too open to absorbing the negative messages around us. I advise having close allies you can trust. I didn't have enough of my own internal controls when Fiona Barrett and I began working together, but she provided wise counsel and reassurance. Equally, when she tells me I have gone too far, I backtrack and apologize. Immediately. She is a rock.

If you don't have those people in your life, find them. And learn to watch what people do, rather than what they say. Someone who is polite to your face but speaks ill of you to others is not your rock. If they are speaking ill of others to you, it is likely that they speak about you like that when you are not around. There's a fine line between gossip, needing a sounding board and trash talk. **Trust the people who treat you like an adult and bring their concerns about you to you.** I want to underline those last few sentences; they are possibly the most important advice in this whole book. Frequent and unboundaried trash talk is a red flag; it leads to lack of trust and fractured relationships – more on this in Section 3. It drives wedges and creates suspicion. Sometimes it is covert and disguised as care or worry about someone 'not coping'. The key is balance. Find allies who share hopeful stories and appreciative comments more than they share criticism. Find allies who show up when there is a problem, who take responsibility for their mistakes and don't defensively deflect issues to others. I have learned this lesson the hard way, both engaging in and being the topic of trash talk. I hope to save you some tears and some time by being brutally honest about this.

Summary

From synthesizing some well-being and relationship academic litera-ture against mine and my peers' lived experiences, I am reminded that neurodivergent leaders must balance more demands than neurotypicals and non-disabled people might never even notice. We must work hard on relationships – not just between the neurodivergent and neurotypical dynamic, but also within neurodivergence. Our neurotype patterns are not necessarily aligned, and we may create unhealthy dynamics by disagreeing too disagreeably, or by having expectations of each other that are unreal-istic. As a leader you have the power to influence the community you lead and serve by instituting plans and boundaries for managing conflict. In enacting these, you provide reassurance and psychological safety for the group at large, which is a hallmark of great leadership. But we must start with our own boundaries, well-being and psychological safety.

CHAPTER 6

The Reluctant Entrepreneur

I started Genius Within when my twins were five, because my husband and I were both consulting away from home, and one of us needed to be at home for the school run. I took a theme (neurodiversity assessment and coaching) that had run a thread through my consulting and partnership work, and decided to focus on it so that I could reduce the demands on my workload. The initial idea that it was built around was an online practice, but the time wasn't right for that yet, and so that aspect of the business never really got off the ground. As I was working through the ebb and flow of the initial failure, I began subcontracting out the neurodiversity coaching work that seemed to come to me regularly and without much sales effort. Genius Within, a company dedicated to supporting neurodivergent people to thrive in their careers, started to bring in money from services. In the first year I had seven subcontractors; by the second year we had 25. By that second year I was no longer in a micro practice – I had become a company leader by default. It was never my intention to build a services business, but I ran with it as it initially provided the work–life balance I craved and brought in enough money to pay the mortgage. Genius Within now has over 200 subcontractors on four continents with around 50 employees. Our engine is the coaching work that I learned in my twenties and developed via Access to Work since 2002.[1] We also deliver training, HR consulting and assessments, we work on employability contracts and in prisons, and we have a number of e-learning and online personal assessment and development services / apps.

The first few years of Genius Within's growth were exhilarating and exhausting in equal measure. I remember being astounded when I first billed £10,000 in a month; we now bill many times that in a week. It is no longer me, my kitchen table and my cat with occasional advice from my non-exec collaborators; it is a thriving business with a complete management team in which I am no longer CEO. Genius Within initially grew too fast for me to catch up with my leadership skills. There were times when my stress load was so high that in any other job I would have resigned, but I powered through because you don't really have a choice when you own the company – your only out is to sell. About two years in I was no longer able to work solely in school hours and had to work evenings after my kids were in bed. And then I could no longer do that and had to employ childcare. My ambition certainly did not stretch to where we are now, and my leadership skills were inadequate for many years. Being in a job you aren't qualified for is stressful; incompetence is stressful. I thought I could just work my way out of the strain and that we would get to a point where it would become easier. When we have the money to hire a finance person...when we have the money to hire an HR person...when we have the money to hire an IT person... But at each stage, our hires were typically six months after we really needed them, and in the interim it was often yours truly filling the gaps. I was chief cook and bottle washer for many years.

A very stressful part of this rapid growth was the people around me, some of whom came with me, some of whom ran out of steam, and some of whom ran out of patience with me. Some felt that I should have controlled the growth more strategically and provided a calmer environment for us all to catch up. It was hard to maintain the right levels of sustainable workload when every time we hit a new milestone a new opportunity presented itself. In retrospect, those people were often right! I didn't initially have an end goal, an exit strategy or a desire to seek investment to cover the gaps. My own rescuing style of just coping and carrying on was the dominant force in the business. We did it ourselves, often with bits of metaphorical tape to cover the cracks, and sailing on a wing and a prayer. It was very typically ADHD, and a big mistake of mine was to assume that others could hyperfocus through a bottleneck. This is an irony because the initial driver for the business was family-friendliness, and indeed, we have always been flexible about hours, location of work and part-time job sharing. I have learned that family-friendly policies aren't enough if the actual workload is not predictable. It was incongruent, which caused difficulties for me and my colleagues, some of whom assumed that I was being disingenuous when actually I was just lacking in my own personal development and healing journey.

Part of my mistake came from not having an accurate self-appraisal of my own worth. This sounds counterintuitive but bear with me. I did not appreciate that the reason I find some things easy is because they are talents. I can write thousands of words in a day. If I have five diagnostic assessments to write I can do them in a day. Others take a day over each report. I knew I was literate, but I didn't realize I was hyperlexic. I assumed that if I could do it, everyone could do it. I thought if I gave everyone the right encouragement and flexibility, they would be able to match my productivity, because all I needed was encouragement and flexibility. This is not true and I lost good colleagues on the way because I didn't adjust my pace or expectations. I rescued people when they said they were stressed and became resentful because I was already doing more than my fair share. I assumed that, like me, a week or so of downtime would enable them to catch up and then they would carry on at my pace. This isn't because I didn't care about them or was a demanding boss; it is because I didn't realize how unusual some of my skills were.

I don't want to trivialize how personally challenging this period was. I went through cycles of feeling deeply hurt, villainized and let down interspersed with growth and success. This period led to many sleepless nights, ruminating and running over what I could do differently, where my own failings were influencing my decisions, where I was justified and where, as I mentioned in Chapter 5, two people's versions of events were equally valid even when diametrically opposed. I had to hold a lot of this in during my day to day and project a sense of control even when I felt deeply out of control. I had some solid allies, but I also overshared with colleagues who I should have not burdened with my innermost worries or fears, and I made a few mistakes in trusting people who did not have my, or the company's, best interests at heart. I failed to notice when some trusted allies were burned out and needed space, which led to me accepting their fears and worries as true when they were, in fact, catastrophizing. I failed to notice when I was burned out and carried on, while catastrophizing. I sometimes noticed I was burned out and tried to rest but was ricocheted back to reality because in a small business there is no backstop other than the founder.

I also fully expected that at some point we would crash and stop growing so fast, because no one from my background had ever grown an independently successful business from scratch. My peers growing up were always worried about money, the next piece of work, unemployment or businesses going bust. I had no idea we would sustain this so long and remain profitable. And so I took everything on and operated from a position of urgency. My personal lack of psychological safety around money translated into anxiety for all, despite my best efforts to be generous with compliments, time and opportunity.

It is an urban legend that the first few millions of turnover are the hardest journey for any entrepreneur, and I can believe that, because it is the stage where you have very little control and have to deputize all roles in the business. I can truthfully state that the only job at Genius Within I haven't actually done myself is IT manager (I am notoriously bad at IT). One of my non-execs, Justin La Hood, helped me with an offhand comment one day. We were talking about his role in a large international consulting company and I was reflecting on how small fry Genius Within must seem to people in his position, who advise businesses with billion-dollar bottom lines. He looked astonished and replied that no one in his circle could do what I had done, and that they were all secretly in awe of anyone who started from scratch. This helped me to take myself more seriously and start accurately appraising what I had achieved, which, in turn, helped me to more accurately appraise my colleagues. We have done something unusual, and by valuing ourselves in this journey we can equally feel more confident in acknowledging our gaps.

Family life

In true ADHD style, my expectations for growth were so low that when we were turning over about half a million pounds a year, my twins were seven and we had a small pause in growth, I took on a PhD, thinking I needed stimulation from academic growth, but I was also rather obsessed with the lack of decent research in the neurodiversity sector. By the time I finished, five years later, the business had grown fivefold. In those years I exceeded my capacity so many times, I have no idea, looking back, how I managed it. I also filmed three series of *Employable Me* for the BBC in the UK and USA, which raised the public profile of neurodivergent talent, and indeed my own career, leading to heavy news coverage and more writing tasks. I tried to take a break and spent a year living in the USA with my family, homeschooling my kids, including two months' hiking and camping across the Rocky Mountains and California. However, the reality was often waking at 4am and working several hours of a UK day before the rest of the family were up. When we returned from this trip, I had a thesis deadline, a financial crisis and a personal crisis. I remember asking one of my sons, who had just started secondary school and had lost his PE kit three times before Christmas, if he would rather have a normal mother who worked the same hours every week and made dinner every night. God bless him – he looked me right in the eye and told me that my work was important and I should carry on helping people. As a female, the question of family life and career is drummed into us. I am aware that many men writing this book would not feel the need to write this section, but as a mother, I feel I cannot adequately relate my journey without explaining how this is possible. Other women ask me all the time, so here's my considered thoughts on making a career and family work.

Women fall away from their careers in the middle years, where a lot of the growth happens, or they take a long pause and find it hard to get going again. These inequalities have a massive impact on women's financial independence and therefore their ability to plan a well-resourced retirement, leaving them destitute in old age if they get divorced. Research shows that this is in large part due to inequality in the home, and not just at work.[2] Women still take disproportionately more of the childcare burden and the cognitive labour of remembering things like PE kits. This wasn't true for me. The year we were in the USA my husband didn't work at all, which is where I got the majority of the cognitive break I needed to sustain the CEO role and finish my PhD. On our return he handled all the school communication, laundry and weekend activities. I wasn't doing nothing (I am always in charge of healthcare and dentists), but he was easily doing more than his fair share while I finished my thesis. He picked up the slack again when I became ill with a chronic health condition in 2021, and in 2022, when both Jacqui and I were unwell, her critically so.

My husband is a different neurotype to me, and has a good grasp on planning, time management and logistics, way beyond my own skills. In our cognitive profiles and personalities we have many of the reverse traits to our gender role expectations. The accolades he receives for this and the judgement I receive for not having his organizational skills are a reflection of what we have accepted as 'normal' in society. In Sheryl Sandberg's book *Lean In*[3] she references the homelife dynamic and makes the point that gender roles at home are essential for gender roles at work. As women we need to expect support and state our boundaries clearly; we can't wait passively for it to be bestowed upon us – that is counterintuitive to empowerment. I watched my mother's generation try to 'do it all' and wind up miserable, smoking endless cigarettes through bitter resentment and anger while their marriages fell apart.

Madonna's lyrics from 'Express Yourself' about not going for second best inspired many in my generation to take their space as equals in a marriage, through financial empowerment ('Material Girl') and career success ('Blonde Ambition'). I didn't absorb this message as commercialism and greed; I absorbed it as being brave enough to be independent as an adult and to not need to rely on others. I confess to being terrified about this, worried that I would never feel financially competent or secure. I still don't at times. I imagine a lot of men have this fear too. Getting to a place where I can feel less terrified about money required both our incomes and, just as my husband never saw childrearing as my sole responsibility, I haven't seen money as his. We have taken turns at different points to put our careers first, based on the needs of the whole family rather than constructed gender roles. This included seven years of part-time work for me and one year of not working for him. However you break it up, my considered advice is to make it a discussion and a choice, rather than a default position that you may grow to resent. Money makes it hard – I earned more than my husband the year we got pregnant, but by the time the kids were two he was on double, so we had to prioritize his income in order to afford a home. Again, research shows that when men become parents they get bigger pay rises whereas women flatline.[4] That was true for me, and my income didn't start to improve from becoming a mother in 2006 until 2017. Such disparities are why gender pay gap reporting is necessary and paid family time off for men is such a big deal.

After shouting the message about equal partnership at home from the rooftops, Sheryl Sandberg sadly lost her husband suddenly and prematurely when her children were still young. Her second book, *Option B*,[5] is much more humble about the way a woman can resource her career singlehandedly. As a newly bereaved single parent, she was fortunate to have wealth, a supportive boss and an existing career identity with which to move forward. If you are raising your children alone while pursuing a leadership journey, you have my total respect. You might need to take more time over it than I did, you might need to pace yourself to handle the intense childrearing years or, if you can afford it, pay for help. I know many women who struggle with this concept, so just notice if you are having any internalized responses to that as an idea! You might be neurotypical or have a top assistant. You might need to stop for a while if your kids have additional needs, but every experience you are having is building your portfolio of expertise and skill.

So in summary, I reflect (now that my twins are about to leave home) that my coping mechanism for working and having a family life is largely due to having an equal partner as a husband. My career wasn't always at a healthy pace of work, but it wasn't stymied because of an unequal marriage. There is a balance of luck and choice about this situation. Not every marriage starts out unequal or indeed equal; we change. Many people change after becoming parents, wanting more equality or indeed feeling more com-pelled to hold opposite roles, but in balance. To a large extent it depends on the needs of your children, the number you have, when and with what amount of resources. You may go into the journey with expectations that become unrealistic as things change, so we need to hold a non-judgemental attitude to the capacities and choices of our colleagues who are parents, of all genders. I have seen many colleagues better off alone than with an extra weight of a bystander co-parent who doesn't contribute their fair share. I equally realize that a choice to go alone has significant privilege built into it with regard to poverty, community support, disability and more. It is a complex, intersectional picture when the choices we make or the situations we are forced into are such a complex picture of intrinsic and extrinsic factors.

The takeaway point that I make is to appreciate that all leaders – men, women and non-binary – need a good family support system to thrive. The idea of a support system can be part of the wider community rather than the sole duty of wife or husband or partner. It can be a religious group, extended family, colleagues and flexible working, wealth, health and so much more. I have combined working and parenthood with the resources of non-disabled children and a non-disabled committed partner, a tipping point where we had money to afford childcare and a home, enough middle-class resources and white privilege to obtain an education that allowed me to work flexibly, and my own health remaining good enough to sustain some fairly hard years. Add to that being self-employed and running my own company to a schedule that accommodated the school day. Remember my point about social comparison and jealousy from chapter 2? Remember my friend who wondered why she hadn't achieved as much as me while solo parenting two children who needed to be home-schooled? Don't compare yourself to others who may have more resources in these ways. Compare yourself to the person you want to be. Every tiny step you take will add up, and leading sustainably might mean a career break. Managing family life and work for people assigned female at birth is socially loaded and judged, and we are generally criticized no matter what we do. People assigned male at birth escape some of the criticism but can also feel as torn on a personal level and are more judged for their earning power. We won't manage the complexity of leading while caring by comparing each other; we manage by working together in our family units and our communities.

Vivienne Isebor, founder of ADHD Babes, concurs that self-acceptance and compassion are essential for holding leading within a social justice context and how she leans into the mutual care of her community:

When I think about leadership I think about serving the many parts that make up who I am as an individual. My journey with leadership has naturally been in response and in resistance to systems of oppression including sexism, racism, ableism and discrimination. As a disabled Woman of the global majority my sensitivity to the ills of the world is high and deeply personal. This serves as a double-edged sword, a deep empathy that drives me towards change that is collective and equitable. However, being so closely connected to the cause leaves me often in a state of vicarious trauma and disillusionment. Above it all, leadership for me has been a cyclical journey of learning, acceptance and purpose, both for myself and my community. A subtle yet persistent current that has carried me through despite the challenges and is painted with joy, connection and healing along the way. The learning never stops and feels more like a way of leading than a destination. The acceptance serves as an anchor and grounding tool to serve from where I am and believe that that is enough, despite perfectionism and the societal pressures placed on me. Purpose is the driving force and motivation that contains and guides me through it all. While there are many things to overcome, being able to lead while holding in appreciation the many parts of who I am means I have full access to the beauty of my identity. To be Black, disabled, Woman, I get to name it for myself out loud and therefore tap into the resources of the community that exists within that paradigm. In doing so, I can allow others to see for themselves that we exist, we are enough, and if it serves them, they can join us on the journey too.

Burnout

Despite all my relative advantages, by the time it came to finish my PhD we were turning over several million and I had a burnout breakdown. I caught myself one day with a dangerous thought: 'I am so miserable and tired they would be better off without me.' Now, I have had enough psychology training to know that is a warning sign, a precursor to suicidal thoughts. I took myself to the doctor to ask for medication, because there was no way I was going to consider slowing down! My GP was amazing. He told me that I had been bouncing in and out of his office with stress-related ailments for years, and when was I going to address my underlying patterns of over-work and stress? By this time, I was taking thyroid medication and I have had chronic insomnia and periods of stress alopecia since childhood. I had severe gastritis and irritable bowel syndrome, bad enough to have had three endoscopies to screen for cancer and a couple of cardiac assessments to rule out heart disease. I was also starting perimenopause but didn't recognize the symptoms because they were atypical. I broke down in his office and he called the receptionist to divert his next four appointments while he helped me work out the impact of childhood trauma on my current health. I recognize this is also an event of luck and privilege. Right when I needed professional intervention, I got it. I'm aware that this doesn't happen to the same degree for women of colour, working-class women, for transgender women and women with little access to healthcare.[6] He stayed with me until I had a plan for getting therapy. I found a therapist who was incredibly effective and got me into taking ADHD medication properly for the first time. She helped me realize that I was holding myself to an unrealistic ideal, a level of perfectionism that would be unhealthy for anyone, let alone an ADHDer who is coming to terms with her identity, childhood trauma and finishing a PhD. She helped me break down the internalized 'ideal' of the perfect leader, mother and friend, and find a better balance between self-awareness and self-consciousness.

Medicating in burnout is a tertiary response. It gets you through, but it doesn't solve the underlying causes. It isn't for everyone, but it was for me. I realized I had a lot of internalized ableism about ADHD that wasn't resolved. Medicating gave me enough of a cognitive and emotional break to start working on the patterns of unsustainability and, importantly, the attention span I needed to finish my PhD thesis. When my therapist initially suggested ADHD meds I retorted with the hard neurodiversity paradigm argument, 'But I am not broken and I do not need fixing! When I was living in the US I was hiking, running and skiing under a wide blue sky and didn't need anything!' Her response was epic. 'Yes, Nancy, but you're not living in the USA. You're living in an English winter with grey skies, and you need to sit still for 10 hours a day and write.' Ah, yes. Good point. I found a decent psychiatrist and worked on finding the right dose and medication pattern for my needs. ADHDers are not necessarily broken, neurodivergents are not broken, but we are different and we do have different needs. Sometimes those needs are disabling. This is a paradox in the neurodiversity community at the moment and this was one of the moments when I had to grapple with two truths being equally reasoned. I am a whole person AND I am disabled in many contexts because my neurophysiology is different. To be fair, the neoliberal capitalist employment context is rough on most people (see Robert Chapman's *Empire of Normality*[7] for more on this), but we neurodivergents do seem to have a more heightened sensitivity to the hardships of modern employment conventions. Even with all the advantages I have outlined and created, I had hit my ceiling.

I carried on working through burnout. I don't recommend it and it was only possible because of the incredible people I have in my family, community and company. It was like going from being an alcoholic to a moderate drinker without a period of abstinence. I have slowly learned to find a more sustainable pace and to make healthier choices. In doing so, I have created a much-improved level of psychological safety in my community. I underestimated how stressful it was for my colleagues to witness how close

I was to the edge and not panic about their own job security. It wasn't an easy time, and I write this to encourage you to avoid such a situation rather than to send the message that you should power through. If, like me, you have an aura of confidence and strength, there may be very few people who can tell you to slow down. People may be frightened to challenge you. Not everyone has the same confidence to interrupt a careening, hyperfocused go-getter. You need to have a close circle of people who are not intimidated by you and who can give you the feedback when you need it. Leaders need other leaders to share their space and buffer them. In my journey I have found those people, the ones with the sticking power to work with me through those times and who had enough faith in my character that I would prevail. These are my colleagues, my mentors, my friends and my family. Now that I see this pattern, I make a point of supporting the other strong ambitious copers in my circle and holding space for them to give themselves permission to rest.

Are you a human doing or a human being?

A theme running through the early stages of my career for me is simultaneously having the power and having no power. As a chaotic and unself-aware young person, I had no idea of the effect I was having on others; I couldn't see beyond my own anxiety. Surely I couldn't affect anyone because I had nothing to offer, right? I meet people from this period in my life and they tell me that they thought I was a role model, they thought I was fierce, badass and / or arrogant. In true ADHD style I interrupted people, disagreed disagreeably and would break the rules if they didn't suit my mood, including avoiding school entirely for nearly two years. In my defence, I also worked as a caregiver and would regularly go to the ends of the earth for my friends. In my personal development growth, I became incredibly self-conscious of this effect and worried about offending people, it was paralysing. I lost a lot of faith in myself and my ability to lead; I internalized a narrative that I was a harridan, that I was dangerous.

I became incredibly socially anxious and assumed that people would only put up with me if I was of great assistance to them, which laid the foundations for a rescuing pattern that persisted into Genius Within's journey. I became addicted to the validation of being needed and helpful – my entire sense of self-worth was based on being useful. My yoga teacher told me once that I was a horrific commitment honourer! I was perplexed. What could possibly be horrific about honouring commitments? Well, everything if honouring those commitments makes you ill. When the circumstances under which you made the commitments changes, it is okay to update expectations. Thank you, Vikki. Took me 10 years to figure out what you meant. I thought my power came from doing, but it actually comes from being.

People who feel powerless when they have power and influence over others are going to struggle with leadership. This is a bind that affects leaders from marginalized backgrounds more than others. The best leadership book I have ever read is called *Power* by Kemi Nekvapil.[8] She discusses her experience as a Black woman leading in white spaces, and her journey of overcoming the external messaging of systemic racism and sexism to centre herself in her own journey and strength. If you're not enjoying this book, go and read hers. It might well be better for you, and I can only aspire to this book doing a similar job. I bought a copy for all Genius Within's leaders. Not realizing our power makes us do stupid things, like taking on too much work or acting like a burning martyr. Realizing our power gives us strength to choose healthy responses and set boundaries on our resources. The people you lead don't think you are powerless, but equally, neither are they. They can manipulate you from the victim position, and I have seen many marginalized leaders be bullied with passive aggression. It was only when I saw it happening to others that I realized I had experienced the same and was able to reflect back on past conflicts with renewed self-compassion. You have the power to make decisions, to change conditions, but members can take tacit power back by ignoring your requests, disrespecting the responsibilities you hold or trash talk. You might feel like you are powerless to manage the performance of a struggling team, but you actually do have the power to put a stop to it.

Another solid influence on my life is the HR expert Gill Rudge. She has mentored me through many tricky HR journeys and relentlessly reinforced to me that I wasn't being unfair, that it was, in fact, my job to set boundaries and limits. She told me that I gave too much away and that I needed to take more power over situations, not less. Her metaphor is the iron hand in the velvet glove. I was conflating style over substance. In overcorrecting my bombastic nature I let too many real issues go; I was an iron glove with jelly underneath. In being too worried that people would accuse me of persecuting, I rescued. I needed to take more action but to do it in a softer, kinder voice. I needed to not wait until it was a crisis and then let frustration propel me through the hard conversations.

The first time I held a hard boundary properly I felt dizzy and my heart rate went through the roof. I had sleepless nights before and after. But Gill was right. And people know when things aren't working, they're not unaware. They're waiting for you to raise it, to take the initiative. The longer you leave a difficult situation, the more people will resent you when you finally take the lead. The longer you leave an underperforming team, the more they will find ways to justify the issues and fire it back at you. And it might indeed be your job to fix it, for not structuring the work well, or not providing training, or making a bad hiring decision, or not communicating effectively. But you won't get to the bottom of these nuances by avoiding the conversation. At first, I thought this was just me and my lack of skill. But the more managers I train, the more workshops about neuroinclusive management I lead, the more I realize this is a common issue.

I have successfully navigated this journey as a third party now, patiently explaining to my team of marginalized leaders that they need to set boundaries and that the way their teams are operating is not sustainable for them or their staff. One of the reasons I am writing this book is because I now see this pattern everywhere – rescuing manager patterns leading to as much harm as the archetypal mean boss. We have to find our power and use it wisely, not hide from it or be scared of it. Directness without kindness is indeed bullying, but kindness without honesty is manipulation. I have found that balance very hard to pin down, and I am sure I still fail sometimes.

We're running a script in our narratives that power comes with glory; this is not necessary. In her book *Women & Power*, Professor Mary Beard[9] explains that some women have exercised significant power without necessarily placing themselves on a pedestal. She names Alicia Garza, Patrisse Cullors and Opal Tometi as three women who created change and influence on a global level, but who avoided fame.* Their lack of fame is both a symptom of a racist culture in which Black women are rarely valued for their achievements, but also a model for power without fame. It may not have served these women to be famed for their achievements. Mary Beard's book asks us to question these relationships and consider the extent to which power as inseparable from glory is a masculine concept, derived from millennia of war stories dating back as far as the Siege of Troy. If we were to consider power as a positive, generous, egalitarian, facilitative process, what would we make of heroes? What is the difference between power and selfishness or greed, and where is the fine line between valuing the contribution you have made and seeking glory? The more we unpick hierarchical cultures, the harder this becomes to conceptualize. Most companies operate as dictatorships – this is incongruent with democracy – but few companies could operate with each decision made democratically – this is incongruent with efficiency. It's time for a new model of power and to reframe power as something that exists systemically, rather than individually.

Self-care and ambition

I had a huge transformation when I realized that I did not want to be the leader of my company anymore because the role had become too corporate as the company had grown. The constriction of everyday consistency and constantly policing my emotions was draining my ADHD brain. At that point I realized how unsustainable the business was, that it didn't have a culture or brand without me in the middle, and that I had no exit strategy. My sense of power was accountability without sufficient influence. In 2019 we had a strategy meeting and, with support from our non-executive directors, started planning five years in advance. At this point turnover was £2.5 million and I had never written a business plan. A budget, yes, but not a strategy. In the meeting I was suddenly struck by how my role as CEO had forced me into a corner, that my creativity and enthusiasm were waning because the role had grown too big around me. I am an entrepreneur, a starter. I can do finishing roles because I hate things being unfinished – they take up too much cognitive space and make me forgetful. But my motivation for finishing things was 'away from' rather than 'towards'. In

* See https://blacklivesmatter.com/herstory

the CEO role, finishing and ensuring projects are completed is an everyday experience. Too much of the job was compliance and rules for me, and not enough was ideas and innovation. We created four categories for business strategy planning: self-care and ambition; culture and communication; mission and money; and infrastructure and size.

In neoliberal economies, putting self-care and ambition together seems oxymoronic. We force ourselves into dichotomies like work OR rest, work OR life, as if these are opposites. People crow about their jobs being demanding because they like to feel indispensable; there is a corporate commando culture that starts with the large companies and filters down to the rest of us. We asked ourselves: What if that isn't true? What if the only way to create a neuroinclusive culture is to succeed by being well? What if the most successful people are the ones who can do their jobs without overworking? What if the best companies are the ones where the staff delivering the support are themselves getting the support they need? What if the long-term structure for people who love to work hard is to first facilitate solid rest periods? The balance of self-care and ambition was born as two sides of one strategic coin. For me to self-care, I do like to work a lot, but I need to do work that suits me and have long restorative breaks.

We decided to find a leader for Genius Within who was a professional manager rather than a subject matter expert, and to move me into a role in which I could thrive. We realized that this was essential to our company mission and that the incongruency of Genius Within's founder being in a role that didn't suit her Genius Within was a blight on our cohesion as a company. My other directors didn't want the role either; Fiona was clear that her Genius Within was being the power behind the throne, and one of our colleagues realized that her Genius Within wasn't within the company at all. We hired externally and found a leader whose Genius Within was to be the boss of the company, Jacqui. And then we had a pandemic, two serious health crises and a massive restructure of our business model and finances! But we survived to tell the tale because we are in roles that suit us, playing to our strengths and taking care of ourselves.

I've learned that there is no point in stopping me working in bursts with periods of rest. If I try to do even a 40-hour week I can't think. I lose my thread and productivity grinds to a halt. When I am on a roll, I will happily do a series of 14-hour days. But I have something called the red flag protocol, which is when I sense I am near the edge of a burst. It is a list of actions that my colleagues can put into place that immediately takes the pressure off and stops me cracking. Our admin support team go into my emails and social media and put an out-of-office responder on. They cancel everything in my diary for the next week that can be moved. They then go through my diary and emails and make a list of all my obligations so that I can talk them through where they can be delegated or deferred, leaving me with a much smaller burden. This happens about three times a year. But it keeps me sane and stops my ADHD-style inconsistency from being a risk to my health or the obligations of the business.

For me, having enough money has also been a large part of self-care. The point where we had enough money in the business to provide the infrastructure and size we needed to resource all the specialisms was a pivotal point. With online influencers and leaders, I can see that they need to remain present in the community through evenings and weekends, even though they may desperately need a break, because the engagement is what pays the bills. It only takes one month off one of these networking sites to lose your seniority in the algorithm. It's a lot of pressure. Fear of, or actual, financial insecurity is also a driver of unhealthy behaviours in relationships and can bring out the worst in us. It is hard to prioritize self-care when you are worried about money and can't relax in your time off. And this is why the two go together, for my colleagues and myself. We need enough ambition to generate sufficient financial sustainability to relax. When we are relaxed, we set health goals, and these resource us to do our best work, which is financially beneficial. It's a virtuous circle. Some of my worst moments as a leader came when I was worried about money, and conversely, when I am not worried about money, some of my best moments.

In social justice work, as minoritized leaders, such as women or people from working-class communities, we are discouraged from talking about money. It's considered crass, or selfish. This varies by culture, too; in some countries haggling is encouraged, but for some reason, in the UK the best approach to sales is to pretend you don't need the business! The UK is particularly odd, in my opinion, but not alone. In learning how to survive as a leader, I have learned how to talk about money. I've learned how to bill properly for my time, valuing not just the effort on the day, but the value of the expertise I bring to each interaction. I've had to force myself through conversations with my heart beating loudly in order to make offers, accept offers, turn down offers that undersold my value and negotiate compromises. I've learned the hard way the resentments that build up when some people are under- or overpaid, when you realize you have given too much away and need to reset a fair share. It is not easy to overcome these ingrained aversions, but they go hand in hand with leadership.

Feeling confidently able to predict and control where the money to pay the bills is coming from and being able to have straightforward conversations about cash are connected to having the confidence to lead. Your staff might be concerned about money but feel unable to say so, and instead bring niggles about communication or workload because they don't know how to ask. If you can get in there and speak transparently, you could provide the reassurance they need. Financing is the security that you provide for yourself and your team in order to thrive. Recognizing the extent to which money drives good health and relationships is a tough transition for those of us wedded to egalitarian principles, but here is yet another place where self-sacrifice doesn't bring us long-term success. We can't solve the inequality in the world, but we can make sure we operate fairly within it.

Genius Within has a legal status of community interest company (CIC), which is the same legal structure as a limited liability company but with two caveats: first, your company mission has to be aligned to some sort of public, sustainable service or product; and second, every time you make a payment to shareholders, you have to make double the payment to a service for your community. It's like a B Corp but with actual legal and financial safeguards. A few years into Genius Within's journey we changed the company legal structure to CIC so that we had these ethical principles locked into the company's articles of association. I didn't want us to be a charity, because I believe that our work adds value to companies and saves the public purse – we should charge and be paid fairly for the work that we do. And as minoritized leaders I feel it is important to set an example of being paid appropriately for our work – economic inequality is a tool of exclusion. Equally, we felt that to profit excessively from social justice work was unreasonable. We pay ourselves appropriately to the level of responsibility, training and expertise we bring to the jobs we take on, but we also invest in research, pro bono services and donations to charities and services for young people and their families. Finding the balance between risk and reward, self-sacrifice and selfishness has become an important discussion at Genius Within, and we live in polarized times. I do not pretend to have the answer to this conundrum but I do not take the responsibility of financial security lightly. It is easy to be generous when you have enough to go round, and I was never more proud of us than during the pandemic when we could be clear about expectations and had enough tucked away to last the wobbly months that followed, keeping all employees and associates in enough work to stay safe.

Psychological safety in practice

In Section 3 we will discuss more about creating psychological safety in your community, but for this chapter our focus is on how you experience it, behave with or without it, and what it brings up for you. Psychological safety is hard to acquire and easy to lose. As a leader, you have a dispro-portionate impact on the psychological safety of the group, and you need to prepare for this. Coming from a neurodivergent background, we may have experienced sharing an 'out of the box' idea and been ridiculed or chastised by our classmates. We may have preferred unusual music, fashion or literature and been ostracized for being weird. We may have found an unusual way of doing something and been 'corrected'. I know many neuro-divergent mathematicians who can just 'see' an answer straight away but who lose marks for not following the right pathway or writing down their workings. We might be excited about a sudden insight and be told off for not putting our hand up first. We seek unusual careers as entrepreneurs, creatives and sole traders because we cannot find psychological safety in the neuronormative world.

However, finding our own path is not a straight line to psychological safety, and neither are our own communities always a safe space. Increasingly, the online forums that were so pivotal in the early days of the internet to community engagement[10] have become places where newly diagnosed people are 'told off' for using the wrong language or wanting to identify themselves with words that aren't fashionable. Their first forays into their new 'in-group' are immediately met with judgement and disparagement.

We've become terrified of getting it wrong, and some community leaders have strayed from their inclusive values. A healing process that is necessary for you to lead from a place of sharing your voice and listening to others is not a given; you will have to seek it out and work on it. I have found this to be an ongoing lifetime's work, but when we give ourselves and each other room to grow, we can truly find an inclusive community.

A positive role model for me is the Black Excellence and Leadership in Neurodiversity group (BLeND), run by Jannett Morgan and Marcia Brissett-Bailey. At one of their events, I witnessed a beautiful example of group leadership and facilitation that promoted psychological safety for all. A speaker had shared her story of being raised by immigrant parents who had pushed her to succeed. She was expressing her frustration as a neurodivergent with the dual experience of exclusion by neurotype and race. This sentiment spilled over into her delivery, which was both fierce and poignant. Her hurt and anger were palpable; it was a powerful oration. Afterwards Jannett stood up and thanked her for sharing her truth, and invited the group to notice that we are all at different stages of healing, of processing and of experiencing the emotions of systemic racism and academic barriers. In these words, she made the speaker's story an appropriate risk to share and simultaneously resettled the emotions in the room. It was a skilled piece of leadership.

Both the speaker and Jannett role modelled psychological safety: not by avoiding the edge, but by being present at the very truthful, raw edge and having that be okay with each other.

JANNETT MORGAN

2020 forced many organizations to hold the mirror up to themselves in relation to race, racism and equity. There is much more work to do (and this is why we do what we do), but it would be disingenuous not to acknowledge there have been some positive steps forwards in terms of recognizing racism as structural and deeply embedded within systems and process in society, including our education institutions and our workplaces. Many marginalized groups, including people who identify as neurodivergent, have aligned with the struggle for race equity and have benefited directly and indirectly from some of the changes we are seeing.

When my training began in the early 2000s, the focus was almost all on dyslexia – no one was using the term 'neurodiversity' back then. Thanks to the activism of a few individuals and groups, the neurodiversity movement has grown exponentially and the narrative is changing. As an ally, this ground-up evolution has been exciting to be part of. Now, we see a lot more about neurodiversity on our television screens; progressive employers are being intentional in their efforts to be 'neuroinclusive'; social media has enabled neurodivergent people to find their voice; Gen Zers have ripped up the invisible rule book about work and are turning their side hustles into successful careers in a fraction of the time it took their Gen X and baby-boomer parents and grandparents. Those who argue that 'we've done race' (aka 'we're done with race') see neurodiversity as, well, The New Black!

What's the big deal with that? As a neurodiversity tutor and workplace coach I am a member of several of the main professional organizations. I'm disappointed, although not altogether surprised, at the response of the (white) leadership when it comes to race. The lack of understanding about the added barriers when discrimination on the grounds of visible difference (i.e., race) intersects with discrimination on the grounds of hidden difference (neurodivergence) will be evident to anyone with a passing interest. **How dare we divert people's attention away from neurodiversity by talking about race?** It is indicative of a marginalized movement that is still coming to grips with its own identity and fragility, so does not see itself as psychologically unsafe for many people of colour. Unfortunately, the 'Angry Black Woman' trope has silenced some of us who have a legitimate critique for the leaders – crowned and self-proclaimed – in the neurodiversity community. Overemphasis on 'superpower' narratives that focus on individual Black stories – **if Lewis Hamilton / Jason Arday / Malorie Blackman can do it, so can you** – ignores the everyday experiences of Black people at work who face racism and ableism. The gains that are being made are not evenly distributed. It also ignores the value that Black practitioners, well versed in the practice of Ubuntu, bring beyond their lived experience.

It's been my pleasure to coach hundreds of clients and see the impact of coaching on their well-being and career progression. When compared to other professions like counselling, coaching is still in its embryonic stage. 'Specialist' neurodiversity workplace coaching is a niche area, and there is a need to grow capacity to meet the increasing demand for support. Workplace coaching (particularly for those in the UK who have successfully navigated the government's Access to Work process – no mean feat) has been transformational for many employees and entrepreneurs, but I have had to fight for clients to have the intersectional complexities included in their needs assessment reports, to make the case for a having a coach with the lived experience of racism. Unfortunately, because of homogenous leadership in the most influential organizations, we see the same examples of systemic racism in the coaching profession that exist elsewhere.

MARCIA BRISSETT-BAILEY

I was always the person people didn't want to sit with. I had the ideas, but this wasn't seen as a leadership quality. As a result, I often found myself isolated. The intersection of my race and my neurodivergence is complex. As a child, the culture in my house was rooted in compliance, and school was somewhere you did as you were told (based on the naive assumption that **all** teachers cared about **all** children). This meant speaking up for yourself or challenging authority was frowned upon at school and at home.

The extra work you have to do to navigate the additional intersectional challenges impact deeply on your sense of self and your understanding of what leadership looks like. How do I 'show up' at work? Will I be seen as the 'Angry Black Woman' because I'm being assertive, or am I not given opportunities for career progression because my manager focuses more on my spelling errors than the solutions I bring?

These two women share experiences of leading psychologically safe work, which means for them that there must be a space where they can be their full authentic selves, rather than masking one to fit in with the other. They facilitate psychological safety more widely because they are speaking openly about the fears that many in their community hold, and because they have done their own work to be in a place of self-compassion and acknowledging the difficulties they have faced. Feeling able to name difficulties and verbalize our emotions, without judgement, is a great basis for psychological safety.

Conflict can be purposeful

I was reminded of the sometimes-fractious debates in the neurodiversity world by a workshop leader who discussed how the transgender community debated their language terms about 20 years ago, and how unsafe it felt at the time, with people arguing and disagreeing openly. However, she spoke about how necessary the dissent had been to establishing agency and cohesion for the community, and how they had arrived at a healing consensus around terms and remained inclusive over the long term. She taught me that we need to ride the current waves in new self-advocacy movements and be comfortable with leaning into the trajectory of the community as a whole. I am reminded by this example that sometimes the best way to create psychological safety is to not try and take control, but to let the discussion happen and trust the process – managing my own state in response, rather than trying to manage the fears or angers of others. I remember being rightfully challenged when using my *Forbes* magazine column to put forward my own interpretation of language in a way that dismissed others who had as much right to their own truth as I did. I edited the article. On another occasion I used a phrase that was a microaggression for Black and Brown women (naming one 'articulate'). Articulate is sometimes used to describe Black people with a sense of comparison – 'You are so articulate **for a Black person**' is the implied ending of the sentence. I was able to do these pivots because I had become aware of my influence and was able to accept criticism – my internal sense of psychological safety was sufficiently healed and developed.

This hasn't always been the case, and I will likely fail at this again. There have been times when my internal equilibrium could not accept criticism and I have acted defensively, which resulted in destabilizing those around me. I felt like a victim and treated the challenges like persecution, even when they were well meaning. Like the wider community at large, Genius Within has been through forming, storming, norming and performing cycles. At first, having felt so unfairly excluded in education, the idea of having a team of people like me felt like finally fitting in, finally being able to unmask, was a sense of relief. But we didn't and don't agree all the time, and we carry trauma responses to conflict. The first major wobbles and people leaving were felt deeply. Some schisms I liken to divorce. As a leader in creating a neurodivergent company I was put on a pedestal, expected to be perfect, and as a founder in creating a neurodivergent company I put it on a pedestal and expected it to be perfect. Expectations such as these can only fail; there is no room for growth and safety has to come from disagreeing without rupture, or with elegant decisions to part ways. I couldn't create psychological safety in my company without creating it for myself. As a neurodivergent leader, creating psychological safety in your environment depends on resolving your own triggers and surrounding yourself with co-leaders who can hold the space for you when you cannot. You need to learn when to intervene and when to trust your colleagues to resolve. Your own well-being is paramount – the balance between the resources you have and the demands you take on or that are foisted upon you. Creating a culture of psychological safety for others is hard when you don't understand it yourself. Your own healing journey, love and compassion for yourself is a precursor for compassion for others.

CHAPTER 7

Advice

☑ **DO** take an inventory of your resources.

Your personal resilience in overcoming barriers, your hopes, dreams and strengths are resources. Your social circle, ancestry, family, religious group, community group, these are all resources. The space you inhabit and how you can make it as conducive to working and resting as possible are resources. You might have creative abilities like making scrap books, project plans, vision boards and playlists of great music. There are obviously also adjustments like assistive technology – if you've not dived into these, you might find them helpful. For me, medication was a resource right when I needed it, but ongoing the resources I need are healthy, protein-packed food and time in outside space. Write a list of all the ways you can control your work and reflect on these when you are overwhelmed. Sometimes, even a very small change, such as putting on an oil burner to indulge in a beautiful scent, is enough to trip the switch of feeling in control.

☒ **DON'T** assume the demands of your work are the same as everyone else's.

You might be used to getting lost / forgetting things / taking time over literacy / suppressing tics or stims / sitting on your hands to stop talking / holding yourself in or up or back. However, consider that this isn't true for everyone and give yourself some kudos for being amazing. Think about any wider identities that you hold that create demands; think about the responsibilities you are holding as a leader and give yourself credit for carrying them. Since developing a chronic illness I've had days where I had to give myself kudos for not getting out of bed and prioritizing rest. Get into the habit of praising self-care.

☑ **DO** consider the personal relationships in your life as an essential part of your journey.

Not everyone wants to be a parent and not everyone is able to be a parent, but we can all have relationships with our families, recovery communities, online communities and religious or community groups where we express mentoring and being mentored. Consider how to pace your work around these relationships and think of them as an essential part of your learning. Consider where you have already developed leadership value and strengths, and what experiences you have had that contribute to the confidence and skills you bring to your leadership role. Being a parent of twin boys was essential development for me in terms of emotional regulation. Being an aunt and godparent is essential in terms of thinking about how I mentor young women. Being a sister is nothing but joy and has been a great support to me in my leadership journey. My siblings for sure have seen the very worst sides of me, and yet they appreciate the work I have put into my leadership journey. Your personal relationships are both a demand and a resource.

☒ **DON'T** accept second best in your home.

I've mentioned this because I feel compelled to as a woman, because I see so many women crush their own lights under the burden of an imbalanced partnership. I don't mean taking turns and doing the work, carrying the load for your partner when they need you to. But a lifetime of unfairness and ingratitude is too common in our society. That said, I was enlightened by the author Mikki Kendall in her seminal work *Hood Feminism*,[1] that when you come from a demographic that cannot trust in institutions like the police, health and social care, it is harder to extricate yourself from imbalanced relationships. I acknowledge my privilege as a white woman with middle-class social mobility in this regard, and one without a disabled husband or family. It might not be within your control to change your situation right now, but I hope I have inspired you to consider these dynamics, and if you can't make it even, you can at least give yourself some kudos. Adding home pressures to your inventory of demands rather than accepting imbalance as something that a partner should bear without question will support you in self-compassion. In our society we each move this dial as far as we can, with the resources we have available at the time. In doing so we make iterative changes for the next generation and, importantly, we don't damage ourselves by making unfair social comparisons to others who don't face the same obstacles.

☑ **DO** ask yourself if you have had enough rest to do your best work.

Ah, rest as a precursor to work rather than respite from work! Consider this. When you are working at your best, what are the conditions? As an ADHDer, I sometimes thrive on the pressure of a crisis, a deadline, some urgency. But that doesn't negate the need for rest, and before I hurl myself into a hyperfocus I can make sure I have had good sleep, fresh air, have bought healthy food to snack on and cleared my other responsibilities. This allows me the privilege of being fixated without feeling guilty or ill. Being diagnosed with a long-term chronic health condition has forced my hand on this matter; if I had learned it earlier in life, perhaps I would have weathered the midlife health crash with less distress.

☒ **DON'T** think you have to earn a break by overworking.

Hello there, rescuer complex! Are you feeding your need to feel valued by taking too much on? Do you need to justify a day off for yourself by smashing out some purposeful action beforehand? Those of us who work in social justice have a saying that self-care is the work. When the world demands so much of our bodies, our minds and our souls, resting is revolutionary. My Board colleague and peer mentor, Whitney Iles, reminds me to 'protect my peace'. I was struck by a thought a few years ago, which is that if we have to work over and above expectation all the time, our work is not part of anyone's healing journey. My role is to create neuroin-clusive and disability-friendly environments. I cannot do that if I cannot live that – it is incongruent. When I can't deliver my work in a reasonable timeframe, either I am attempting something beyond my competence, or I haven't resourced the task well enough, or I haven't planned well. None of those three are good leadership qualities. We cannot expect to create sustainable, healthy environments for others if we have no idea how to do it for ourselves.

☑ **DO** learn how to talk about money.

It is no accident that marginalized people find it hard to talk about money. How on earth will we ever achieve economic equality if the people without cannot confidently negotiate? This has been a 'feel the fear and do it anyway' mission for me, and it is something I encourage you to learn. Find people to role model for you. Invite collaboration from people who do this well. When Jacqui Wallis joined our leadership team from media tech, the three of us who had always worked in social justice and the public sector were astounded by her feedback on what we should be billing for our time. Her confidence in getting businesses to pay us our full value has been a sea change in our attitude and financial stability as a company. At Genius Within we have an open pay policy and we run ethnicity pay gap analyses, inspired by Dianne Greyson's campaign. These open, transparent conversations let everyone know where they stand. My view is that if we hide salaries and pay awards, we run the risk of being unfair. We keep it open and share our community interest reinvestments and annual accounts with our colleagues to encourage a culture where no one is afraid to talk about money.

☒ **DON'T** be frightened of turning down work if it undervalues your worth.

The first time I did this I was in my twenties and I had just had a miscarriage. The person on the other end of the bargain told me I was lucky to be offered a job since he knew I was trying to get pregnant. It was only a short interim role! I was offered a middle-of-the-road pay package, which reflected the priority that the business was putting to the role, and which I instinctively knew meant I wouldn't also have the leverage to make the role work. I turned it down, which felt like a risk at the time as I was paying down student debt and saving for a mortgage, but I don't regret it. I also get asked to deliver work for free a lot, which can feel difficult. I ask companies what their budgets are and, if they say they don't have one, I make a point of quantifying the commercial opportunity for 'exposure' and have them commit to public platforming. If they are a charity or underfunded themselves, I will sometimes do the work, but not always. Phrases like 'I'm afraid I don't have any time left this month for pro bono work' are a good exit strategy if you find it hard to say 'no'. I've also learned to directly question whether a resourced company should ask disabled people to educate them on disability inclusion for free, whether they feel that is appropriate. I can assure you this is more embarrassing for them than me! I recommend it.

☑ **DO** learn how to plan and manage money.

Resourcing your leadership journey is self-care. You cannot pour from an empty cup. If you are worried about money all the time, you will make survival-based decisions, and these are stressful and can undermine your passion. When I was self-employed, I put a third of all my earnings into a savings account for tax and then, each year, when I did my tax return, I would have a bonus after taking off my expenses. As a business, Genius Within has a tax account where we put all VAT income and then have the same bonus each quarter. We also have a 'squirrel account' where we save our surplus for a rainy day. A good aim is to have six months' running costs available at any one time; this is a good buffer for most situations – it gives you time to think as well as make changes to income and outgoings. I always plan a worst-case scenario budget that makes sure we can honour commitments as well as one that shows what we can achieve if things go our way. At the start of 2020, when we were budget planning for the upcoming financial year (ours starts in May), I remember saying to my team, 'Given what's going on in China, I think we should forget this exercise and instead work out how long we can last with no income.' Through the first few months while we were working out how to deliver coaching and assessments remotely, this budget kept everyone's morale high. We went out to all our subcontractors and asked who had income and who was dependent on our referrals, and prioritized work for those with no alternative. It was strong financial management from a 90 per cent female team.

☒ **DON'T** underestimate the importance of money for your confidence.

If you don't come from wealth and, like me, were raised to think of saving money as something greedy or counter to egalitarian values, it can be hard to prioritize it. But financial stability brings confidence to you and your whole community, whether you are leading a small business like me, or you are an influencer, sole trader or team leader. It buys you confidence. People who say money doesn't matter haven't had to choose between essentials or go without. If you are a business leader or a self-employed advocate,

I hereby vocalize that it is okay to seek a decent amount of cash, and try to build up a six-month buffer, as a minimum. Even starting to save £10 a month will build up over time. The habit is important. Be disciplined and detailed in your accounting and revenue pipeline predictions, and encourage the same from your colleagues. We grow in confidence as we shed the sense of precariousness that comes from inadequate funding or feeling in the dark about whether we will still have a job in a few months. The choices we gain when we have enough to go round are rewarding and stimulate creativity. No one wants to feel dependent. I once made a massive flow chart of how each role and team at Genius Within contributes to the financial health of the company, with the finance team in the middle, but clear links to marketing, sales, delivery, HR, IT, administration, supervision, etc. Let everyone know how they contribute to the end result. The finances might not be the goal of your leadership, but they are the engine that propels you forward. You need to be resourced.

☑ **DO** consider whether you are in drama before you act.

I can tell when I am in drama because I have a tense, urgent feeling in my solar plexus – I call it my emotional hook. It lets me know that something is triggering me related to my previous experiences, and not necessarily related to the person or situation in front of me. I have worked very, very, very hard on not acting until I have understood the link and separated it from the present context. I sometimes fall short of this aspiration, and those are the times I usually end up making apologies. It is okay to ask for a pause, for a break in dialogue or response; you shouldn't feel obliged to respond to the situation immediately. However, it is right to let people know that you are doing this. Something like 'I'm sorry, there's something in this which I am finding triggering / uncomfortable / confusing and I'd like to think and process before I get back to you.' If someone won't give you that space, feel free to send them elsewhere for support, but do not feel obligated to rush your process to accommodate their anxiety.

☒ **DON'T** act before you have resolved the emotional hook.

I have a number of ways of dealing with this. Sometimes I write a really grumpy email and don't press send, going back to it a day / week later and reflecting from a calmer space. If I am really upset, I might send it to a trusted ally for feedback, or I might call someone. But I have learned to keep this circle small out of respect for the relationships. There's nothing more likely to create drama than complaining about people to people they know – particularly if you are a leader and the people know each other, have to work with each other and you don't circle back to let your sounding board know that the matter is resolved. Complaining gossip loops are the short cut to psychological unsafety. Role model giving people the benefit of the doubt, at least until you have spoken to them. If you catch yourself engaging in badmouthing people, stop. If you do it accidentally in a moment of stress, return to the person who was listening and take accountability for it, apologize and make it clear that you have changed your mind, so that you don't leave them hanging and anxious.

☑ **DO** find your allies.

If you don't have people in your life who can be a safe sounding board, find them. Learn to watch what people do, rather than what they say. Someone who is polite to your face but speaks ill of you to others is not your rock. **Trust the people who treat you like an adult and bring their concerns about you, to you.** I want to underline those last few sentences. I know I am repeating them, but they are possibly the most important advice in this whole book! You need a wise and trusted counsel of people who will tell you straight up when you have pushed a boundary and help you make amends, as well as those who will help you buffer undue criticism. I have mentioned some of my allies, but there are many more. I have always had non-exec directors who can challenge and support in equal measure.

☒ **DON'T** take criticism from anyone you wouldn't ask for advice.

As you advance your leadership career, you will inspire criticism from a wide range of sources. As a neurodivergent leader, you will trigger people's feelings of injustice simply by existing. They might hold negative stereotypes about who should and should not be in leadership roles. They might see your success as evidence that neurodivergence is made up. They may be neurodivergent themselves and seek to diminish your efforts because you make them feel inadequate. But do not hide your light under a bushel to make other people feel better; celebrate yourself, others around you, and create space for other people to shine. You will also find yourself unable to please everyone all the time. Some people won't like your decisions. As a neurodivergent leader, approval from others might be something that you seek for your self-worth, but you need to find a way to make peace with criticism and respond to it from an adult ego. Reflective practice and allies are essential.

☑ **DO** consider your own psychological safety.

What do you need to feel psychologically safe? Consider in which spaces you experience (or experienced) a sense of being able to make mistakes without being penalized unfairly. It might be that in your leadership journey you don't feel this right now – the exposure of leadership and the implicit beliefs that our cultures enact regarding the heroic leader can make leadership very psychologically unsafe. Many leaders feel unable to admit or talk openly about failure or mistakes. Just look at our politicians. But also look at our leaders who do, congruently, own their mistakes and make amends. It IS possible with authenticity and the right levels of community safety and cultural competence. If you don't have psychological safety in your leadership space right now, it is a sign that you need some different people around you, to delegate some work, to find some quiet space / time for planning or admin – whatever it is, prioritize this.

☒ **DON'T** assume that what works for you will work for everyone else.

I've already mentioned that I sought to create psychological safety with encouragement and flexible working hours because that is what works for me – I missed how essential some people find routine and consistency because I find it paralysing. In supporting my own working practices, I inhibited others from sharing their voice. This is an area in which you need to seek regular feedback and temperature check the experiences of the group at large.

☑ **DO** notice when there is silence.

Silence is not a good sign! Many of us as neurodivergents miss those social cues and might not notice if people are withdrawing or demotivated. I always assume that people will tell me if they are not happy, because I would say so immediately! I find it very destabilizing to find out that someone I haven't heard from for a week / month wasn't 'just busy' but was actually harbouring a massive grudge and didn't tell me! Interestingly, this pattern was an overcorrection from my teenage years and early twenties when I would assume by default I had upset someone. I recoiled from this after being told once 'It's not all about you, Nancy' and then headed in the exact opposite direction! If you, like me, find yourself on the extreme end of this cognitive bias, you might need to build some sort of listening session / anonymous survey into your routine to collect this data manually. That's okay, you can do that, and then you have given people every opportunity to enter into co-creating psychological safety. And the best way to generate more psychological safety is to act on what you hear and avoid showing defensiveness if you have missed something. This will send an implicit signal that it is fine for the group to ask for change and get it, so you set up the conditions for people to ask directly next time.

⊠ **DON'T** expect magic when you prioritize psychological safety.

As you have seen, there are a wide variety of antecedents, and not all of these are in your sphere of influence. If you are trying to encourage team members to voice their fears, you may be battling a lifetime of them hiding and avoiding conflict, and you might be battling clashes in personality. The only person you are actually in control of is yourself. So focus on acting in a psychologically safe manner by responding elegantly to problems that are raised, creating solutions when people share their fears and anxieties and supporting these with structures and methods of communication that will suit all – some direct, some anonymous, some formal, some informal. Take responsibility for any managers you hire; if you have psychological safety nailed but they don't, it will create incongruence. You want co-leaders who can enact this essential community safety skill and also support you in times when you are struggling.

☑ **DO** judge people by their actions and not their words.

I have already said this, but I am saying it again. It applies not just to how you select your allies but also how you manage your colleagues and teams. Genius Within is a majority neurodivergent company, and if I had fired or disciplined everyone who had ever said anything negative, I would have no staff! I have learned the odd overspill or overwhelm is not the most important aspect of our communication, but that the actions of people who are putting in the work are where your attention should be. I see so many neurodivergent leaders being swayed by charming words and missing the clear actions of people who do not support them, pay lip service and have put in no effort. We want people saying the negative things out loud so that we can resolve them. Feeling negative isn't in and of itself a problem – resistance to resolving issues is more problematic – but the naysayers are often the people with solid risk insight, and you don't want to inadvertently create silence because you have prioritized politeness over candour and surrounded yourself with 'yes' people. Instead, watch what people do. Who will go out of their way to support you with time, money, resources, creativity, ideas and challenge? Those are your allies.

☒ **DON'T** ignore your instincts.

I've personally stopped using the word 'instinct' and replaced it with the word 'judgement', as it has a gender trigger for me. Some people use the phrase 'feminine instincts' to make something very rational and observational seem like a magical witchcraft that has less basis in reality than unicorn. I reject the separation of the two. I think our integrity and so-called spidey senses operate through clear, very real mechanisms in our body. Our conscious brains are there to interpret the meaning, not to ignore them. The instincts are real and their meaning is important. Listen to your inner voice, your inner direction and your moral code. You didn't get them by accident. If you're struggling to listen to your inner voice and find that you err on the side of distrust too often, this is a sign that you need to heal. Find a group or therapist that will gently challenge you to identify exactly what is going on, rather than dismissing you or indulging you.

CHAPTER 8

Doing the Work

Demands / resources

What is your leadership role? Use this page to make an inventory of your demands and resources.

Demands	Resources

— 163 —

Now go through the list and highlight all the ones that are within your control, and resolve to make your own life easier one step at a time.

The following list comprises the typical disability adjustments that neurodivergent people find valuable. Consider this list for yourself and make some notes:

Adjustment	Yes / No	Notes
Choosing where you work, including availability of distraction-free space		
Standing desk		
Wobble stools / kneeler chairs, etc.		
Extra wide or dual screens		
Ergonomic mouse / keyboard		
Flexibility of hours		
Ability to share tasks with co-workers		
Access to a laptop, table or voice recorder		
Speech-to-text software		
Text-to-speech software		
Mind-mapping software		
Time and organization software		
A personal assistant or support worker		
Coaching for organizational skills		
Coaching for time management		
Coaching for memory skills		

Coaching for communication skills			
Coaching for well-being support			
Additional support with changes like IT			

Now consider the demands and resources in your home life:

Activity	Hours per month	Who does it	Notes
Shopping			
Cooking			
Kitchen tidying and cleaning			
Bathroom tidying and cleaning			
Shared areas tidying and cleaning			
Bedroom areas tidying and cleaning			
Garbage and recycling			
Window cleaning			
Cupboard cleaning			
Gardening			

cont.

Activity	Hours per month	Who does it	Notes
Home repairs, carpets and furniture			
Decorating			
Water bill			
Energy bill			
Mortgage or rent organizing			
Insurance organizing			
Phone bills			
TV subscriptions and licences			
Electrical items maintenance			
Car maintenance and insurance			
Travel planning			
Birthdays of friends and relatives			
Organizing social events including annual festivals like Christmas			
Buying presents			
Healthcare coordination			
Dentist coordination			
Laundry			
Buying clothes			
Pet care coordination			

Voting register			
Fire safety			
Neighbourhood communication			
School liaison and parents' evening			
Homework monitoring			
Dealing with conflict between family members			
Supporting the wider family / friends who have needs			
Managing banks and finances			
Add your own examples that I might not have thought of...			

cont.

Activity	Hours per month	Who does it	Notes

Now that you have done all that, appreciate either your own effort or your family's efforts!

And use the Oldenburg Burnout Inventory* if you need to see how close to the edge you are.

Fostering well-being

Now it is time to do some serious thinking about how you can set up the conditions to support yourself.

Primary: what are the conditions of work that set you up for success?

1. Do you, like me, thrive on variety and flexibility, or do you crave routine and structure?

   ....

   ....

2. Are you well-resourced in terms of headcount as a ratio of turnover in your team / company?

   Or do you have enough work as a sole trader? Too much?

---

* https://www.mdapp.co/oldenburg-burnout-inventory-olbi-calculator-606/

. . . .

. . . .

3. Do the people in your life take their fair share of the load, or are you picking up what they can't manage? Is this temporary or long-lasting?

. . . .

. . . .

4. If you don't have anyone to share with, what aspects of your role would you like to work towards delegating? How much income do you need to afford this, and where can it come from?

. . . .

. . . .

5. Do you have the disability adjustments you need and, if not, can you acquire them through a scheme like the UK's Access to Work?

. . . .

. . . .

6. Is your environment psychologically safe, or is there drama?

. . . .

. . . .

7. What can you do to improve psychological safety?

. . . .

. . . .

8. Who are your allies, and do you get enough time with them?

. . . .

. . . .

Secondary: how do you plan for and manage your own well-being?

1. How is your general health and well-being? Do you have time for exercise and / or being outside?

    . . . .

    . . . .

2. What is your sleep hygiene like? How can you improve this?

    . . . .

    . . . .

3. How much variety is there in your diet, your ability to eat non-processed food and good proteins?

    . . . .

    . . . .

4. Do you / can you take part in any focused relaxation work, such as yoga, meditation or long walks?

    . . . .

    . . . .

5. Do you have the healthcare you need? Can you prioritize this?

    . . . .

    . . . .

6. Does your diary have time / provision for social events, reading, gaming, listening to music or other human connection activities?

    . . . .

    . . . .

7. Do you have a sense of annual and seasonal demands? Can you

put breaks in your diary before and after busy periods to get the rest you need?

....
....

8. Are there any hobbies or crafts in your life that bring you joy?

....
....

Tertiary: how do you respond to problems when they arrive?

1. Do you have people you can call on for additional support?

....
....

2. Do you have access to counselling coaching or therapy?

....
....

3. Can you take breaks and have other people cover your work when you are ill or overwhelmed?

....
....

4. Do you have sensory care plans, such as a weighted blanket, candles, food, ear defenders or soft clothes that make you feel safe?

....
....

5. Can you take breaks from social media and / or put boundaries on the time you are on social media if this is distracting or distressing?

. . . .

. . . .

6. Can you recognize your warning signs before a crash? Spend some time thinking about times you have crashed and the precursors. Write them down here:

. . . .

. . . .

. . . .

. . . .

7. Do you need a red flag protocol that goes into action when you crash or just before you crash? Write it down here:

. . . .

. . . .

8. What is the most important priority for recovery for you? Sleep? Good food? Human connection?

. . . .

. . . .

Drama relationships

Consider the four drama roles and an example of when you have recently felt in all four of these positions:

Victim – unable to act, unfairly blamed or put upon.

. . . .

. . . .

. . . .

Bystander – unable to act, without confidence to intervene.

. . . .

. . . .

. . . .

Persecutor – fed up with other people not acting or acting incorrectly.

. . . .

. . . .

. . . .

Rescuer – forced to act, because no one else can do it.

. . . .

. . . .

. . . .

How does this dynamic play out in your leadership space? Who goes where? Do you have any teams that operate in a drama loop?

. . . .

. . . .

Now think of a time you have felt in a drama but resolved it well. What changed? Take some time to work through how to extricate yourself from drama and what strategies might work for you.

I'll give you an example. When I feel like a rescuer, I hear myself offering to do things for people that they haven't asked for and haven't expressly said they can't do. I start actions that aren't on my 'to do' list and could be done by someone else. What helps is for me to think about the person in a year from now, and the kind of empowerment I want for them. What helps is to pause and ask them 'What would you like to have happen?' or 'What is the best way to support you right now?' and to listen to what they say rather than assuming I know best, which could be insulting.

When I feel like a...	This is what I say and do	This is what helps
Victim		
Bystander		
Persecutor		
Rescuer		

What are three things, within your control, that you can do to take more responsibility for your drama responses?

1. ....

2. ....

3. ....

Your psychological safety

Consider the thought of psychological safety as feeling able to get things wrong without undue reprisal.

What have you done wrong recently? What happened?

....

Were you able to make things right?

....

Have you held yourself to a higher standard of account that you would anyone else?

....

How did people respond?

. . . .

Write down here the things you need to feel psychologically safe as a leader:

1. . . . .

2. . . . .

3. . . . .

Write down three people who you admire for their ability to admit their mistakes, take accountability for them and maintain their dignity:

1. . . . .

2. . . . .

3. . . . .

Remember how I explained that I need flexibility but I realized that other people need predictability. This intersects with power – it is easier to thrive without predictability if you have more power over the direction and plan. Who in your team needs different structures or communication to you? What do they need and where can it come from?

Silence

Think back to the section on psychological safety and take an inventory for yourself of your own behaviour.

Can you think of a time you have been silent because:

1. You planned to resign?

. . . .

2. You were worried about being told off for raising a problem?

. . . .

3. You were worried about getting a colleague into trouble or losing business?

. . . .

4. You were angry and wanted to undermine someone?

. . . .

5. You were too nervous and self-conscious to think you could be right?

. . . .

Now consider the features of the communities / companies you lead, and how these promote or inhibit psychological safety.

1. Personalities: are there sufficient conscientious people in the group thinking about the whole, or too many people focused on self? Are people extraverted or timid? Does this lead to some voices being heard louder than others?

. . . .

. . . .

. . . .

2. Do people understand their remit, and what is expected of them with regard to voicing concerns?

. . . .

. . . .

. . . .

3. Are leaders (including you) role modelling openness, consultation and commitment to fixing problems?

....

....

....

4. Are there any features of your context that make it hard for people to voice concerns? Is there a caring climate?

....

....

....

Power

Are you comfortable with power?

Consider my journey of not realizing the power I wielded and the impact of my words. Can you relate to this at all?

Reflect back to Chapter 1 in Section 1 on coercive controlling traits. Are you worried about these traits? You can take an online test if you are – just search online in any browser. Have you been on the receiving end of misuse of power? How has this affected your implicit beliefs about power and leadership?

Let's consider a positive frame of power. List three people who are powerful, whose work you admire:

1. ....

2. ....

3. ....

Michelle Obama would be in my list. Consider Michelle's insight: 'I have been at every powerful table you can think of... They are not that smart!'[1] What does this bring up for you?

Consider my colleague Fiona's self-awareness about power being the throne rather than the public face of leadership. Interestingly, in the four years since she made that statement, she has challenged herself more to give talks and presentations and to chair committees. She has become much more comfortable with visible power. What would you do differently if you felt you had more power?

Who helps you feel more powerful AND comfortable?

. . . .

. . . .

Money

1. Do you feel confident to talk about money? If not, who do you know who does? Can you talk to them about their journey?

   . . . .

   . . . .

2. Did you worry about money when you were a child? How does this affect you as an adult?

   . . . .

   . . . .

3. Do you feel you have a good grasp on money?

   . . . .

   . . . .

4. Do / can you have a savings account and do / can you put something in it every month, even £10 to get started? What would you like to have happen here?

   . . . .

   . . . .

5. Have you worked out how much money you need to feel resourced? What does that look / sound / feel like?

   . . . .

   . . . .

6. Is it possible in the current role and routine of your leadership journey? What would need to change if it is not?

   . . . .

   . . . .

7. How much of your work is currently for free?

   . . . .

   . . . .

8. What would need to change for you to charge more?

   . . . .

   . . . .

Protect your peace

Lastly, take a moment to reflect on your peace.

1. Where do you find you are able to protect your peace? What kind of environments fill up your reserves?

   . . . .

   . . . .

2. What do you do to protect your peace?

   . . . .

   . . . .

3. Do you have any skills or hobbies that help you to protect your peace?

....

....

4. Unpack any beliefs you hold that limit or facilitate your ability to protect your peace:

....

....

5. What are you capable of when your peace has been protected?

....

....

Use the space below to make notes, or sketch a diagram or metaphor about a peaceful you, who is engaged, relaxed and leading at your best:

Section 3

SUSTAINABLE LEADERSHIP

Sustainable leadership for neurodivergent leaders revolves around creating sustainable teams. I have had periods in Genius Within where turnover of staff was problematic, times when it has been stable, and times when it was a relief! Attracting and retaining the right team is the pot of gold at the end of the rainbow that all organizational psychologists and management scientists are chasing. Like the end of the rainbow, though, it is a moving target. The reasons people are motivated to work and stay with you are complex and overlapping. You can start well, and one hiring mistake can destroy a culture and take months or even years to rebuild. When we are replacing and retraining staff, we are spending money, time and our own effort, and it can be exhausting. Psychologically safe, engaging cultures are harder than they look – remember my insights that all I thought I had to do was be nice to people and fair! My naivety was quickly corrected when I was faced with the myriad of perceptions from which people assess fairness. We're in a good place right now, but after a LOT of hard work, reflection, personal development and balancing the roles within the leadership team. And I am well aware of the fragility and need to continually check in on our workplace culture. It is an essential leadership task.

CHAPTER 9

Creating a Sustainable Culture

Professor of Management Edgar Schein proposed that organizational culture is built on three layers.[1] First, there are underlying, perhaps unspoken or unacknowledged, beliefs and presuppositions about the mission, communication style and expectations of staff. Those pesky unwritten rules again! Second, there are espoused values, which may or may not be congruent with underlying beliefs – for example when we say we value diversity but then do not address lack of representation. On top of these he placed artefacts, the overt and visible aspects of the organization such as branding, logos, company policies and codes of conduct. An important lesson in leadership is how to align all three and reduce incongruence, lest it be perceived as mixed messages or hypocrisy. In this chapter I will introduce you to some of the organizational theory literature that I have found helpful in creating a positive working culture; I assume you can adapt the examples to the team, group or relationships that you lead if they are outside the workplace. As an ADHDer, I have always been fascinated by motivational theories, how we inspire ourselves and others to commit and engage. As someone growing up with limited power or money, with significant symptoms of pathological demand avoidance (PDA[2]), I have also been intrigued by how imbalances in power operate to limit permission, fairness and consent. As well as motivational theories, I will introduce the concept of the psychological contract[3] and research regarding giving and receiving feedback. These can help us craft artefacts that match our values, as well as unpicking how our tacit, unconscious beliefs might drive divergence from our core beliefs.

Motivational theories

Motivational theory has deep roots in the psychology of the early 20th century, where it entwines with political thought and social movements. As factory work became more automated and the production lines were implemented, Frederick Taylor proposed 'scientific management theory'[4] in which he advised that the best way to encourage productivity was fourfold. First, break down the task to find the most efficient way to execute the component parts. Second, ensure that responsibilities are clearly divided. Third, pay people according to their performance, that is, they get paid per widget produced rather than by the hour for producing widgets. Last, he suggested that there should be a rigid hierarchy and strict surveillance of workers to ensure no slacking. Although we may be far from the sweatshops of the Victorian era in the Western world, many businesses still operate in this vein across the world and in distribution centres, call centres and more. Even some remote knowledge workers have had devices attached to their laptops to measure key stroke per hour. This is intense monitoring and micromanagement.

In the 1960s, philosopher Douglas McGregor named Taylor's view Theory X, and defined it as holding the underlying belief that humans are innately lacking in motivation and need to be externally motivated to perform. McGregor proposed a counter, Theory Y, that humans are intrinsically motivated to perform and that leadership's role is to create the right conditions for success by clearing blocks, rather than instigating control and surveillance.[5] While these two theories are quite nebulous in psychological terms, they are still very much in play in our modern thinking – they map neatly onto the psychological world views underpinning some authoritarian versus democratic politics, right wing versus left wing. In my early management career, I was wedded to Theory Y. This is, of course, because I am intrinsically motivated and was raised in a democratic culture. My position reflects my naivety. I was shocked by people who would obstruct, delay and avoid. I found it very difficult to comprehend, but of course motivation is more complex than this simple dichotomy. A good culture can inspire a natural shirker, and a toxic culture can demotivate a naturally diligent colleague. As a leader, it is your job to understand the conditions that create conflicting directions.

I am a big fan of Professor Frederick Herzberg's two-factor theory[6] in which he describes that some aspects of work motivate by driving people towards them whereas others demotivate if not present by driving people away from them. Famously, he suggested that pay wasn't motivational, but the absence of decent pay was demotivational. This position has since been found to be widespread at the individual level (with some exceptions such as investment banking and also at the collective level, where working to a common financial goal can enhance performance).[7] Herzberg called his two factors 'motivators' and 'hygiene factors'. A hygiene factor is a metaphor – imagine if you stayed at a fabulous hotel. It had beautiful views from the room window, friendly staff and a great restaurant. You might commend these things in the review – they are motivators. You wouldn't mention that the bathroom was clean because you expect that at a foundational level – it is a hygiene factor. However, if the bathroom was unclean, this is the first thing you would mention in a negative review. In our research looking at neurodivergent experiences at work, Professor Almuth McDowall, Dr Meg Kiseleva and I found that workplace adjustments work a little like hygiene factors. The absence of adjustments explains some of the reasons why people might want to leave, but actually psychological safety, good relationships with the boss and career progression are more motivating.[8]

Around the same period as Theory Y and the two-factor theory came equity theory from Dr Stacy Adams,[9] who proposed that productivity had a linear relationship with the amount of effort expended with the value of the reward (either extrinsic, like pay, or intrinsic, such as feeling satisfied and valued). In other words, as the expectation of rewards increase, so does the effort expended. Rather than just a rehash of Taylor's scientific management, equity theory included the proposition that comparing our efforts and rewards with our colleagues can reduce or enhance our motivation depending on whether or not we feel there is a fair balance. And herein lies the reason why one essential task for a manager or leader is to ensure a fair and equal division of labour.

One of the biggest issues I see in neurodiversity / disability management training is when an employee has disclosed a disability or neurodivergent condition to their boss but not the team. Or the team know, but they don't understand. The team can perceive adjustments as unfair, which leads to demotivation. Balancing this takes skill. One useful outcome of inclusion training for the whole team can be to set a baseline expectation that some people have confidential diagnoses that require us to make adjustments, and that you might not know why your colleague is getting certain permissions such as a specialized chair, but to trust that there are good reasons. Such differences are easier for your team to accept if there is a good balance of work in other areas, when each member's talents are celebrated, and when the boss is generally perceived to be fair.

The *Harvard Business Review* reports that unfairness perceptions between team members is a huge driver of people leaving.[10] Unfairness is sometimes characterized as justice in the organizational psychology literature. The concept of 'organizational justice' refers to the sense that your organization behaves in a fair way, or not.[11] There are different categories of justice, such as procedural, distributive and interrelational. Procedural justice is about how decisions are made, which is something that I had to learn the hard way. In a micro business, you know everyone, and it is really easy to share and swap tasks, roles and positions. You are the only people in the group, and therefore you can move easily between conversations and sharing. As my organization grew, we needed to agree processes for decisions that would be perceived as fair, including hiring and promotion, performance appraisal and annual pay decisions. Balancing a transparent process while avoiding too many forms is tricky! But decisions need to be transparent and open, and as neurodivergent people we are sometimes very sensitive to injustice – it creates an anxiety and fear of rejection.[12] Distributive justice benefits from actions like open pay policies and being clear about roles, remits and responsibilities. There's also informational injustice, for example when we have to maintain secrecy to protect confidentiality in HR events, which can be a massive conflict for a company trying to role model transparency. I have learned to stretch some of these conventions. I know I have driven some of my colleagues up the wall in the past with keeping organization charts up to date and open pay policies, but this is why. The artefacts of the organization have to match the values. Interrelational justice is about differences in the strength of leader–member exchange (LMX) between team members, which is both natural and problematic. You will obviously click more with some people than others, and there will be people you find easy to work with and people who challenge you, but this is where you really have to be aware of your biases and make additional efforts to build rapport.

These aspects are the hard work of leadership, the second-guessing, responding to criticisms, looking beyond a colleague's withdrawal to identify why they might be justified in their withdrawal. We start, at Genius Within, with Theory Y, a presumption of positive intent and intrinsic motivation. We observe our colleagues and look for how we can remove blocks for them so that they can fly. When things go wrong, we look for where we haven't communicated our rationale, where we might have offered people inequitable rewards, or required inequitable contributions. We ask those questions of our teams. As a new leader, and when mentoring new leaders, I notice the same pattern, which is that you need to consciously add space and time in your diary to take care of company culture and psychological safety. If you don't do it in advance, you *will* be doing it as a repair. It is a short-term pain to put down the deadlines and admin to focus on people and relationships, but it is much harder to unpick unfairness once trust has broken down.

The psychological contract

'The term *psychological contract* refers to an individual's beliefs regarding the terms and conditions of a reciprocal exchange agreement between that focal person and another party,' wrote Professor Denise Rousseau in 1989.[13] These are distinct from the terms and conditions of employment, or implied contracts such as that between members of the same community or religious group. A psychological contract can exist between a member and leader, a member and the organization itself, and between members. It is more nuanced than your typical code of conduct, which tends to be too vague and too standardized to affect the nuances of social expectations. Psychological contracts affect commitment to the leader, to the team, to the mission. They can be broken, leading to disengagement, rupture and stress. Psychological contracts also include the biases and stereotypes of leadership beliefs, about what a boss should do for you and what you should do for your boss, as well as member beliefs such as what an employee should and shouldn't do as standard. Psychological contracts therefore vary between cultures, political persuasions, genders, generations and, indeed, neurotypes. They are a labyrinth of unwritten rules.

Rousseau painted psychological contract violation as distinct from perceptions of inequity – a more severe breakdown in a relationship that cannot easily be remedied with review and recompense. She used the metaphor of a bank robber: if you have stolen money from a bank, you can't just give it back and all is fine. You have to pay a different level of debt to the fear and harm caused by the process. It is more than transactional; it is deeply relational, more like an infidelity in marriage, a rupture. She also points out that the psychological contract is in the eye of the beholder, that one person can feel as if the contract is violated whereas another can perceive the situation as a misunderstanding or difference of opinion. This has happened to me more than once, from both sides, where I felt a contract with me was violated, and where another person experienced this and I did not. Whichever way round, it caused deep anguish and soul searching for both parties.

The psychological contract is a useful framework for the neurodivergent leader, as neurodivergent people are frequently misunderstood. We have experiences of making assumptions that don't match the responses we get when we act on those assumptions. These rifts can be understood and framed through the lens of the psychological contract, which acts as a metaphor for unspoken social rules. We might inadvertently break psychological contracts by acting in unexpected ways, or others might break them by acting differently to the expectations we had. Remember the example from previous sections about my tendency to jump in with a solution before offering sympathy? This act, with someone who isn't happy with being rescued, can result in a rift akin to a contract break. So can changing your behaviour. I am a very different leader when I am resourced to when I am / we are in crisis mode. The switch from generous, servant leadership style to commander-in-chief can feel like a break in the psychological contract, particularly when relationships are new. It has been experienced by my staff as a fundamental shift in my worldview, or personality, which wrenches a gap in the psychological contract. I do not undertake such shifts lightly and would argue that whenever I have done so there have been severe potential consequences for the business's survival if I had not, but I also know that this is very stressful for some people, particularly my autistic cousins, who prefer consistency and find rule / pace changes destabilizing. Others welcome my ability to switch gears and take immediate decisions that lead to the business remaining sustainable during times of crisis.

The ability to switch leadership styles in response to varying conditions is known as situational leadership. However, if people are carrying beliefs about heroic leadership and the style conflicts with the members' implicit beliefs about good leadership, it can look like a hero falling off their pedestal. It can feel like this from the leader's perspective too. Falling from grace is a current theme in modern society – we have seen so many of our leaders truly disgrace themselves it has become a template with expectations. The #MeToo movement, the rise of political populism, religious fundamentalism, antisemitism, transgender exclusion and all these made public with ill-advised social media feuds. While many falls from grace are justified, we are now primed to take down our leaders. But, just as there are problems with unaccountable, impervious hero leaders, there is also something deeply problematic for society about needing heroes in the first place.

We can't relitigate the past, and certainly in psychology if we removed everyone with misogynistic beliefs or who tended towards eugenics we would lose much foundational knowledge! White feminists have been fairly criticized for failing to make room for the experience of Black, Brown and Indigenous women, but this doesn't negate the success of equal pay legislation in the 1960s and 1970s. The family planning movement was started by a desire to prevent disabled people from being born and disabled women from bearing children, yet reproductive freedom has enabled women to gain financial independence and passage out of toxic marriages. The civil rights movement in the USA has been criticized for sexism, but this does not diminish its achievements in voting rights and legal desegregation in the USA. As intersectional inequities become visible, we learn from them and improve – this is progress.

Marcia Brissett-Bailey and Jannett Morgan call us to action when they ask for self-reflection and humility from white leaders in the neurodiversity space. This requires us to own our failures, not brush them under the carpet and move on to the next hero:

> If we look beyond what our eyes are used to seeing as the norm when it comes to dominant narratives about neurodiversity, we see the possibility of what authentic neurodivergent leadership could and should look like. For too long, the Eurocentric leadership paradigm has been

privileged in a way that is not fit for the world we live in – it never was. We only have to look at the homogeneity of leadership in the C-suite or on the board of trustees of most organizations. While there have undoubtedly been positive changes, the higher up the organization you go, the less likely you are to see leaders from neurodiverse and global majority backgrounds. This is not an 'either / or' but a 'both / and' call to action; the neurodiversity movement must be open to understanding how privilege means that the leadership tips and strategies, even by those who are neurodivergent, can reinforce structural racism.

Of course, not every neurodivergent person of colour will feel marginalized, but our work tells us this is the exception rather than the rule. With that in mind, what's needed, we think, is work on at least four simultaneous fronts:

- The equity work leaders must undertake to enable neuroinclusion that is fully informed by the intersections of neurodivergent people.
- The healing that those directly affected must do in their own restorative spaces, so they maintain their well-being in the face of multiple oppressions.
- The work neurodivergent leaders / influencers must do to better understand how they and their peers (while themselves experiencing oppression from systemic ableism) have benefited from white privilege.
- The radical collaboration that is needed for these groups to work together to enable sustainability.

I experience Jannett and Marcia's comments as calling me in to join the work. We live in fear of social media for weaponizing call-outs and leaving less room for reconnection and learning, which hampers our ability to benefit from the transparent egalitarian ideals of the early internet creators. I encourage you to watch the 2020 documentary *The Social Dilemma** to help you reflect on where this ultimately could end if we continue to allow ourselves to be facilitated to outrage in order to support advertising revenue. We are currently leaving inadequate space for failed leaders to

---

* www.thesocialdilemma.com

take accountability and move on, and focusing on the examples where the failures were criminal and rightly brought to justice – this risks translation into expectations of perfectionism for all leaders. And yes, I know that the advertising model of social media originated from Sheryl Sandberg, who I have quoted favourably earlier in this book. These are the cognitive dissonances we need to learn to live with in respect to our leaders. Two things can be true at the same time, as Marcia and Jannett point out – all of us are a rich complex bundle of right and wrong, triumphant and humble, kind and unkind. Reductive application of good / bad binaries is not helpful in establishing sustainable cultures and communities.

Cancel events are rifts in the psychological contracts we have with our heroes. But one of the reasons this keeps happening is because we mistake leaders for heroes. People are ultimately fallible. Differences in social values are pain points but, until we cross the Rubicon of seeking harm to or erasure of people because we disagree, we remain in civil discourse. These are difficult times, as Dr Lewis so rightly points out in her 'Surviving Society' transcript in Chapter 5. Even well-intentioned actions have multiple interpretations and not all of them good. You are going to fall off your pedestal as a leader. You might not want to be put there in the first place. Unquestioning appreciation is not healthy; as leaders we have to find ways to fail safely and to be fallible, as long as we are not actively harming. One of my esteemed colleagues, Angelica Simpson, our HR leader, gently challenged me in her first week when I was singing her praises: 'Don't put me on a pedestal, Nancy.' This was a clear signal, to me, of someone who had done her personal development work and operated from a place of psychological safety.

Psychological contracts are formed with pre-existing beliefs, but they are also co-constructed with cultural norms in your organization. Onboarding new people with training, mentoring and buddying, the materials you send them, all these communicate implicit psychological contracts. In my Master's dissertation I explored mixed messages between induction training and the organizational behaviour of the leaders in the business. They communicated overtly the ideal style of coaching-based leadership, prioritizing justice and autonomy. However, in practice, employees were left with very strict targets, rules and expectations of putting in extra hours to avoid failure. This caused stress to the employees, who found they were performing according to training expectations with their clients, but not receiving the same from their leaders. At Genius Within we are continually working on the language we use in our policies and procedures, and a job that never quite makes it to the top of the 'to do' list is to change them from written documents to videos, to be neuroinclusive. For many of our staff who work remotely, the written documents are how they form their beliefs about us. We can't just download example policies from HR websites; we have to make them our own in order to maintain consistency in the psychological contract and our company culture. As remote working increases, so does the reliance on the tone in written contracts. The staid, soulless wording of most corporate documentation will not connect the gap left by the absence of rapport without considerable thought and effort.

A good example of psychological contracts where explicit and implicit rules can conflict is work–life balance. We all have our own underlying presuppositions about how much and when we like to work. We experience these as our values, our work ethic. At Genius Within we have company policies about hours of business and contracted hours. These may conflict sometimes, particularly if there is a crisis or a large project on the go. I have mentioned before that we encourage people to work flexibly, but to use the delayed send function when they are emailing outside of office hours. I have found that if I, as leader, make one slip, it will encourage people to join me, as if the one slip has changed the psychological contract for all. What are you doing even checking your emails at the weekend, I used to wonder! But because our culture here is so very different from other businesses, my faux pas immediately plays to pre-existing expectations and is very hard to undo. An ADHD forgetful moment of pressing send instead of delayed send is an easy mistake for me. I then have to be extra-diligent in recovery.

People are used to getting mixed messages from their leaders; hypocrisy and incongruency are the norm when policy states well-being aspirations but the behaviour of leaders role models corporate commando, where the status is linked to how long you stay at work and how much you can take on. A difficult thing to accept is that when you make a mistake, people will assume it is intended and will read all kinds of meaning into it. They come with what I call 'pre-employment trauma disorder', having experienced lack of safety in other organizations. As a leader you have a disproportionate impact on what others think is the right thing to do; you have to take care of your boundaries if you want others to do the same. Rousseau's work on the psychological contract recommends being explicit when you are breaking a norm, owning it, and explaining why it is necessary as a one-off. I have not always managed this, but I have had good results when I do. I recommend radical candour to mitigate a violation of contract experience.

Fiona always says we must 'fess up', and she role models this beautifully:

> I have worked at Genius Within now for nine years. When I first started, I was an experienced leader; I was very experienced in managing geo-graphically dispersed teams, which is what my teams at Genius Within were. I thought I had that covered. However, I hadn't factored in leading a majority ND [neurodivergent] team; this was completely new to me.
>
> My teams at Genius Within are usually 80 per cent neurodivergent, which is wonderful; people in my teams are creative and have a can-do attitude, but there is a but...if your communication is ambiguous and not delivered in the format that works for the individual, all this crea-tivity can be lost in confusion.
>
> On reflection this is what I realize went wrong:
>
> - A lot of communication I sent was via email – we didn't have Teams then.
> - I found that a lot of the emails I sent were misinterpreted, and I was confused and so were the team. I thought I was being explicit.
> - This led to what I called 'ping pong back and forth', and was not very productive. Worse, sometimes, sending an ambiguous email can put people in overwhelm, or upset them, and this takes time and energy to then resolve.
>
> Looking back now I also realize that there was a great deal of time wasting.
>
> What I do differently now:
>
> - If I need to communicate a new task or instruction the first

thing I do is pick up the phone or have a Teams call immediately and then follow up with an email. This avoids the back-and-forth emails occurring, as I can check out if I have been understood.

- If I see the 'ping pong' emails occurring with other team members, I do not watch this happen. I learned I have a tendency to take the bystander role in the 'drama to calmer' model, so I have taught myself to instigate a three-way call now to prevent the confusion.

- I use the clean feedback model [see the next section] right from the beginning when I'm working with a team, and encourage that I get this back, frequently. This builds up the trust and rapport lightly, so that when we run into a real problem, we have a system that everyone feels safe with to resolve the difficulty.

One really important thing for me, that I have always done as a leader, is to acknowledge if I am the one who has made a mistake – I fess up. We all do it, and as a leader in Genius Within I know I have to own this, and I'm not afraid to do so. Fessing up is a powerful sign of your own confidence and signals that I am human and that you can trust me.

Giving and receiving feedback

In their seminal work, Professor Avraham Kluger and Professor Angelo DeNisi[14] reviewed the academic literature on giving and receiving feedback and how it affects people at work. Their summary was fairly damning. They found that most performance feedback leads to demotivation rather than motivation, and it is reasonably likely to break psychological contracts of trust and appreciation. Yet performance appraisals remain in force in many large organizations and represent an annual faff of paperwork, with two very uncomfortable people trying very hard to be honest with each other, without coming across as unduly harsh, unduly lenient, unduly ungrateful or unduly defensive! Kluger and DeNisi named an issue in feedback, the problem of 'cognitive elaboration'. They explained that when there is an exchange of feedback information, the giver tends to use ambiguous, inferential language such as 'confident' or 'lacking attention to detail'. The receiver then has to work out what that means and think of examples that might fit the feedback; they have to do the work of cognitive elaboration.

The problem with cognitive elaboration is that the receiver often gets it wrong. People delete, distort and generalize the feedback they receive, and it is more likely to end up confirming their existing beliefs. Their beliefs may be that they are amazing, and so they attribute negative feedback to an unreasonable boss and remember the positive comments. Conversely their beliefs might be that they lack value, and therefore the negative feedback confirms their worst fears and positive feedback is overlooked, and all the variations and nuances in between.

From a neurodivergent perspective, it is said that ADHD children (for example) receive 20,000 times more negative feedback by the time they reach secondary school.[15] Such a heavy additional load of negative messaging takes its toll over the decades, which makes marginalized people more vulnerable to even neutral or balanced feedback. Professor Kluger and a different colleague, Dr Nina Nir, came up with a process called the 'Feedforward Interview'[16] that prioritizes the positive actions a person has taken and deconstructs work performance from the perspective of mastery. This technique is good for building self-efficacy,[17] which means your belief in your own ability to act. The Feedforward Interview is easy to learn and can be instituted quite easily as part of a review process to build a positive relationship around strengths. It is certainly true that we can build psychological safety, strong psychological contracts and motivation when we focus on success. It is also true that psychology has historically focused on the negatives, as the full diagnosis labels awarded to many of our neurodiversity community can attest! Attention **deficit** and hyperactivity **disorder, dys**lexia, **dys**praxia – each condition could equally have been defined by the many strengths that they bring – hyperpassion and creativity syndrome, visual thinking dominance, verbal skills thinking dominance. The Feedforward Interview can help recalibrate for individuals who have had their entire education / work identity constructed according to their struggles.

At Genius Within, we have found it necessary to augment the Feedforward Interview with a process called 'clean feedback',[18] which breaks down the cognitive elaboration for the feedback receiver. It also gives us a framework for having difficult discussions around performance or relationships. 'Clean' refers to the idea that you can reduce or remove the bias that you have inserted into your language based on your inference and interpretation.

Clean language was developed by Māori psychotherapist David Grove,[19] and taught to me by Dr Caitlin Walker, Penny Tompkins and James Lawley, among others. Clean feedback involves separating the inference from the observation. Instead of saying that someone is 'confident', you would state your observation, in context, first:

> You stood at the front of the room and smiled. From this, I inferred that you were confident. The impact this had was to make me feel relaxed.

> I noticed that the form was only filled out in three columns and that you hadn't written in the fourth column. From that I inferred that you didn't have enough detail to understand the audit. The impact is that we need to go back and get more detail and provide more explanation.

Using the clean feedback model, we can break down communication, behaviour and emotions while holding the space for intention to be positive. We give even more detail for a neurodivergent colleague to fully understand when they have done great things, which helps recover self-efficacy. We also give neurodivergent colleagues the ability to unpick cognitive mismatches in expectations which can repair breaks in psychological contracts. Clean feedback operates on positive intentions; if we use it to remain curious and gain understanding of what was happening for others, it can build trust – you have to have this baseline before you can use it safely. However, the level of detail it requires means we have to pay attention and remember what was being actually said and done. We tend to remember how people made us feel, but the details of what was happening can be vague memories. In clean feedback, we are encouraged to make a note of these straight away, so that we can bring them to a discussion when the time is right.

We have found this a necessary part of our culture when we have so many overlapping and intersecting differences in our staff. It creates safety by letting everyone know, from the start, how they can raise issues and deal with difficulties. By preparing for them, we prevent people from feeling unsafe when they have had a surprise or negative experience. We train all staff – not just our coaches, but admin and back office staff as well – in giving and receiving feedback. As leaders, we open ourselves to it ad hoc, but also in surveys and meetings. We role model accepting clean feedback and sending the signal that it is safe to raise criticisms as well as making it clear that as leaders we expect to fail. We intend this to go some way to correcting the leader as hero, on a pedestal issue, but it requires skill because accurate feedback can create unsafety if not implemented with care for those with the least power in the organization.

Rejection and hostility

There are two concepts I want to talk about which crop up when creating sustainable neurodiverse cultures: rejection-sensitive dysphoria and hostile attribution bias. I have a reaction to both these terms, because they are literally the opposite of my maxim 'you're not messed up if you feel messed up in a messed-up situation', but let me explain them. So, rejection-sensitive dysphoria (also known as rejection sensitivity) refers to an intense and overwhelming fear response to rejection.[20] It can sometimes go hand in hand with justice sensitivity,[21] which is a hyperfocus on whether or not something is fair, and results in people finding it hard to let something go that wouldn't trouble others. Rejection sensitivity is (logically) increased for people who have been excluded in education, community, family and workplaces. It often comes from a rational self-consciousness following repeated experiences of rejection, and leads to intense bodily experiences of emotions (heart racing, butterflies in stomach) as well as obsessive thoughts and replaying events over and over. It can feel traumatizing and relate to prior history of trauma.

Hostile attribution bias[22] is part of the wider concept of attribution theory, which is the idea that we make attributions of other people's intentions (inferences, interpretations) that are not accurate, but are instead based on our own experiences. We might make more positive attributions towards someone in our social group or with similar demographics – these are the basic cognitive processes that lead to prejudice and in-group / out-group connections. Hostile attribution bias is when we are primed for people to be negative, even when they are neutral, forgetful or even positive in their communication and behaviour. Like rejection sensitivity, hostile attribution bias is a defence mechanism, often born from experiencing hostility and trauma. Now, not all neurodivergent or otherwise marginalized people are traumatized, but we are more likely to have experienced this than the general population, and more so in workplace contexts. So hostile attribution bias is more likely to be a hurdle in the cultures of inclusion that we seek, and the natural diversity of communication may inadvertently activate hostility. I call this activation the neurodivergent 'switch' that we experience when we flick from seeing someone as 'motivated to be on our side' to 'not on our side'. The same shock that I experienced when I realized that not everyone was intrinsically motivated can lead to an overcorrection if we don't have safe spaces to deconstruct the experience and revise our shock with contextualization of the bigger picture. We start sorting through our memories for negative experiences and build up a wall of hostility that others find impenetrable. They experience it as disproportionate punishment for human error. We experience it as a rupture in the psychological contract.

Rejection sensitivity and hostile attribution bias lead to a bit of a conundrum. They are similar to drama responses, but could come across as victim, persecutor or indeed rescuer and bystander. A person expecting to be rescued could perceive adult ego management as rejection or hostility. As a leader reading this book, you most likely have positive intentions, but you may not always be perceived positively. By this I mean more so than the justified misunderstandings that arise, or the subtle slights that emerge when you are not grounded in your power or stuck in neurodivergent discomfort, as already discussed. I mean this can happen even when you are doing all the right things. You might give a beautifully clean Feedforward Interview, and still inadvertently trigger a response. It can be a 'them thing', not a 'you thing'. It can be hard to take and can trigger your own defences; I certainly have spent hours wondering what I did to offend when actually it was nothing to do with me.

Equally, you cannot assume you are faultless and use these psychological constructs to minimize your role in a problem. I have merrily left people to process what I assumed was something in their own emotional development when actually they were harbouring a grudge, and it would have been better for me to reach out. This is again a great reason why you need supervision, allies and a tight team of colleagues, because you need to separate your own responses from those of your staff or members. In the next chapter we will talk more about strategies for resolving hostility and handling rejection sensitivity, but for now, just note that they are deeply incongruent with psychological safety. You need a strategy in place for handling difficulties, and you can't merrily plan feedback or feedforward without some guardrails. The depths of psychological safety needed to successfully include neurodivergent employees in honest feedback exchanges might require more effort than you are used to providing.

Professor Amanda Kirby, a long-time peer on the journey of the Neurodiversity at Work movement, shared her experience and advice on handling these tricky aspects of neuroinclusion:

> The term 'psychological safety' is one I hear being banded around often by organizations wanting to do the right thing, and has been related to good team functioning. A standard definition interpreted from a neurotypical perspective may exclude those where there is a challenge in interpretation. The concept, which has some sound principles, is often used as a descriptor to say it is safe here to speak your mind, without considering, in fact, if that is true. The lack of clarity in meaning is something that I have discussed with many neurodivergent folks, especially when they have also been told they can be their 'authentic self'.
>
> When there are power differentials within teams it can be difficult to know when to speak and when not to; also for some people processing and interpreting information may be more challenging. All this makes it harder to know how much to say and what to leave at home. I find this grading sometimes challenging myself. I am quite forthright and want to be open and friendly but then may reveal parts about myself that I later regret sharing. This has then been replayed later and then taken out of context.
>
> Ironically, by opening ourselves up to others, this can result in a lowered level of trust as colleagues may believe you have not always been honest in who you really are. The reality is that we often can mask as a survival method to fit in. The challenge is understanding when it is safe to speak and it not being rhetoric. If we say something that doesn't fit with the group, how do we assess whether this is inappropriate or not? Part of being in a safe environment is taking risks, failing and learning from them. I wonder if this is being taken from a neurotypical perspective. It may also be seen from a position of resilience. The

reality is that so many of us have had poor past experiences in school and workplaces and we are starting from a position of low self-esteem and self-confidence. A fear of failing again and again can be a massive hurdle to overcome and why so many individuals decide to remain quiet and not rock the boat...and masking continues.

I believe that leadership requires the need to ensure if we use terms like psychological safety we have a responsibility to consider the potential risks that this brings as well as gains. There needs to be a safety net of support. We all have a responsibility that while intending to do good we do not, in reality, expose someone to greater harm.

Job crafting

A long-time model of performance in organizational psychology is person–environment fit theory,[23] which states that the quality of work performance is defined by the extent to which the person fits their role and environment. For example, I am a competent leader in an entrepreneurial role, but would be a terrible political or corporate leader. These theories have been refined over the years, and the myriad of factors included have morphed and changed. From a neurodivergent perspective, of course adjustments moderate the impact of an environment / role, such as ear defenders or assistive technology. In coaching, we typically work on the different behaviours, thinking processes and emotional responses to help an individual take control of their environment and role.[24] One of the more recent iterations of person–environment fit theory is job crafting,[25] in which the person crafts their role, rather than a person found to fit the role. This heralds a new direction for leaders interested in neuroinclusion, because it gives us a foundation on which to allow differentiation within teams, so that they can perform at their best. The important thing about job crafting is that it is bottom-up, giving employees the agency to bring their unique skills and passions to the organization.

Job crafting happens naturally, over time, as roles evolve with organizational change, and a top tip here for neuroinclusion is to review roles frequently to avoid taking people for granted. People who can't function in ambiguity will appreciate an annual review where the job description is updated to include the reality of what the person is actually doing now, rather than their original contract. This gives both parties a chance to consider whether the remuneration and job title are still fair, and unpick any issues. Job crafting can be done at the team level, allowing diverse members to play to their strengths, but needs to be balanced across the needs of the team function; job crafting isn't an excuse to avoid the general housekeeping or more dull tasks that no one wants to do. For example, I have said that I am a good finisher, because I don't like things being left as they take up too much space in my limited attention. However, I have worked in teams where no one liked being the finisher and those tasks were left to me, without appreciation. I floundered and became increasingly demotivated and resentful. Conversely, job crafting done well can lead to increased engagement and career fulfilment. It works best when people are intrinsically motivated and there is some freedom around how the demands and resources of the job can be planned.[26]

If you remember my explanation of Dr Helen Taylor's complementary cognition from Chapter 1, you will see how job crafting can blend with neurodiverse teams beautifully. Advocate and health economist Tumi Sotire comes at this same concept from the perspective of an old economic theory, the theory of comparative advantage,[27] which relates to nations collaborating to exchange trade according to what they are naturally able to deliver. Sotire and colleague Charles Freeman devised a simple graphic for explaining how this can work in diverse teams:[28]

If we do what we are good at, we are all better off

Janet 1 day work   John 1 day work

Combined total 4 Iron 4 Cakes

Janet specializes in Iron   John specializes in Cake

Combined total 6 Iron 4 Cakes

DAVID RICARDO – THEORY OF COMPARATIVE ADVANTAGE

My colleague Jacqui Wallis says that we should all do what we uniquely do first, before we then work out what's left and divide the remaining tasks. Job crafting is an interactional process; it isn't static and allows us to be flexible according to the demands of the wider field in which we work. It does, however, require us to know what we are good at. As we have already discussed, that can be hard for marginalized people to identify, let alone offer up in a debate. I see a lot of neurodivergent people still hiding their proverbial lights under a bushel, fearful of critique and putting themselves out there. At Genius Within we have created an online assessment of strengths, comprising cognitive, emotional and sensory skills, to allow people to work this out. It is called the Genius Finder™, and provides your own spiky profile, pulling out the things that come naturally to you. We offer a team view, so that you can see where your team skills chime and where they diverge.

When we did this a few years ago, we saw how few people reported a talent in numeracy, which gave me the impetus for revisiting finance training. We could see that there was a general lack of self-organization skills, which led to hiring dedicated project managers. We could see that verbal presentation skills, literacy, creativity and visual skills were well split across the company. We noted that emotional resilience was lacking across the business, but stronger in our HR team. An honest appraisal of where the skills are in your organization will facilitate strengths-based job crafting; this is a solid plan for neuroinclusion and company culture.

An overarching theme in career theory is the contrast between the extent to which your career is a result of your own efforts and 'agency' versus the extent to which it is limited to the resources in your environmental structures. The reality is both, and the interplay is relevant. Like leadership, some career theories focus on personality, intelligence and accurate vocational choice. Also within the research on career development is a deep repository of narrative and interview-based studies, which draw on the experiences of underserved communities and their psychological barriers and breakthroughs. Such stories play deep into the underpinning belief systems of our sociopolitical culture. On the one hand we have the espoused value of the 'American Dream' and 'pulling oneself up by the bootstraps'. On the other we have the issue of few role models who are 'like me' and the psychology of 'you can't be what you can't see'. We have narratives of hardship for those who break through their class, gender, race, ethnicity, sexuality and disability, where their novelty as leaders attracts additional criticism and even hate speech.

Dr Holly Slay and Professor Delmonize Smith evaluated the career narratives of historical leaders from Black communities and their speeches, written works and interviews.[29] They found a theme of uncertainty, a sense of being the 'token hire' and vacillating between advantage and disadvantage, never knowing who will perceive which aspects of you. Blending job crafting with the Feedforward Interview is a strategy for authentic communication around the strengths of your neurodivergent or marginalized colleagues, which will do more than raise the efficiency of the workload; it will signal a deep respect for their talents. This may start to overcome some of the structural deficits acquired by being from an underserved community and bring a creative agency,[30] which will, in turn, facilitate engagement, psychological safety and a strong contract.

Summary

Sustainable leadership is built on a strong culture, but cultures are defined by unwritten rules, which can be both unintelligible and conflicting for neurodivergent people. As a leader, I encourage you to spend some hyperfocus on culture, because the impact of culture is persistent. An urban legend in industrial / organizational psychology is management consultant Peter Drucker, who coined the phrase 'Culture eats strategy for breakfast'.[31] Most of you will find strategy easy, along with your neurodivergent problem-solving creative genius. But culture is a wider, bigger-picture problem and it needs your conscious attention. I worked on an MBA programme for a while with Dr Paul Tosey, who led the course at the University of Surrey. He used to tell students an allegoric tale about three monkeys, which I think encapsulates the way rules, psychological contracts and motivations can be embodied in a company culture.[32]

Imagine this: three monkeys are in a cage. There is a stepladder. At the top of the stepladder, a researcher places a banana. Immediately the monkeys climb the ladder to reach the banana, and as soon as they do, they are hosed down with cold water (poor monkeys, but don't worry, this is a thought experiment, not a real one). They try again; they are hosed down again. Eventually they stop trying. Then one of the monkeys is removed and replaced with a new monkey. The new monkey heads straight up the stepladder, but the first two monkeys pull them back until they stop trying. Then a second monkey from the original group is replaced by a new monkey. The new monkey again heads up the stepladder and is pulled back until they stop trying. Finally, the third monkey is replaced. The new monkey is again stopped from reaching the banana, even though their cage mates have never been hosed with cold water. They have simply learned the rules of the cage.

Dr Martin Seligman coined the term 'learned helplessness',[33] when we learn to stop trying because it is fruitless. This is the opposite of self-efficacy, and the monkey story shows how organizational cultures can persist with learned helplessness even though the negative event is far from current experience. It is a cautionary tale, which inspires me to debrief, reflect and give feedback regularly, so that we can learn and move on from bad times. Unless we find ways to communicate and bring into our conscious minds the unwritten rules that are preventing growth and progress, we will stagnate.

I have outlined some of the models we use in organizational psychology to understand and frame workplace engagement, which is the foundational basis for workplace culture. In a safe and productive culture, there is room for taking risks, diversity of thought, diversity of culture, gender experiences and ages. Indeed, such diversity is a creative advantage and allows us to hold internal knowledge about the diverse client base we may serve. The difficulty is creating organizational structures and processes that hold these values in check and give us the format of resolving misunderstanding and conflict, particularly when these are loaded with pre-employment stress, rejection sensitivity and hostility bias.

Understanding that there is a psychological contract, which is in the eye of the beholder, is an important frame for sustainable leadership, as is knowing that we may inadvertently break it when we make mistakes or act differently without explanation. Working with marginalized colleagues may result in more intense emotional responses to psychological contract breaches, and a default position of learned helplessness,[34] which we need to counter as leaders. Instead of typical awkward performance appraisals we can build trust and self-efficacy by using Feedforward Interviews. Giving and receiving clean feedback can be a way back from ruptures and a way to bring into the light the unwritten rules that are holding us back. You can use Feedforward Interviews to identify people's Genius Within and align their formal role to their stand-out strengths.

CHAPTER 10

The Genius Within Operating System

I called Section 3 'Sustainable Leadership' because once you have mastered the psychological journey of self-care and ambition, you need to work out how to institute this in your community or organization to create a sustainable culture. 'Do as I say, not as I do' will not work; the unwritten rules of culture will prevail, and as I have said before, people are watching you. They will interpret what you do and say as the rules, whether you like it or not, and whether it is intentional or not. This can be hard for neurodivergent leaders, because we make mistakes and have overspills that we find hard to control. Trying to be perfect all the time is constricting – it costs too much and leads to burnout. So, having diligently worked through some of your challenges, what else can you do? I prefer the approach of radical candour. It is a bit like authentic leadership, but with boundaries and caveats to help you walk the fine line between healthy vulnerability and toxic victimhood. Once you are established as a leader, you need to accept the identity of Goliath and not David. This can feel very weird if you have battled from the margins to a position of power and find it odd that people see you that way. I find it very difficult to process the power I have sometimes, which doesn't chime with my inner child. When people behave towards me as a powerful person, there is still a quiet voice calling 'Hold on a second, don't you know I am a 14-year-old who is too scared to go to school?' With power comes accountability, and, given that you can't always rely on your own emotional regulation to buffer the inner child, you need to set up systems, accountability and psychological safety in your wider environment so that it holds you, and your group, safe. There are a series of steps to this, which I have approached by building a coaching culture, appropriate to a coaching-based company, but I think it would work for all – both workplace and community contexts.

Everyone at Genius Within undertakes what we call 'core models training' as part of their induction. This includes: transactional analysis (drama roles, as in Section 2), clean feedback, the drama to calmer model and double loop learning. This sounds easy, but it is not always! Some people learn these models immediately and they make total sense. Some people find they make sense but are hard to embed in everyday behaviour. Others wonder why, as a member of the finance or admin team, they have to learn all this 'hippy' stuff. It used to be the case that only the client-facing staff were well versed in these coaching psychology style approaches; however, as the 'back office' staff team grew, we realized how important it was to provide a level playing field for all.

Clean feedback

Clean feedback training as a standard skill for all at work sets a fundamental rule for communication in your organization – that it is possible for two people to have the same experience and make wholly different interpretations. This truth seems self-evident, but the depth at which we need to accept it is not. The majority of people assume that their inferences and interpretations are correct, even with considerable evidence to the contrary. Unpicking co-cognitive dissonance is vital for understanding social rules. I have provided many examples of this from my own experience of misunderstanding and being misunderstood, but these reverberate across every interaction point in your community.

Some examples of mismatched interpretations I have seen include:

- Anxious perfectionist neurodivergents upset with colleagues who send them emails full of typos because they interpret it as carelessness, whereas the behaviour is prompted by dyslexics thinking that they are in a safe space and don't need to overly police their thought flow.

- Earnest dyslexics having trigger responses to co-editing documents where the changes are tracked in red, which reminds them of school experiences, and becoming fearful around colleagues who didn't notice the microaggression.

- Thoughtful dyspraxic people worrying that they are going to be late and let people down because they can't find a venue, including on their way to an interview with us, who then need a lot of reassurance, which can be misinterpreted as self-centredness.

- Passionate ADHDers speaking quickly and enthusiastically being interpreted as show-offs or arrogant.

- Caring autistic people withdrawing and being interpreted as rude when they are in an overwhelm.

- Loyal colleagues with long-term chronic health issues being interpreted as grumpy when they are, in fact, exhausted.

Mismatches cause psychological contract breaches when they aren't debriefed, even in a neurodiversity-literate organization. They cause irrevocable ruptures if they are left unattended. People have a natural tendency to assume that the drivers behind the behaviour of others are the same as their own motivations if they were exhibiting such behaviour. People who only raise their voice when they are furious find it hard to interpret loudness as enthusiasm. People who only make text errors when they don't care about the recipient find it hard to understand people who can't control typos even when they care deeply. People who only get lost when they haven't planned a journey properly think that arriving late and in a flap is driven by carelessness. People who need to see faces on video calls to engage think that those who have their cameras off must be doing something else. People who need to turn their cameras off to listen well think that those who have their cameras on are too intense. People who find maths easy think that those who don't deliver their figures on time are lacking accountability. It goes on and on and on.

Unpicking through these layers of learned social rules, which intersect and mismatch across neurotypes, age groups, cultures and genders, requires some boundaries, and we have found clean language[1] an essential framework for working in multiple, intersectional diversity. Clean language is a style of interviewing, used in therapy,[2] coaching[3] and qualitative research,[4] and its fundamental principle involves limiting the influence of the facilitator upon the client, coachee or interviewee. From this principle, emerged clean feedback emerged, which seeks not to limit the influence of the giver or receiver, but to separate it from the event and to provide a framework for investigating how different versions of the same event emerge.

To learn clean feedback, you first need to be able to cognitively separate the information that has been presented from your inferences. This is the clean context and the beginning of psychological safety, when you can agree between you that two truths are possible, that two opposite things can be true at the same time. You need to be able to cognitively process that your inference may not match the intention of the other party.

Let's unpack a few of the examples:

Presented information	Negative interpretation	Impact	Benefit of the doubt alternative
Email with at least one typo in each line	Doesn't consider me a professional colleague or isn't able to write professional emails	Worried that this might happen with external customers	Was in a hurry and didn't want to break flow for spell check
One-liner email	Impolite or angry	Worried that it might be that I had done something wrong	Was in a hurry and wanted to get the information over in order to not hold up the recipient
Camera off in video meeting	Doing something else	Worried I wasn't interesting or had mistimed the meeting	Finds face and eye contact intense and wanted to devote listening ability to the call
Arrived 15 minutes after the start time and saying things like 'Oh gosh, this was a really tricky place to find'	Hadn't planned properly or read the instructions; thought the directions I sent weren't good enough	Thinks less of the colleague's professionalism OR feels blamed for not sending good enough directions	Finds directions very difficult and anxiety over the importance of the meeting caused an overwhelm

These examples show the way you can use clean principles to separate your inferences from another's intention and hold space for them to be 'okay', even when they have transgressed one of your personal rules for communication. It can take many iterations of practice to get the first column right, as we are not all practised at remembering detailed words, actions and expressions. We tend to remember our emotional response instead; however, this is what we need to work on. I have seen people give feedback that an email was 'curt' – this is an inference. Or that the person arrived late and was 'self-conscious' – but this isn't entirely clean either.

First, people have different models for 'late' – some people think on the dot is late because you should arrive with time to take your coat off and sit down before the start time. Second, 'self-conscious' is an inference unless you are a mind reader. What did the person actually say? Were they apologetic? Apologetic doesn't automatically infer self-consciousness. To get good at clean feedback you need to train your brain to notice the actual words people use, their body language and the circumstances around the event. It can be hard to remember, so we encourage people to note things down when they have a reaction, to help their memory so that they can give the feedback cleanly.

Pre-forgiveness

In the earlier days of Genius Within, we used to think that everyone knowing how to separate presented information from inferences was enough of a guardrail to keep people psychologically safe when breaking down conflict. This turned out to be naive, and actually much more is needed. Clean feedback, given without thought to the person receiving it, can feel just as disruptive as any feedback, but actually even more intense because it is so accurate. We call this 'clean bashing'! We have also found that the negative interpretations, even if you are holding the space for your interpretation to be untrue, can cut deeply, particularly when accompanied by a power imbalance. I remember a colleague receiving some feedback with negative interpretations and she said, 'Wow, I didn't know clean feedback could be weaponized.' I think this is a reasonable statement, and it really taught me how careful we need to be with a powerful and accurate communication device like clean feedback. If you can't be sure that people know how to do this, it might be better to give no feedback at all. To address this, we are working on ensuring that our core models training establishes the clean context, and that when we teach clean feedback, we show the difference between a 'benefit of the doubt' interpretation and a hostile attribution. We sometimes call this 'pre-forgiveness'.

People Director for Birmingham Pride Char Bailey explains her approach:

> It's not easy to give people the benefit of the doubt, but it gets easier with practice. It's become part of my way of life to expect that people are trying to do good. I used to expect and then accept poor treatment from others, minimizing the impact because I had predicted it. Giving the benefit of the doubt is partly about believing in the good of others and also in believing I deserve kindness and the best from others. It's nicer on my brain to assume that if something went wrong that it was as a result of a mistake or misjudgement rather than malice.
>
> I learned to give people the benefit of the doubt by unlearning the rules or narratives imposed on me about how people work in society. What if everyone is just doing their best? What if I can use my empathy here? Is it easier for me to believe in love or hate? When you ask a better quality of question you get a better quality of answer. The benefit of the doubt is like giving myself a chance to land on a positive thought. It means if I need to find out more information, I can make a gentle, caring and curious enquiry. I believe successful communication is about achieving the intended result. I learned, through trial and error mostly, that to get the best from people, it's important to show them you believe in them and see the best in them.

If you are lacking in self-efficacy and don't know how to change your behaviour, it can create a sense of learned helplessness and divide people. In the original clean feedback model we set the rule that any time you give a piece of developmental feedback, you have to do the cognitive elaboration on what you would prefer. For example:

What didn't work well	What I would prefer	How I would interpret that
Email with typos	For you to let me know you are in a hurry with a short note: 'Sorry, in a hurry... XYZ'	That you are taking care of my emotional response in your communication with me
One-liner email	For you to have a conversation with me to agree that one-liner emails relate to the urgency of the task, not the mood you are in	I would know how to interpret the changes in your style and not take it personally
Camera off in video meeting	A note in the chat: 'Camera off so that I can concentrate'	That you care about whether I feel heard in the meeting
Arrived 15 minutes after the start time and saying things like 'Oh gosh, this was a really tricky place to find'	For you to pull over and send a brief message to let me know you were on your way Or that when you arrived you said, 'I'm sorry, I was really looking forward to this meeting; I got myself into a muddle with the directions because it was so important'	Lets me know that you care that I am waiting and not knowing if you are okay Or lets me know that you don't blame me for not sending good enough directions

Providing people with the feedback of what you would prefer leaves the feedback receiver clear on what they can do. The feedback becomes a negotiation:

I will try to remember to mention I am in a rush when I send an email, but if I forget, perhaps you could just jot back to me to ask if I am in a rush, rather than assume I am being rude or curt?
Yes, I can do that.
Great.

And now those pair of colleagues have taken the sting out of the mismatch in preferences and they can communicate even when they clash values. As you can see, breaking everyday communication down like this takes time and energy. It is not something you can do in a rush, and for some people joining Genius Within it has felt arduous and like a waste of time. Until, that is, something goes wrong and they need to lean into the process to resolve something they feel strongly about! All these negotiations work much better when feedback is regular and exchanged over positive events as well as to resolve problems.

We try to combine clean feedback with feedforward to ensure that people don't see it only as a stick to beat them with, but just a language tool that is neutral in intention. We have tried to institute clean feedback and feed-forward into everyday meetings, events, annual surveys, ISO 9001 incident reports, evaluation of services, projects, supervision meetings, appraisals, probation progress meetings, company meetings and more. By placing it everywhere, we are continually role modelling the process and getting everyone up to speed. It becomes normal to give and receive accurate, insightful feedback. We learn more about how other people think and the diversity of interpretations that are possible, rather than be wedded to our own assumptions about each other. This builds confidence in working in diversity and a clean context.

I learned this process in my early twenties, when my husband and I first became a couple. We used it to learn how to respect each other's communication style, because our neurotypes are quite diverse and our family communication is very different. We came into the relationship with dia-metrically opposed underlying beliefs about communication. My husband, for example, if he has had a bad day, prefers to be left in peace to process his thoughts and feelings. I prefer to talk mine out. If I came home cross, he would go out and leave me to it! I would be furious by the time he got home. Conversely, if he came home cross, I would follow him around the house trying to ask him about it. He got totally overwhelmed! By doing what we thought was best for each other and trying to be supportive, we were both doing exactly the wrong thing. Management works like this. I have explained how I need the odd bit of encouragement and then a lot of flexibility, but to some this looks like abandonment. The kind of support they needed I would experience as micromanagement and so it wouldn't be my natural style. So, by providing to others what works best for me, I might look like I am unsupportive, even when I am trying to be supportive. Knowing this can also result in an overcorrection, which then appears like meddling.

Clean feedback works best when it is part of a culture of positive regard, the 'clean context'. In my marriage, we have always had a foundation of trust and positive regard, so the exchange of feedback is amusing and endearing; it has strengthened our relationship. However, having the foundation of positive regard isn't a given, particularly when you have a team with historic marginalization, which can lead to rejection-sensitive dysphoria and hostile attribution bias. Further, clean feedback is a communication device, and won't be sufficient for unpicking breaches in the psychological contract. When someone has let you down, caused a crisis, failed to avert a crisis, lied, stayed silent when they should have spoken up, committed gross misconduct or covered up a problem – these things are more serious. Clean feedback might open the discussion, but you need a more expansive framework in which to hold the feedback exchanges when they are within a drama dynamic. A simple two-way exchange might lead to worsening relations and a third party might be needed to unpack the drama, cleanly and respectfully.

My colleague Kate Omonigho Pearson explains how pre-forgiveness helps her negotiate her typically neurodivergent self-doubt and overanalysis patterns through feeling safe with her team:

> Starting my leadership journey, or rather my attempt to start my leadership journey, in my previous roles was extremely difficult. My interpretation was that I had to just be the best worker – don't moan, work as hard as possible, and hope that I would be promoted, because surely being the best worker would mean that I would seemingly walk in one day and be told I was promoted?! I had the inner belief that if I did exactly what my boss wanted me to, then this would be rewarded with the start of management roles. This was completely wrong, I was saying 'yes' to everything, and it led to burnout, resentment, and exacerbated my anxiety.

> Joining another organization, and becoming a leader within a year, opened my eyes to what leaders should be, and exactly what was wrong and not working for the management I had encountered in the past. I started with a 'I want to be liked by my team' attitude, and this quickly became ineffective as being liked and leading a team to perform well isn't always a great alignment. What I discovered is that a team has a togetherness, and all parts need to work in synergy. This book mentions

Ubuntu ('I am because we are'), and I couldn't agree more with this concept. Being neurodivergent (but not diagnosed at that point) and leading a majority neurodivergent team was so rewarding when we worked together, and I quickly learned that I didn't need to work at being liked by my team; being liked was a consequence of being fair. Fair in how I communicated, managed tasks, managed performance, led the team, pushed them, but allowed for them to complete the work in the ways that worked best for them. And also holding my hands up when I made a mistake – this definitely created greater trust and acceptance. We are managers, not robots! In this team we had a togetherness that absolutely rocked!

Things changed again when, four years after becoming a leader, I entered into a senior leadership, and I gained a diagnosis of bipolar and the following year ADHD, to go along with my anxiety disorder. I managed a team of seven team leaders with a continuous voice of 'Yes! But what if...?' and then every negative possibility running through my mind. This was alongside periods of being overly confident and shooting off in many directions with hundreds of ideas, and then having a moment a couple of weeks later where I realized that they were utter shite. Overconfidence and exaggerated self-belief was just as damaging as the lack of belief and anxiety. I had to learn to check in with myself and assess my mood, energy, thinking, resources and plan of what next. I would have spurts of energy for days or weeks even, creative, excelling, delivering, driving my teams well, and then complete lack of faith in myself and in a state where I was unable to talk coherently, take care of myself or my family, or do any basic life tasks. I needed to establish a 'what works well for me' to ensure that I pace my energy, manage my emotions, and do not negatively impact on my team. For me, learning to manage myself was top priority, followed very closely by the key to being an effective leader – clean communication. Clean communication with my team, my boss and myself. What is actually going on? What needs to happen? How is that going to happen? There will be peaks and troughs in energy and output, but that is for my team also. From my experience of managing different teams, the most successful ones are those that have pre-forgiveness, accepting that people work well in different ways, and understanding that as a team we are together – we cover each other, we support each other, we can bounce off each other and create something brilliant, and we can stretch to pick up for people when they are unable, as they then return this for us.

Naming drama

When I was working with my previous company, we were training a struggling school in both the clean feedback and drama models. One day I had a bit of an 'Aha' moment when I realized that the clean feedback and some clean questions were ideal for coaching someone who was stuck in drama roles. The standard questions used in clean feedback can map neatly onto the different roles to help someone shift their position. Let me explain, with some examples of clean questions after each drama role:

Victim: What would you prefer? What would you see or hear that would let you know it was working better? What would you like to have happen? [And then work with them on what is in their direct control, or how to advocate for what they would like with others.]

Persecutor: What did you actually see or hear that let you know [the person was wrong / the thing wasn't good enough]? What would you prefer? [And then work with them on how to express this factually, using concrete examples rather than judgemental language.]

Rescuer: What did you see or hear that let you know it was your job to jump in, or that only you could do it? What would you prefer? What would work better next time? [And then work with them on how to express this factually, using concrete examples rather than presumptive language.]

Bystander: What did you see or hear that let you know it was not your job to contribute? What would you prefer? What would work better next time? [And then work with them on how to express this factually, using concrete examples rather than presumptive language.]

I have tried my darndest to get these questions instituted at Genius Within so that we ask these questions instead of going along with drama. It is often a lot easier for people to sit back and run their ingrained patterns or distract themselves with admin, easy tasks that are well within their control. It is also hard to get everyone trained to such a high level in terms of clean feedback and understanding their own drama patterns.

So, things naturally bubble over sometimes, and we can get into a loop of rejection-sensitive employees triggering rejection-sensitive managers, and relationships can become strained. This is usually manageable, but in 2021, after a long hard year of lockdowns and very little time to build relationships (we all had Zoom fatigue), things started to unravel. Our staff were acting as de facto safeguarding leads for many of our clients – we went from a couple of safeguarding events a month to several in a week. As that emotional labour took its toll it was rolled up the management lines and we had several teams in drama states, with psychological safety starting to unravel, particularly in the teams with the highest contact with the most vulnerable clients. We already had an employee assistance programme, but this was a tertiary, neurotypical response. We already had a solid HR leader, Angelica Simpson, who was well versed in unpicking drama, but she was only one person! We had some very highly skilled managers, but most of them were also neurodivergent plus one other marginalizing identity, and they were at their limits. We needed preventative action.

My husband provided the most amazing metaphor. We were talking about how high the stress levels were at Genius Within with the world in crisis around us, and he said, 'Your company is like a Formula One racing team. The cars either go at 200 miles an hour, or they're smashing into the wall. What you need is a tyre wall to soften the impact, some gravel traps and some chicanes to slow things down.' He was so right! Now that might sound like more secondary and tertiary responses, but actually it also gave rise to a primary response. I discussed this with my colleagues and we realized that we had a whole bunch of neurotypical boundaries that worked for regular cars, but not for Formula One speeds. We had some bespoke practices, like clean feedback and drama insight training for everyone, but we didn't have a clear process that anyone could instigate or follow. Everyone knew what could be done to resolve drama, but not everyone knew what the rules or boundaries were about when it should happen. More junior staff didn't feel they had the power to initiate a resolution, so felt ill at ease when there was a difference of opinion. It's very hard to give clean feedback when there is a power imbalance. There were different rules around behaviour – what some would characterize as a bit of emotional overspill others would experience as malicious gossip. When should we intervene to facilitate a conversation away from drama and into a calmer space? When the majority of the team are in drama, whose job is it to press the 'adult' button? Can anyone do it, or should it only be managers and HR who intervene? Yes, that's right. A whole company of neurodivergent people who find unwritten rules challenging had some unwritten rules.

I went into a problem-solving hyperfocus. I wrote down the unwritten rules. Using the clean feedback framework, I reflected on some of the unprofessional behaviour I had seen / heard, such as:

- Eye rolling in meetings or answering questions with one-word answers and a sigh.

- People leaving online meetings without providing warning or an explanation.

- People scheduling meetings with less than 24 hours' notice and then verbally expressing anger when colleagues couldn't come.

- People sharing their frustrations with each other in messages and private calls and not bringing it to the person concerned to resolve.

- People frequently sharing frustrations and concerns with friends in the business who are not directly involved and can't help.

- WhatsApp groups communicating out of office hours with issues and problems that should be resolved within the working day.

- An increase in overwhelm – including making negative or accusatory comments in open meetings, followed by the group remaining silent rather than asking questions.

- Staff undermining their managers by failing to complete tasks without advance notice or apology.

- Leaders staying silent about concerns they had about and for others.

I want to be really clear here for a minute. I do not think that having a neuroinclusive culture means you have to put up with these things. These examples are actually pretty common in most communities and workplaces. You do not have to accept unprofessional or unhelpful communication in any group. Yes, neurodivergent people might struggle more with social communication and overwhelm. But these examples are indicators of psychological unsafety. It is your express job to prevent these examples of hostility and passive aggression. I have come to the conclusion that rather than brushing things under the carpet and looking the other way because someone might be struggling, neuroinclusive cultures acknowledge and seek to resolve communication issues swiftly and, critically, kindly.

I know some neurodivergent people think that they should be permitted to behave in these ways as a reasonable adjustment, but actually case law shows otherwise.* And as a majority neurodivergent company, it is not a case of better-resourced people accommodating those with a disability. Condoning unreasonable, unprofessional behaviour from people is not neuroinclusive; it is weak leadership. We can forgive each other, we can seek to prevent rather than chastise, but this has to be reciprocal. The neurodivergent person overspilling has to understand the effect they have on others and be accountable for it. An apology, acknowledgement, discussion and conversation is required to recover the situation, openly and transparently. Neurodivergence is not an excuse to treat people badly. Allowing hostile environments to perpetuate is not safe and will violate the psychological contract of those around this behaviour. What is neuroinclusive, however, is avoiding going straight to a disciplinary or any other formal procedure – this creates more hostility and unsafety, particularly when the behaviour is coming from a problem in context or a relationship. The examples I provided happen when there is a problem. Your job is to find out what the problem is and resolve it, which is much harder to do when people are fearful of losing their job...

When people are behaving as the examples in this list, it doesn't tend to

---

* See *Philip McQueen vs. General Optical Council Employment Appeal Tribunal 2023* for an example, at www.gov.uk/employment-appeal-tribunal-decisions/philip-mcqueen-v-general-optical-council-2023-eat-36

get better on its own. Ignoring it until it is so bad that people leave or need to be disciplined is not a time-saver. I'm being very directive here because finding it hard to hold a clear boundary on what is okay and not okay in a workplace is very hard for leaders who have been trained to fear conflict, dissent or exits. I have struggled with this time and time again, as I have shared openly in this book so far. All my neurodivergent leader colleagues struggle the same. However, we have worked hard at personal development in coaching to transform our emotional intelligence and come to a place of healing, loyalty and trust. The ultimate test of a neuroinclusive culture is providing a framework in which conflicts and hostility can be resolved within the team. This is the boundary we have chosen to apply at Genius Within – we don't have to accept it, but we do have to create space for resolution before turning to formal HR processes that might lead to an exit or a rupture in the psychological contract. Everyone gets a chance to resolve. If they choose not to or are unable to, they need a different response, but we start with an assumption that resolution is possible. We call our process the 'Eight "drama to calmer"' responses, which has three informal stages before we start making formal notes, in which most drama can be, and is, resolved.*

In 2021, when we found ourselves in a period of crisis and drama, I wrote an expansive document, rather like a code of conduct but more detailed, which listed some of the examples above and many more. In columns, I debriefed each piece of evidence into what the positive intention might be behind each, what the risks to psychological safety were, and how you could address them from a clean feedback and drama perspective. The table on the following pages presents some examples, and there are many more in the neurodiversity coaching books that I co-wrote with Professor Almuth McDowall.[5] The key element is separating the actions / words from the intention, and considering a positive intention behind each behaviour, rather than making assumptions about colleagues that are negative.

* https://geniuswithin.org/avoiding-workplace-drama-4-steps-to-being-an-ally-not-a-rescuer-victim-or-persecutor

Behaviour	Positive intent	Risk	What we do	When to ask for support
Raising volume and speed of voice when communicating, expressing anger, frustration or fear about something. Can be in a meeting or email	This usually happens when someone feels passionately about something; could be in defence of a client or colleague, or a sense of injustice This could also be a culmination of many disparate events, which again, if work-related, could provide insight, but also might be related to personal difficulties	Creates 'walking on eggshells' fears in colleagues who are triggered by or the target of intense emotions Sets unsafe precedent if ignored; worries those who come from neurotypical fields where emotional outbursts are taboo at work and those for whom calm and courtesy are a high priority for workplace well-being, as well as being triggering for people with high levels of conflict in their personal lives There's a risk the individual has something valuable to contribute but this is not heard because the tone has overshadowed the insight	• Use stages 1–3 of the 'Eight "drama to calmer"' (8D2C) strategies (explained below) to unpack what is happening • Consider a group session to resolve and share apologies if this is appropriate • Coaching and group coaching to improve awareness of triggers from all parties	• If the regularity means that team relations are compromised; however, this is also a personal boundary level • If the individual is in distress • If the outbursts are triggering distress in others • If 8D2C stages 1–3 have not addressed the issue, or have not been appropriately applied, any party involved or observing can confidentially enquire to HR about instigating stages 4–7

cont.

Behaviour	Positive intent	Risk	What we do	When to ask for support
Speaking / messaging significantly less than normal in team meetings or projects; saying the minimum only Might include under the breath mutterings, eye rolling and asides when others are speaking; can also be present in email communication as well as meetings	Usually caused by similar to the above, a strong emotion, but this is a different, more passive style of expression	All the above risks apply to passive displays just as direct displays Both in-person and written passive displays create tension in a team. Where many are neurominorities, who may struggle to identify, vocalize and resolve emotion, the impact can create significant distress Also as above, there's a risk of dismissing the cause of the distress because the communication method is unwelcome	• Use stages 1–3 of the 8D2C strategies to unpack what is happening • Consider a group session to resolve and share apologies if this is appropriate • Coaching and group coaching to improve awareness of triggers from all parties	• If the regularity means that team relations are compromised • If the individual is in distress • If the outbursts are triggering distress in others • If stages 1–3 of the 8D2C have not addressed the issue, or have not been appropriately applied, any party involved or observing can confidentially enquire to HR about instigating stages 4–7
Abruptly leaving or ending a meeting; not answering emails or not picking up the phone when called	Emotional overwhelm, a decision to withdraw (flight) rather than express strong emotions in front of colleagues Has important information to share but doesn't know how to share it, or feel safe enough to do so	Creates tension and upset for remaining colleagues, wondering what happened and if the person is okay; indicates a precedent of how to behave, which may cause alarm to new or junior colleagues Safeguarding issue if an individual becomes not contactable There is a risk that important information will be forgotten if the individual doesn't circle back when ready to do so	• An individual always has permission to leave or withdraw if needs be. If this can be done with an explanation of 'overwhelm', great; if not, an 'overwhelm' can be given retrospectively to explain to colleagues rather than leave them hanging or wondering • This may also require an exchange of apologies if the silence created a negative effect on the group • Use stages 1–3 of the 8D2C strategies to unpack what is happening	• If the regularity means that team relations are compromised • If the individual is in distress • If the outbursts are triggering distress in others • If stages 1–3 of the 8D2C have not addressed the issue, or have not been appropriately applied, any party involved or observing can confidentially enquire to HR about instigating stages 4–7

Typical triggers for emotional overwhelm

- Sensory sensitivity to light, noise, feelings, taste, smell, temperature

- Lack of sleep

- Hunger

- Alcohol and drugs, including prescribed drugs if inappropriately prescribed or no longer needed such as ADHD meds and antidepressants

- Misophonia

- Rejection-sensitive dysphoria

- Pain

- Past anxieties and triggers

- Draining of the 'social battery', which may happen quicker in neurodiverse teams where people have different styles

- Short notice changes to plans

- New IT software or a new process that isn't easy to understand

- Lack of adjustments or accommodations from others

- Changes to staffing structures without being aware of the confidential details behind the news

- Blame or chastisement for events in which you tried your best

- Being accused of harm when you didn't intend harm

- Feeling like the 'only one' who will take action even when you have asked for help

- Too much or too little communication (personal preference here, we will get this wrong a lot)

- Difficulties outside work – caring responsibilities, moving house, financial changes, family or friendship breakdown, health and disability leading to reduced capacity

- Racism, homophobia, transphobia, sexism, ableism, ageism, classism – discrimination either at work or experience of it in wider society, directly and indirectly

- Microaggressions and incivilities

- Clients' experiences triggering our own memories or experiences

- When rules are inconsistent or clash depending on who is asking

- Too many Zooms

- Waiting for others to 'notice' your state and intervene

- Feeling like you can't take action to resolve

- Disagreeing with a colleague and lacking the processing space to explain yourself

- Disagreeing with colleagues and being overruled or outvoted

- Disagreeing with colleagues and having your way but worrying about what they think

- Making a mistake and worrying about the impact

- Interpretation anxiety – wondering what others intended or meant by their actions and not being sure

- Worrying about clients' welfare

- Paperwork and processes

- Too many deadlines

- Not enough space for informal relationship building

- Being put on the spot

- Having to wait to check in or resolve

- Persistent lateness

- Aggressive and passive aggressive comments

- Not knowing when to stop, and taking on more than you need to without a break

- Rescuing others at work or home until you've reached your limit.

Eight 'drama to calmer' stages

After I had listed all the difficult behaviours and potential causes, I then charted the options that were open to all employees to raise and recover from difficulties. I outlined an eight-stage approach, the 'Eight "drama to calmer"' strategies:

1. Give and receive clean feedback in the moment, or set aside time to do so soon after the event.

2. Ask the team manager to run a clean feedback timeline to unpack the intentions and interpretations on both sides.

3. Ask a manager from a different team or HR to run the clean feedback timeline debrief.

4. Review reasonable adjustments to assess if the issue is about resources and being overstretched.

5. Ask to have some co-coaching, where an external or uninvolved, mutually trusted coach can work through the difficulties with all parties over a few sessions.

6. External, occupational health or counselling referral.

7. Instigate a disciplinary or grievance procedure.

8. Work out a fair and reasonable separation – could be a move or an exit.

Stages 1, 4 and 6–8 are what happens in most companies, albeit not cleanly. Stages 2, 3 and 5 are particular to us and, I argued, the things we need to keep a neurodivergent community emotionally safe, given our over-lapping and sometimes conflicting drama roles. They are, using my husband's metaphor, the gravel traps and tyre walls. To be clear, we were already doing this. But we had neglected to write it down so that those in remote locations or not in management could feel reassured or able to instigate easily. I sent the document confidentially to two trusted autistic women in my wider community for their feedback. One got back to me and said it was the best thing I had ever written. The other responded that it was terrible, and if a leader in her workplace shared something like that, she would resign immediately! I worked through the latter reviewer's edits and came up with a version that accommodated her main critiques. I then sent it out as a discussion paper and ran several workshops and an anonymous survey to gather insights from the team as to what they would prefer and how they felt they could implement the process. I diligently addressed each concern, acknowledging them all even when they were in a minority. We then made the revised documents live, thus producing a tyre wall, a gravel trap and some chicanes to prevent harm when fast-paced cars come off the tracks.

You might think, from my description, that the 'Eight "drama to calmer"' stages (or the 8D2C, as we call them) are tertiary (reactive) responses rather than primary (preventative). But they are both, because, first, they act as a guide to nip things in the bud before they go irreparably wrong (tertiary). Further, and most importantly for prevention, knowing that there is a clear process, which exists before something formal starts in an HR context, is also very reassuring if you are the kind of person who worries about what might happen if things go wrong, as they have many times before (primary). Sharing these unwritten rules with all employees, rather than just asking managers to stick to them, empowers those employees to instigate a resolution if their manager is too busy, in drama themselves, or isn't aware of how worried they are. It places power in the hands of all employees, rather than them being at the mercy of their manager's skill and attention span. Knowing what the stages are means that everyone knows there is a step before, or after; they can work up or down the stages to escalate assistance and de-escalate drama.

Many employers I consult for have asked me how we do this at Genius Within when they find out how neurodivergent our staff team is. They want to adopt this policy for themselves and institute it. I always say no. They can't have it, because it needs to be co-produced with their teams. Their in-house rules will be different. They aren't likely to be able to give and receive clean feedback, or give feedforward accurately, and may not have a strong HR team who can facilitate drama resolutions. They may have a performance appraisal process that is poorly linked to pay and causing organizational injustice issues that are far too complex to unravel like this, particularly when the team level managers can't change the bureaucracy around the policies. I tell them that I can facilitate them to come up with their own process, but they need HR buy-in and ownership. They wince. They want a quick fix, a few workshops, but this is culture change, not learning needs. To embed a process like this it needs to be role modelled at every level, most of the time, and needs Ubuntu-style community empowerment to ensure that those with the least senior roles have enough psychological safety to bring their experiences and gripes into a discussion without fear of reprisal. Few people are happy to start a formal HR process. You need something boundaried before that starts, to catch the wobbles before they become entrenched, but you also need to signal that this won't automatically become formal. But just because you don't have the latitude to embed a comprehensive process like ours doesn't mean you can't act positively.

Jacqui Wallis, whose corporate leadership experience is more recent than my own, advises that the place to start is with healthy acknowledgement of strengths and struggles, while prioritizing sustainable work patterns. She shares the feedforward that she would have given herself in her corporate role:

When I speak to other employers now, I often hear that they WANT to help their employees to reach their full potential. They are often stumped as to how to put disability adjustments in place, and what to choose for the best effect. We need to open up this conversation; allow individuals to admit to areas they struggle in, and employers to offer tools and ideas that support them, or to move tasks around to suit the strengths of others in the team. Employers need to invest in tools and platforms that identify the individual's needs while at the same time looking for the system-level changes that mean more of their employees can access support at a time when they might need a bit more support – be that temporary or long term. Changes will happen, to us, to those around us, and to workplaces. The ability to adapt to that change is the difference that makes the difference.

We need to trust that we all have a shared aim, to be able to be our best, most productive self that advances the company's AND our personal goals symbolically.

So, if I could skip back in time, and could go back, as my own line manager, I would tell my previous self these things:

- Your strengths are amazing – trust yourself and them and follow your dreams.
- You do struggle with some tasks. This is not failure; this is balance and you admitting this in itself is a strength.
- Overworking will not, in the long run, deliver your dreams.
- Assistive technology can make your dyslexia feel obsolete.
- Disclose – not just for you, but for those who come after you. Open the door for those who do not have the power of leadership or who cannot advocate for themselves and make it okay to talk about our cognitive differences.
- Direct the negative energy into positive actions. When I stopped masking, I was amazed at the amount of energy I suddenly had for everything else. Trying to be someone else is incredibly cognitively draining.

If I was my line manager, the behaviour I would be asking me about was my overworking. What is going on for me that is leading to that behaviour? I still worry that overworking is hard-wired into me, learned in all those hard-won moments of success and promotion. These days, however, I am better at putting in boundaries – I will NOT put my emails on iPhone, for example. That has taken the most enormous amount of self-discipline, because I know that left to my own devices, and without healthy boundaries, my default is still to overwork.

Being able to be your most authentic self is a gift at work. I realize I am lucky to be able to experience that every day. However, what I do know is that if you are a neurodivergent leader, or you lead neurodivergent employees, spending time understanding how you or they can work at their best will be some of the best investment you ever make!

On the following page I've shared the graphic we use to show the stages. I've differentiated the 'normal' HR processes from the Genius Within ones; these are the chicanes in stages 1–3 where we just try and slow things down before they risk going off the track, as well as the gravel trap of having a good reasonable adjustments framework and co-coaching options before people hit the wall. You can go up or down the eight stages depending on what has happened. An elegant exit is a tyre wall; this is much harder, but still possible. When we finished these two policies, we went through all our other documents – whistleblowing, grievance, disciplinary, performance management, etc. – and aligned and referenced them back to each other. It was an in-depth activity. But like building and sustaining a leadership career, leading a sustainable culture involves work. There are no short cuts here – you are either in or you are performative. These detailed plans take time to implement and to role model, but I sincerely think they are worth it in the long run if you want a high performing, intersectionally diverse team to thrive. We are still learning. Drama still happens. A process like this won't prevent all drama, but it adds significant confidence to those who seek to avoid or resolve drama.

My colleague Angelica Simpson, an HR professional, shares her thoughts on the small but essential 'benefit of the doubt' questions before we start any formal process:

Having worked predominantly in HR for eight years when I started my journey at Genius Within, the thing that stood out to me were the steps

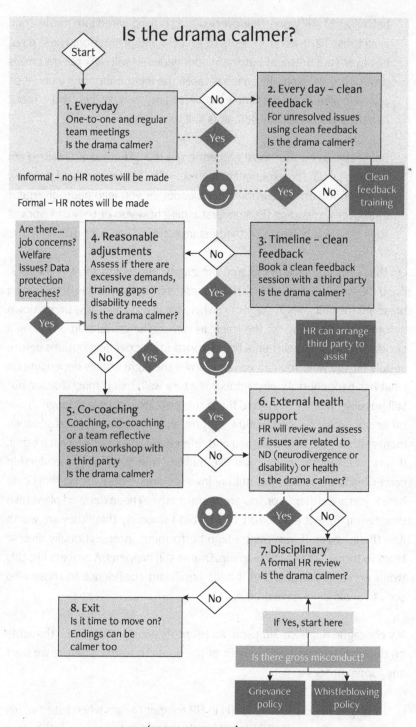

Is the drama calmer?

Start

1. Everyday
One-to-one and regular team meetings
Is the drama calmer?

No → **2. Every day – clean feedback**
For unresolved issues using clean feedback
Is the drama calmer?

Yes

Informal – no HR notes will be made

Formal – HR notes will be made

Yes / No

Clean feedback training

4. Reasonable adjustments
Assess if there are excessive demands, training gaps or disability needs
Is the drama calmer?

No ← **3. Timeline – clean feedback**
Book a clean feedback session with a third party
Is the drama calmer?

Yes

Are there... job concerns? Welfare issues? Data protection breaches?

Yes

HR can arrange third party to assist

No / Yes

Yes

5. Co-coaching
Coaching, co-coaching or a team reflective session workshop with a third party
Is the drama calmer?

Yes

No

6. External health support
HR will review and assess if issues are related to ND (neurodivergence or disability) or health
Is the drama calmer?

Yes / No

7. Disciplinary
A formal HR review
Is the drama calmer?

No

8. Exit
Is it time to move on?
Endings can be calmer too

If Yes, start here

Is there gross misconduct?

Grievance policy

Whistleblowing policy

EIGHT 'DRAMA TO CALMER' RESPONSES

the organization took before going anywhere near a formal HR process. Coming from environments where those employees who 'didn't fit in' or 'caused too much trouble' were swiftly removed from the organization and many protected conversations were had and money was used freely as a 'get out of jail' card, this was alien to me. I remember speaking to my old HR colleagues and asking, 'What have I done?!' My old colleagues, on hearing Genius Within's process, concluded that was just too much unnecessary work!

But now, three years on, it's those very processes that make my job the most enjoyable role I've had, a role where I give my all with no resentment, I get to work with the most amazing people, and my voice is not only heard but welcomed!

What are those steps I hear you ask...

- We should always check that the role is properly resourced, and that the employee has received sufficient training and induction.
- If performance has not improved, we should ensure that the employee has been offered reasonable adjustments via a formal workplace needs assessment (WPNA). This should always be provided, even if no condition is disclosed.
- Reasonable adjustments should be given one month to bed in.

Nothing unusual there but you'd be surprised how little these steps are even glanced at let alone deeply thought about in most HR departments. These steps make such a difference to an individual who is probably dealing with a myriad of things, from masking their neurodivergence, not understanding their neurodivergence or maybe not even knowing they are neurodivergent. For those individuals to know that their employer wants to support them to work at their best and provide support, equipment and coaching if required has a huge impact!

So what? The difference those steps make is not spending hours on employee relations case management calls as I've done previously, and being able to count on less than two hands the amount of employee relations cases I have managed in my three-year tenure! I also think about those 'protected conversations' I used to have and what a difference the aforementioned steps could have made to those individuals.

Whose pattern wins?

This question comes up a lot in a team where neurodivergent patterns clash and both stakeholders in a conflict are entitled to flexibility. If you are an ADHDer who likes spontaneity and have an autistic colleague who prefers routine, for example, you have been through drama resolution, you know that each other is coming from a position of positive regard, but on a day-to-day level, one person is going to have to shift their pattern to accommodate the other. I asked who this person should be to a group of undergraduate students recently and there was an immediate response – 'the line manager'. I can see why; this is built on a solid principle that the person with the most resources should be the one to compromise, and the embedded cultural norm is that the manager will have more resources than the employee. I certainly tried to be the one to accommodate and adapt for the early years of Genius Within, but found it was impossible – it is a tempting decision, but actually a reflection of parent–child relationships, not adult to adult. The reality is that resources are more complex than organizational hierarchies. There's a tendency to assume that the neuro-divergent is the employee and the manager will be neurotypical.

Naomi Johnson, an ADHDer in multinational technology settings, found herself the neurodivergent leader in a predominantly neurotypical space:

> Navigating through many industries, roles and then into leadership as someone neurodivergent has been a huge mountain to climb, partly as I didn't know I was neurodivergent for 75 per cent of it. I was lucky to have had, in that time, some awesome leadership, while not know-ing I was neurodivergent. They were leaders who recognized people work and communicate differently, and therefore were teaching me by example even if they weren't realizing how supportive they were being.
>
> I've also had some absolutely terrible managers and leaders who, if nothing else, taught me how things really shouldn't be done, and

have given me toolsets and understanding that I wouldn't have had otherwise.

I went on a leadership course very early on, before neurodiversity coaching was available, which was all around communication styles and soft skills. For somebody neurodivergent, it was probably one of the best lessons I could have had. In teaching me more about different communication styles or personality types, seeing the world through other people's point of view, it helped me to understand that it gave me a basic set of tools around communication, which for somebody autistic was incredibly helpful.

The communication journey was expanded when I moved into the international space, where all of a sudden intersectionality caused all of my knowledge on communication to be out of date. As an autistic person, the discovery that working across 40 plus countries had completely different verbal and non-verbal communication styles was an enormous adjustment, and had my brain working many times harder for a long time while I processed all the additional information and learned how to lead and communicate successfully with an international audience.

Another challenge I have faced is my masking tendencies, which, for a long time, caused me to chameleon into different leadership types rather than finding my own style. I was becoming the leader I perceived that person I was with or the team I was with at the time wanted me to be, reflecting their needs as opposed to my actual authentic self, and flexing my leadership to what the team needed from me. My over-empathy and people-pleasing due to my ND [neurodivergent] profile meant I was not being myself as a leader; I was being what I thought everyone wanted or needed me to be, which is a very different thing.

However, being a neurodivergent leader should not just be about us navigating the neurotypical world and adapting our leadership and communication. I spend so much time accommodating and adjusting to support the neurotypical world in flexing my communication styles and my way of doing things that it holds me back at times and makes me less effective. The neurotypical leaders and team members also need to flex, check their biases and increase their knowledge. In that way, we begin to meet in the middle, as opposed to the neurodivergent leadership always having to do the legwork and always having to be the one accommodating the neurotypicals.

Don't be seduced into a trap of thinking that making a culture neuroinclusive means sacrificing yourself, or you will have to start this book again from the beginning! Naomi's experience reminds me that in sharing our vulnerabilities and negotiating through feedback and drama, we can avoid default expectations that the most senior person in the room should always defer (rescuer) or indeed insist on having it their way (persecutor). Let's instead aim to arrive at a place where we can pragmatically negotiate compromise on an ongoing basis, in a light-hearted and respectful discourse. In a clean timeline debrief, both parties have to accept each other's version of the truth, even when it is unpalatable, and find a way to work together that might involve compromise. Sometimes it will be you who needs to shift; sometimes others. If this isn't working and you've both given it your best shot, we have to learn how to construct an elegant exit, which can be extra-sensitive for those of us with histories of rejection-sensitive dysphoria and / or relationship rupture.

Elegant exits

Since unpacking miscommunications doesn't always work, and there have been occasions when I have failed to do it in time, I have sometimes carried great lumps of grief in my stomach for months, even years, as I ruminate on what I might have said differently or what they failed to understand about my intention. Stuck, conflicted relationships rarely happen because one or other party is solely 'good' or 'bad'; more that the relationship didn't work anymore, or the particular styles of both bring out the worst in each other. I've found that in these cases, the longer I spend dissecting the conflict, the more aggrieved I can become. Sometimes in ruptures the drama continues, and as a leader I've had to hold a dignified silence, knowing full well that to revisit it would exacerbate the drama and that it is better to quietly move on. This can feel risky from a leadership position, because sometimes joint colleagues have split loyalties. But believe me when I say no good can come from relitigating a rupture with third parties because you are worried about what others might have said about you to them. Excruciating as this is, we have to maintain confidentiality about exits, we have to keep close counsel and stay quiet; the alternative is unprofessional gossip, and failing to lead by example. If you have colleagues who are judging you by what others say about you and not by the way you behave with them, that is on them. You can't control it and you have to let it go. I know, ouch.

Don't confuse a commitment to debriefing and feedback with the need to justify yourself, and learn to notice when others are doing this. As dramas emerge, when trash talk is happening, when people are feeling victimized but projecting blame, when I am being called out harshly instead of called in, or if I am calling out harshly instead of calling in, it is hard for me, as a neurodivergent, not to want to set the record straight. Where feedback loops go wrong is when both parties are trying to use them to establish that their version of truth is the 'correct' one. This inevitably leads to 'clean bashing', as one party insists that their interpretation of hostility was justified. It comes from being externally referenced and undersupported by close allies; we get stuck when we need to feel validated by others for the strong emotions we experienced, and we haven't unpacked that those strong emotions might be projections of our past. I've had to work on this, hard, because I have so many hang-ups about being negatively interpreted in the past. I've had to accept how other people may find me bombastic even when I am vulnerable, and learn to live with it.

Even elegant exits can be hard, particularly when you have been close, when you are mentoring people who are also neurodivergent and when you feel you have not done your best. An often-made mistake at Genius Within, regularly pointed out by Gill Rudge, is that sometimes we try too hard to salvage a relationship that has served its time. When I get stuck here, it's usually because I haven't been blameless. I have now seen this third hand – watching managers in our company wring their hands over a few mistakes they made that they are using to justify giving someone more chances than is necessary. Remember, it is not your job to be perfect! Just fair. If those mistakes mean they deserve a second chance, go for it. But don't avoid calling time on something just because you weren't perfect in response. Some people don't have exit strategies; they only know how to leave or let go when they get to the end of their tether, for example if they have insecure attachment styles. Someone may take your generous acceptance of a blame proportion and use it to cast you as the villain in order to justify a flounce out. You may do this to them. I can honestly admit to being on both sides of this dynamic over the years. Yes, they will probably talk trash about you. Finding a way to live with that is essential self-care. If you are fair, and they are professional, you can exit a relationship from drama without recriminations, and actually, the earlier you do this the better. If the actual or psychological contract isn't working, you do more damage trying to hang on than generously letting go. Elegant exits come from acknowledging the reality of a situation rather than trying to force something together just because you once loved or believed in its longevity. As a leader, the onus is on you to make that call if no one else is brave enough.

Double loop learning and governance

Central to a lot of the feedback, drama and psychological safety themes is double loop learning,[6] which I introduced in Chapter 1, Section 1. To remind, in double loop learning, we don't just solve a problem, we try to unpick the conditions that caused the problem in the first place. In a psychologically safe culture, double loop learning is fundamental because it legitimizes mistakes and problems and recasts them as learning opportunities. I've explained how governance systems can assist you in this process. You don't need to be driven by what others have done; create your own processes and link them to external verification. I had an amazing colleague with quality management expertise who developed our International Standards Organization (ISO 9001) accreditation by starting with what we already had and aligning it to the standards before filling in the gaps, rather than starting with the manual and writing a whole bunch of new policies and procedures for us to learn. In Genius Within, we have embedded the following processes that support ISO 9001 and now ISO 27001, which allow us to reflect and learn as part of everyday routines:

1. Impact data: We have automated emails with survey links for all services, which are timed to go out a few weeks after the delivery. The delay is important – research shows that feedback on the day tells you how likeable the deliverer was, but not how much was learned. We also do telephone follow-ups after longer periods, collecting both rating scores and qualitative feedback. This is summarized in a

monthly spreadsheet that is reviewed by our management team and used to make decisions on hiring particular skills, training for staff and areas where we need to focus account management. It wasn't always automated via our bespoke database; it used to be done manually by our office staff and me, personally. We have picked up serious failures this way, but also the information can be used to promote our work and generate positivity in the team.

2. Incident reporting: When something happens beyond an everyday slip or if there is a safeguarding issue, we write a summary document of the event, the stakeholder impact, corrective action and preventative measures, along with costs. We do the same with near-misses. Each report is summarized in a line on the central issues log, with category drop-down menus. The central issues log is reviewed periodically in leadership meetings and board meetings, to identify themes and patterns, so that we can get a warning when several little mishaps are actually part of a broader theme. This allows us to plan technology fixes to human error issues and again work out training needs or key skills that we may need to hire in specifically.

3. Risk management: We have a risk register, where we categorize risks based on the strength of their impact and the likelihood of them happening. The risk register is updated monthly, with each manager assigned a risk to mitigate. It is also reviewed in board meetings, where themes and patterns can be noted. It was in just such a meeting that we realized it was time to hire a professional HR manager because so many of the risks were related to people issues such as contractual changes associated with large commissions. This process helps us keep abreast of wide-ranging big-picture issues, which are easy to get lost in the day-to-day churn of work. It also helps us to keep focus on things that are important, but not necessarily urgent.

4. An active and engaged non-executive board: I cannot tell you how useful this is and how much support I have received from board members over the years. There are no hard and fast rules on this unless you are a charity; you get to write this up as part of your company memorandum and articles (a posh term for the

structure of decision making and company purpose). Often, people with very senior executive expertise will join the boards of smaller companies to 'give back'. We pay our board members a small fee (two hours per month at the same rate as our executive directors), which is a lot less than many of them get paid elsewhere, but it is a principle, and also allows us to remunerate board members who are not employed at high levels. We review board membership and recruit people who have specific experience that we lack in the leadership team to provide guidance and review, depending on our current strategic plan. They look at our accounts, our risks, our HR summary data, any legal issues, and help us drive strategy. Most recently, one of our board members held us to account for overworking and not walking our own talk in terms of self-care; on other occasions they have led financial reviews and legal checking of complex contracts for which we were out of our depth. Board members share legal responsibility for the company, meaning that they have a vested interest in preventing us from bankruptcy or legal action. It's another check on our good practice and a way to share the burden.

5. Decision-making clarity: When you form a board (and have share-holders), your memorandum and articles (and shareholders' agreement) have to define decision making, responsibilities and how to handle disagreements and problems. Take advice on this. Some of the hardest parts of my leadership journey have been unpicking where I set up teams to fail with lack of clarity on roles and responsibilities, and how we would resolve disputes. I assumed that since we were so small, disputes would be easy, but as we grew, they were not, and these terms of engagement were not written into our company governance. Governance doesn't have to just be for formal disagreements in legal structures like companies. The principles can apply to any group you are leading – be clear and upfront about who is expected to do what, where the decision-making power lies and what is expected in return for participation. Plan for failure, how people will exit, how conflict will be resolved. By creating a written document, you might find that you uncover mismatched expectations from the start.

These are examples of good governance and reduce the drains on the cognitive attention of our leaders and managers. It is all too easy, when you are a neurodivergent leader particularly, to get caught up in daily quick wins and to overlook smouldering issues that might get out of control if they aren't addressed. Governance is a way of taking the pressure off you and your colleagues; you don't have to remember everything, and have those moments where you wake up at 2am with a sudden worry – there is an agreement, a place, a system for handling and storing the knowledge of what happened, and a good audit trail in place. It helps destress unexpected events and takes the emotion out of them, making it much easier to stay in an adult ego state.

The examples I have shared relate to being an entrepreneur and a small- to medium-sized business leader, but the same principles apply to all types of leadership. If you are running a small team or department, if you are a sole trader and influencer, have you agreed terms with your followers? Do you have a code of conduct for engagement? How do you measure the impact of your work? Are there anonymous feedback loops and ways for you to reflect on and rationalize mistakes and failure? Do you keep track of risks and make time to think about them? Do you have active and engaged senior peers or mentors you can call on to review issues and mistakes?

Lyric Rivera, better known for their social media handle Neurodivergent Rebel and author of the fantastic book for managers and employers *Workplace Neurodiversity Rising*,[7] has worked through their own journey to arrive at a place of solid governance of their platform:

> My name is Lyric Rivera, and I am a multiply NeuroDivergent, late-identified adult.
>
> Late-identified, in my case, means I've gone more years of my life than not thinking I was something I wasn't, trapped in my own version of the Ugly Duckling story.
>
> For the past seven years of my life (since my diagnosis), I have been unravelling the trauma that came from almost 30 years of denying my true self.

By the time I was finally diagnosed autistic at the age of 29, I had already been in (workplace) leadership for over 10 years, starting with my first leadership role as assistant manager at a fast food restaurant when I was just 17. After fast food, I moved into management and marketing in retail, before eventually migrating into a more corporate leadership setting several years later. While much of what I learned in business leadership has been helpful in my journey as a community leader, leading a community is different from leading in a workplace setting (for many reasons).

When I started the 'NeuroDivergent Rebel' blog around the time of my autism diagnosis, I didn't know I was in the process of becoming a community leader. Seven years ago, when I started writing about my experiences as a late-identified Autistic Person online, I didn't know how to lead and care for a community. Back then, I could not have imagined that I would be blessed with the community currently surrounding me and my work.

I've made mistakes.

Much of what I know now about advocacy and community leadership I've learned in the years since starting my blog. There have been many mistakes and painful lessons along the way, and undoubtedly, I will make more as I'm still learning new things every day.

One of my personal life goals is not to compete with or compare myself to anyone but myself, a principle I carry into my leadership style as a NeuroDivergent leader.

Have you ever worked with an inflexible leader who refuses to accept new ideas and information? What was working with this person like?

I'm autistic, and while I sometimes need more time to process and accept new information than non-autistics do, I LOVE additional information and widening my understanding of things.

Every day, when I wake up or start a new project or activity, I try to be better than I was before. I also like to challenge myself to learn something new each time I do an activity. This curiosity and willingness to grow is essential for good leaders (of all types). Whether someone is NeuroDivergent or identifies as NeuroTypical, leading with one's strengths can be crucial in leadership. It is also essential for all leaders to be aware of their weaknesses (and when, where and how to get and ask for help when needed).

While everyone on earth benefits from having a clear understanding of their individual profile of strengths and weaknesses, NeuroDivergent People (who often have irregular or spiky skills profiles when compared to the NeuroTypical average) should take extra time getting to know themselves. I owe most of my success as a NeuroDivergent leader to my ability to lean into my strengths (while finding ways to avoid, offload or get help with my weaknesses).

Knowing my strengths allows me to confidently speak up about what I can do to help (and what skills I bring to various teams and situations) in workplaces and beyond.

Understanding my weaknesses has also helped in that I'm no longer afraid to ask for help when needed. I'm quicker to say 'no' to things that aren't good for me, turning projects down when I know I'm not the best fit for them.

I lead with my strengths and what I'm good at (because I know I can do the most good in the world if I play to my skills). I don't feel bad (any more) for passing on projects that aren't well suited to me (or vice versa) because I know there are people with the skills I lack who are better for the work in question.

I was a leader fresh out of corporate America when I started advocating online, sharing my stories and building my community. Like many leaders who grew up in a work setting, I was terrible about neglecting self-care, ignoring my own well-being and having weak and overly permissive boundaries (falsely believing this self-neglect made me a good leader).

What I didn't know for most of my life, before learning of my

NeuroDivergent brain, was that this tendency to neglect myself, letting people violate my boundaries and failing to rest as needed was detrimental not only to me but to those around me (who I thought I was helping by wearing myself thin).

When you fly on an airplane, in the safety speech, they tell you, 'In the event of an emergency, put your own mask on first before offering aid to other people.' The younger me would have thought this was a selfish move, but the older me understands that putting on the mask is to keep you from passing out, too, because if you pass out, you can't help anyone while unconscious.

Another metaphor I like says, 'You can't pour from an empty cup.' This is one of my favourites because, as a visual thinker, the cup metaphor clearly illustrates the problem of taking care of others without caring for yourself until you become 'empty' and have nothing left to give. If you are a person who is inclined to give large parts of yourself to benefit others, you also have to send some of the love, care and compassion that you give others to yourself.

While community leadership is **servant leadership**, even servant leaders are humans with **human needs**, like those they serve and care for.

Additionally, as leaders, whether we mean to or not, our actions set the example for those we lead. Leaders in communities work to empower and build up their community members. If we (leaders) model poor self-care and overly permissive boundaries, these values may be adopted by those who look to us for guidance. This is just one of many ways the unintended behaviours of a leader trickle down, impacting those they care for.

Community leadership is a big responsibility – the larger a community grows, the bigger the obligation for the community's leader(s) becomes. In communities, leaders must be open to taking and acting upon **REASONABLE feedback** from community members.

Leaders must learn how to sit with their traumas and cognitive dissonance that can arise when feedback is offered to them. Leaders must also learn to recognize when feedback is unhelpful, unreasonable or given in bad faith (something that happens a lot online and in larger communities).

As a Queer and NeuroDivergent community leader (with multiple marginalized interesting identities of my own), I am keenly aware that many communities fall short when it comes to considering intersectionality. Multiply marginalized individuals have unique experiences shaped by multiple identities (rather than just one). When leaders consider intersectionality within our communities, we can better understand and address the varied and complex ways the leaders' (or groups') actions can impact marginalized people, helping to minimize harm to those community members. Leaders (both NeuroDivergent and NeuroTypical) will play a key role in driving the changes that must be made to create more inclusive and equitable communities and spaces.

As a NeuroDivergent Community Leader, it is my goal to:

- Always remember, I am here to serve my community, and they are not here to serve me.
- Support my community and make the lives of my community members better (by encouraging them, leading through example, and providing resources that make their lives easier).
- Monitor and moderate the community spaces I tend on social media to keep them as safe as any public forum can be.
- Listen to what the members of my community have to say (about me, their needs and what I could be doing better).
- Be aware of the harm my actions can cause to people I am trusted to support (intentional or not) and hold myself accountable when I fall short / cause harm / make mistakes.

NeuroDivergent leaders have the potential to make a profound impact on society as a whole, driving positive change and breaking down people's barriers and stigmas towards those with brain differences (by building more inclusive and innovative communities that embrace and celebrate our unique and diverse minds).

Though NeuroDivergent leaders have the power to do great things, we often still benefit when we have help from our allies to create environments where our talents and contributions are recognized and celebrated.

Similarly, Vivienne Isebor has set up her ADHD Babes group with a commitment to provide feedback and maintain the boundaries of psychological safety:

My decision to create a space that centres the Black experience of ADHD stems from the unique challenges we face. Navigating life post-diagnosis felt lonely. Trying to access support is incredibly limited, and it felt like I had to leave parts of myself behind when entering certain spaces. ADHD Babes was a labour of self-care that developed into something bigger than me. It was an offering of intended safety, consideration and accommodation that tenderly cherished, valued and celebrated my race, gender and disability. While there are many people and allies that will share experiences and values, having a protected space for this unique intersection serves as a resting space for me and other babes before entering a world that often erases and diminishes our light.

As a community we co-create guidelines for the space and review them on an annual basis. We share them at the start of our sessions and during the sign-up process for our events. One of our important guidelines is making a distinction between recalling traumatic events and discussing the impact they have on us to ensure we can focus on recovery and healing without triggering others in the process. Having a background in applied psychology serves as an anchor for me, starting with trauma-informed care and community psychology principles. We make sure all hosts are supported in their journey with us, with flexible inductions and shadowing processes, regular team check-ins and tailored training sessions based on feedback.

The stories shared by Vivienne and Lyric remind me that neurodivergent leaders can deliver strong, authentic leadership. We have a commitment to justice, and we are not afraid to apply our principles to ourselves when we need to. Working with increasing numbers of neurodivergent leader peers over the years close up and from afar, I see the trend emerging in our styles of radical candour and transparency.

Mentoring, not managing

I am delighted to discover, in the maintenance and succession planning stages of my career, that although I am not organized or tactful enough to be a good line manager, I am actually not a bad mentor. I am finding deep joy in supporting the next generation of psychologists, neurodiversity advocates and employees to find their Genius Within and match their ambition to their potential. I love being a cheerleader. However, like everything, it isn't a straightforward journey and it isn't always easy. I have been lucky to have had very good mentors from whom to role model effectively, my favourite being my then PhD supervisor and now academic best friend, Professor Almuth McDowall. Almuth's mentoring had two tenets that made the most difference for me when I was developing my academic confidence. First, she had clear boundaries on what she would and wouldn't do as supervisor, such that I developed my own independent study. Second, she didn't mollycoddle me. I remember her saying, 'You know Nancy, a PhD doesn't get better the longer it takes.' The key difference between mentoring and management, for me, is that as a mentor your express job is to create an independent equal and, if they don't make it, it is not your job to reallocate the tasks or pick up the work. Without the burden of being responsible for wider outcomes if someone struggles, I feel free and able to be my best, cheerleading self. A mentee is on their own timeline; their job is to come to you, and they don't need nannying. They are in charge, and you can participate in the joy of learning without the level of responsibility you bear within management. By giving me this respect, Almuth created the conditions for me to thrive at the highest level of education, the point at which you become an independent academic. Mentoring and sponsorship are tools by which we can overcome exclusion and can lead to successful leadership career opportunities.[8] We need to find the right mentors and we then pay it forward by becoming the mentors we needed.

Mentoring is a chance for you to reflect on the path you have carved and what barriers remain in place for the next generation. In The Smiths/

Kirsty MacColl song 'You Just Haven't Earned It Yet, Baby' there is a verse about how the world pulls you back and holds you down. There's a layered message in there about rites of passage that we have to overcome. But there's something also about privilege and power, and unhealed patterns that perpetuate intergenerationally. The world doesn't pull everyone down and hold them back. I am sure most of us have heard our elders say, 'Well, I had to deal with it and so can you.' This is sometimes true – lessons about actually doing homework rather than just expecting to magically pass exams, the level of practice needed to be an accomplished pianist, dancer, artist, bricklayer, electrician, hairdresser, surgeon, lawyer, etc. However, sometimes it is just passing on the torture. In medicine, for example, senior doctors might have very little sympathy for junior doctors struggling to perform on three-day shifts with very little sleep. But is this a necessary function of learning medicine? Or is it just a feature of the professional training that all but ensures access only to young, abled people with no children or caring responsibilities outside work? Should children who have been traumatized by being misogynistically and / or racially abused at school simply 'toughen up' and absorb catcalling and bullying because their parents did? Should those with attachment disorders from being sent to boarding school toughen up because their parents managed it? Should our neurodivergent emerging leaders have to battle through the entry levels of careers doing all the jobs that don't suit them just because my generation managed it?

I find this tricky to answer. I've noticed the odd tinge of resentfulness when I think back on some of the hardships I overcame that my younger peers don't appreciate, and to be a good mentor I'm going to have to work that through. In some respects, I am only in a leadership position because I battled through my neurodivergent challenges long enough to get where I am today. In some respects, I can only handle the difficulties of leadership because of those battles to overcome the procrastination, disorganization and time-blindness that comes with ADHD. But on the other hand, it was also those battles that caused my scars, and my greatest advances occurred every time I refused to play the game. I stopped going to school and my grades went UP. I left corporate commando for self-employment and enhanced my productivity by figuring out how to play to my energy routines. I developed self-efficacy and career agency by overcoming things that I thought were out of my reach. I became more influential when I realized the limits of my power and the essentials of being in a balanced team. There is a tendency for humans to assume that our way applies to all. Senior leaders in corporations today have typically gotten their role after battling through middle management, putting in years of corporate compliance and with the large mortgages, divorce rates and peptic ulcers that come with it. Should that be the price we pay for seniority? What kind of businesses are run by people who all spend years having the life blood sucked out of them? Except for the specialists who are joyful middle managers, of course! Those people do exist and certainly deserve their seat at the board table. I find it perplexing that the skills we need for leadership – decisiveness, strategic thinking, problem solving, influencing – are at odds with the skills needed for management – compliance, accuracy, consistency.

What is possible for leaders who start their journey having enough self-efficacy, who have healed their inner children in their twenties and not their forties? Who found their neurodiversity community at the start of their career and not halfway through? Who started their working lives with adjustments provided and the neurodiversity movement narrative of creative strengths as an available identity? My view is that every generation has their own battles, and that human progress happens when we clear the path for the next generation, who then have the energy to go further. You don't have to do all the things you hate in order to get ahead. You will have to find a way to be reliable, to be seen as accountable and accurate. But you don't need to do that by banging your head against a wall! Take the coaching. Take the assistive technology and the tech memory hacks. Take the specialist role instead of the entry-level team leader. In mentoring, we get to choose to pass on the life lessons of value, and we learn what the next set of challenges might be. Our role is not to pass on burdens that we learned from but are ultimately no longer needed. It is to clear the path so that our mentees can go further than we were able. This is my hope for my PhD students and trainee psychologists, my management colleagues and the field of (neuro)diversity inclusion in general.

In recent years, mentoring relationships have begun to question the power dynamics. In reverse mentoring, a typically powerful person will be mentored by a marginalized person (e.g., older, senior leader and younger, junior employee) to develop new and relevant skills. There is also peer mentoring, which is the basis of the relationship I hold with Fiona and Jacqui as my business partners, and represents the evolution of my relationship with Almuth who began as my PhD supervisor but is now my academic partner.

Peer mentoring is also a relationship I have with one of my non-executive directors, Whitney Iles. I invited a contribution from her for this book, but she is an excellent boundary maintainer and has a very full workload right now, so we agreed that I would tell a story on our joint behalf. When I talk about mentoring, and finding your allies, this relationship is a great example of the mutual benefits:

> Whitney and I met in 2015, as we were both small business owners working on projects in the UK prison system. We became close through mutual appreciation of each other's willingness to stick our necks out and complain about unsafe practice (e.g., when illicit use of the drug Spice in prisons was effectively poisoning our staff). Over the years, we came to notice how differently we were treated within that same system, as a white woman (me) and as one of Mixed Heritage (Whitney). This led to a joint journey of mutual personal development – visibility of Whitney's experience of systemic discrimination, opening my eyes to systemic privilege. In 2020 we formalized the relationship by taking a seat on each other's boards to increase our collaboration and share resources in a difficult contractual landscape.

> Whitney said once that I was a pillar in her life, which I took as a great compliment, since she is that for me. As neurodivergent women, we provide each other with a safe, non-judgemental space where we can say hard things, plan out next steps and work through the nuances of our boundaries. Whitney's mentorship regularly calls me in to notice where I am failing to live according to my values, but from a place of appreciative enquiry rather than harm.

> Whitney's work is transformational and has transformed her in my time knowing her. Her prison projects have closed now, a conscious decision made for her own self-protection. In facilitating her team to consider how they would elegantly exit the contract with as much care as possible for themselves and the men they supported, I asked

the question: 'What experience do any of us have in something ending well?' We realized that none of us had experienced positive endings, but that we had the freedom to make this situation the first. Her new direction is an intentional, congruent evolution, following a graceful and peaceful closure of previous work.

Witnessing Whitney's journey in 2022 and 2023 taught me so much about my own motivation for my work and where I was engaged in unhealthy compulsion rather than leading (and letting go) with love. She is the master of congruence, like so many autists and neurodivergents, but unlike many of us, she can see that in herself as well as others. Her diligent commitment to reflexivity has brought me along for the ride and reminded me how much I still needed it, despite my intensive early career training. Whitney always notices when I stray from my values, and rarely shies away from alerting me to the risk. When I talk of good governance, it is often Whitney's voice I hear in my ear when choosing the right, longer path versus the easy short cut.

Neurodivergent overthinkers to the max, we once walked along the River Thames for an hour in the rain talking about life, love and the universe before we realized we were soaked. Neurodivergent to neurodivergent, we thrive on not needing to mask in order to connect and the release that comes from being able to be very raw, real with each other, but still maintain respect.

Where did it all go right?

I have a wonderful colleague, Charlie Eckton, who frequently says, 'Where did it all go right?' As well as being funny, Charlie's question helps to ground me in what we've already achieved. A side effect of trauma and / or marginalization is that sense of being on guard, never quite able to stop and appreciate where you have got to and the hard work it required. In our bi-annual assessments from the British Standards Institute for our ISO 9001 accreditation, the most common feedback we receive is that we don't spend enough time appreciating the positives. Can you relate to this? The trouble is that what you focus your attention on will drive your state and culture. We absolutely suck at this still, but we are getting better!

As a company, we have to work on our collective rejection sensitivity and hostility bias; we need to remember all the good things we do, to which impact data also contributes. We review our impact for faults forensically, and breeze by the continual good news, such as 20–30 per cent of our clients getting promoted within a year of having coaching with us and 75–95 per cent of them keeping their jobs (the other 5–25 per cent move roles, which is actually often the best thing for them). Every year. Since we started measuring this over a decade ago. For our 10-year anniversary, we made an impact report with the stats on how many people we had helped, which featured some client and staff quotes and interviews, to put a marker in the sand for saying, 'Yes, we do a good job.' We also received the Queen's Award for Enterprise in 2022; this is like getting an OBE or a Knighthood for your business – it is an incredibly prestigious award and very hard to achieve. As a leader, it is down to you to bring momentum to these sorts of celebrations. This might not be easy for you, personally, but it is something you need to work on for the greater good.

Do we ever just sit with the joy and let it wash over us? Rarely. I hope this is a work in progress, and just like at the individual level, I eventually learned to appreciate my power, so I hope to get the whole company to that stage as well. A wise woman once advised me to copy and paste all the appreciative DMs that I get via social media into a file that I can re-read when I am feeling low. I remember to do this sometimes, but I have yet to re-read when low. I think I just set myself a new goal? My company, your company or community will never be perfect. There will always be mistakes, and how we respond to these is the mark of quality, not them never happening in the first place. Good governance, feedback loops and learning from errors is enough. You are enough. Letting go of the need to be perfect, the mask of worrying that if you aren't perfect people will disproportionately chastise you because of your neurodivergence, gender, race or ethnicity, sexuality, class or age – these things are a lifetime's work. If you want a role model here, it is probably not me. Try Michelle Obama or Megan Rapinoe, and Google the video of rapper Snoop Dogg thanking himself for all the effort he put in to his career! Or just ask yourself, where did it all go right?

Reflections on this chapter

I'm noticing that this last section about setting up a sustainable culture has been more like an operational manual for small businesses and has less of my self-reflections than the previous two. This might be because I am still very much embedded in the process and have yet to close it, finish and revisit what worked well and what didn't. I don't know the outcome of this stage yet. I do know that I no longer feel alone and like I have sole responsibility for the company. I can adjust the settings on my metaphorical treadmill because I have other people who can take turns to run. I have attention for writing because Jacqui is holding the CEO overview, Fiona the good governance, Helen the financial security, Royston the commitment to customer service, Ian the accessible and ethical technology develop-ment, Kate the enthusiastic horizon scanning, and Angelica the operation of HR with love and respect. This hasn't happened with a few key hires. It wasn't just about getting the right people; it was also about cultivating the right relationships. The past few years have been very turbulent across the whole world, and this looks set to continue as we globally haggle over collectivism versus individualism, over rights versus responsibilities, and handle increasing global challenges. The pandemic was a pivotal time; I have explained how my company adjusted to accommodate the additional levels of overwhelm that threatened to consume us. These adjustments have been effective so far and, teamed with other changes to how we hire, manage, onboard and support performance, have transformed our staff turnover levels. But we also had to have the courage to exit a failing contract. Sometimes it isn't about trying harder, or reviewing relationships; it's that a structure is fundamentally flawed. This has been a hard lesson with consequences for relationships.

We're having a moment of reflection as I write as we work out how to bring on a new staff team from a different sector to support our digital services – these are people who come from better-resourced industries than social justice and have different cultural expectations. There are clashes, but so far our processes of radical candour and regular feedback debriefing are holding up. I don't know how easy it would be for us to onboard a new team at scale. It feels very fragile, like we have just got ourselves to a decent place of sustainability and now we need to hang on while the company grows and evolves again. My colleagues and I spend a lot of time discussing and reviewing these issues; we're rewriting our onboarding process to better acclimatize people to the clean context, and we've noticed that we need to edit it further to accommodate people who aren't used to social enterprises, small businesses and, dare I say, female majority leadership teams.

The advice I have shared with you in this chapter has brought us so far; I am yet to know how to scale them or replicate the practices / processes in other spaces. This is the focus of my research and consultancy right now. If you emulate any features, do please reach out and share; even consider researching with me the impacts. The details may change, but I think the fundamentals of prioritizing psychological safety through establishing a clean, 'benefit of the doubt' context and ensuring psychological contracts are maintained with a clear process for resolving disputes and drama will sustain. These seem to me the essential issues for the neurodivergent clients we have and the companies that are trying to be neuroinclusive, and that are missing from most management training and company policies. The structures we have for pay transparency, performance management and governance will seem burdensome for smaller businesses and difficult to retrospectively implement for larger businesses, but the underlying values of moral management and ethical leadership are transferable to all workplaces, community groups and sole traders. We are not alone – I know other businesses are working on these ideas, and at some point they will start to coalesce. As our sociohistorical paradigm shifts focus away from the heroic leader, the ideas of shared leadership and engaged members will surely grow. I am fully bought into these goals, but still fumbling with the operationalization as I shake off and heal from the embedded power dynamics of my generation. My hope is to have created enough safety and affirmative self-discovery for the next generation to progress the work.

CHAPTER 11

Advice

☑ **DO** trust your people.

We recently onboarded a new customer, and as part of their due diligence they asked us what we did with the CCTV from our offices. 'What CCTV?' we asked. 'Well, how do you manage your staff?' they asked. We were literally gobsmacked. We trust them to do their job. If there are problems, that's a communication issue, not a monitoring problem. Taylorism is not conducive to Ubuntu, community leadership, to the values of the neuro-diversity movement or indeed any diversity and inclusion climate. You will get let down sometimes, but this is better than a culture of fear.

☒ **DON'T** panic when you get let down.

Prepare for it. Expect it. Not everyone will come along for the ride, and that is okay. You need to park your own rejection sensitivity and remember that everyone loves to hate on the boss! It's a cultural narrative even when you've done nothing wrong. If you go chasing after every recalcitrant member of your group you will exhaust all your creativity trying to keep everyone happy. It is NOT possible to keep everyone happy. The greater good and knowing that you've done your best is enough.

☑ **DO** review pay, effort and unseen work as part of your evaluation of hygiene factors in your organization or influence.

Even if you have a strong 'pull' factor of motivation and passion, avoiding these basic caretaking efforts will result in people leaving you. Remember that people might have different hygiene factors to you, such as the hours you work or the sensory profile of the environment in which you work.

⊠ **DON'T** underestimate the fair exchange justice theories.

It is often about the money. Remember, your team are likely similar to you – they are socialized to avoid talking about money. They will talk about admin, effort, overwork and lack of communication, but money is usually underneath or alongside these critiques. Sometimes you need to read between the lines and have straight-up conversations to right the justice balance.

☑ **DO** learn to recognize the importance of the psychological contract.

Ask more questions, be more explicit. Even as a neurodivergent leader with a reputation for directness, you may need to be more explicit. Whether you like it or not, people with less power than you will feel they can't initiate the verbalization of expectations. They will be waiting for you to start the conversation and you need to get over your inhibition. You need to overcommunicate because often people need to hear the same message three or four times before it sticks. This is normal. Expect it.

⊠ **DON'T** mix messages between your behaviour and your rules and, if you do, acknowledge it.

People will follow what you do, not what you say. This is particularly important in work–life balance. If you have terrible work–life balance, your colleagues will either mimic or rebel. You will inspire disrespect if everyone can see you don't practise what you preach. If you, a neurodivergent leader, also have a neurodivergent staff team, they will sniff this out at 20 paces – this is our Genius Within as a minority community. Some have called it 'justice sensitivity', a pathologizing term as ever I heard! But we are unnaturally good at spotting incongruency in others, even when we are blind to our own hypocrisy. So, you need to follow the lead of my dear business partner Fiona and 'fess up'. This is an art. It requires a solid, adult ego state, but around it you will create more safety than pretending to be perfect.

☑ **DO** expect to be knocked off your pedestal.

No matter what you do, some people are going to heroize you; they will look up to you (fine) and be let down when you turn out to be human after all (not fine). We have a culture of hero leaders, and this psychology is normalized in politics, media, the arts and sports. I recently watched a documentary about David Beckham, the world-class footballer, and Victoria Beckham, the singer and fashion designer. It depicted their experience of being very young, becoming parents, while simultaneously being vilified for a millisecond mistake in a lost football match. Their case is extreme, but it follows the pattern. We love to tear our heroes down. The more you can buffer against being on that pedestal with humility, frankness, vulnerability and apology, the easier the fall.

☒ **DON'T** avoid cultural issues.

They almost never get better on their own, and they spread. What might seem like a storm in a teacup to you could be a symptom of something structurally unfair or a serious communication failure between team members. If it flags to you as not congruent with the values you are trying to institute in your sphere of influence, then it needs your attention. An early open conversation is better than unpicking months of building up grudges. This takes courage and is an appropriate use of power. Addressing people's issues promptly and without drama is exactly why you need to do your own work and get comfortable with your power. People will look to you to resolve, and if you ignore, in a bystander role, you will signal unsafety. People will feel unprotected.

☑ **DO** institute feedback and feedforward mechanisms in your organization or community.

Align them to your standard practices, so that the routine is part of the culture. In this way, you set up the right systems for handling problems in a familiar way. If you are regularly exchanging feedback, people will build trust. Institute the practice at multiple levels – interpersonal – but also with routine surveys, impact analysis, anonymous and direct. It needs to be a structure that replicates at all levels and is open to all to work. It won't work if you only give and receive feedback during a crisis.

☒ **DON'T** shy away from fessing up when feedback is valid.

You need to role model psychological safety to your group; this means taking it well. You can send hugely strong signals by simply accepting feedback – positive and negative – with a smile and appreciation for their cognitive elaboration efforts. Do your own work on it if you need to, even if it is a 'them thing' and they have misread you or misunderstood their own part in the problem – it takes courage to bring something to a leader. You need to make it safe to do so by reacting with curiosity and avoiding defensiveness.

☑ **DO** reflect on patterns of feedback or similarities in cultural problems.

If you want to know if it is a 'you thing' or a 'them thing', a key question to consider is whether or not it is a one-off or a repeat. This isn't foolproof but will help you gain some context. Even if it is a repeated 'them thing', the critical reflection is why your community are falling foul of the same risk. Few people get up in the morning with the express intention to create harm or upset. If there is a problem, there is a context. The context question should always follow the crisis resolution.

☒ **DON'T** take on more than your fair share of feedback.

One of the best leadership skills in the book is being open about your own failings, for sure, but there is a limit. I have experienced and seen leaders accept feedback that accounts for 20 per cent of a problem only to then be leapt upon, and this acceptance used as justification for the whole problem. When this happens, take your time but don't leave it hanging. If your colleague or community partner is living true to the values in the culture you are creating, they will accept their part too. Feedback is a reciprocal process; it shouldn't be one-sided.

☑ **DO** review the feedback you give to others.

This will tell you more about yourself than others. Your feedback will be consistent with your values and work ethic. It will let you know your own biases and patterns of inference. This is incredibly useful self-development work for you, and will help you identify the patterns in your assumptions, such as an aversion to brief emails or your impression of timekeeping. For example, I used to be rigid about timekeeping – it was one of my 'do not cross' red lines. I am still very keen for people to not make work for others with lateness. I still expect people to warn me in advance if there is going to be delay. But I have also learned to own that not everyone who is late is deliberately disrespecting me! As a neurodivergent, there is sometimes a sense of 'if I can do it, you can do it', but people have different resources and skills.

❌ **DON'T** implement an intense feedback system where there is no safety.

You need safety first. Start with the Feedforward Interview and build trust. Never give developmental feedback without a culture of positive feedback alongside, unless you are in a specific feedback session that is facilitated and focused. This is not the same as the praise sandwich (aka the shit sandwich), which has been shown to be demotivational.[1] The reality is that people prefer their feedback in different orders and will focus on different aspects. If you only give positive feedback as a precursor to negative feedback, people become primed to ignore the positive feedback and wait for the critique.

☑ **DO** ask people how they would like to receive feedback.

Only recently I sent feedback via email to someone I thought was robust enough to handle an unsolicited email, only to discover that they were not in a great place and the feedback was destabilizing for them. I prefer to read and process before a conversation, but this is not true for everyone. In this instance I got it wrong and had to repair the relationship. Not only does this detract from the content of the feedback; it can make a new drama that wasn't already there. This occasion for me was fixable, but sometimes it isn't.

❌ **DON'T** give feedback that makes negative inferences in a standard clean feedback exchange.

You can own the impact it is having on you, but if you write the negative inference, people will assume that you think this of them, at least at first. Have a check back to the explanation of clean feedback where I have written a negative inference and an alternative 'benefit of the doubt' explanation. The 'benefit of the doubt' explanations are a better fit for building psychological safety. I have learned this the hard way on my feedback journey. If you can provide a 'benefit of the doubt' explanation with your feedback, it will demonstrate that you are operating from an 'I'm okay, you're okay' position. If you can't get there, it is a sign you are in a drama and you may need to do some work before pressing send or starting a conversation.

☑ **DO** make room for more expansive feedback wash-ups, in which you can honestly speak about your interpretation and impacts, with support and facilitation.

It is incredibly liberating to name and speak about what is making us uncomfortable in a style that limits feeding a drama. Giving voice to the subtle anxiety that hostility and passive aggression causes feels frightening when you are conflict-avoidant, but it is actually healthy, adult behaviour. In long-term, trust-based relationships falling out is normal, and so is making up. People who don't have this lived experience in their private lives find it very hard to replicate at work, but that doesn't mean they get a free pass; it means you have a wonderful opportunity to role model psychological safety.

☒ **DON'T** shy away from tackling conflict if it doesn't work first time.

Simply naming the issue can produce the opposite response to the one you want first time, particularly for those who experience candour as a threat and not as an opportunity to learn. But shying away will not help you create a sustainable culture. People will look to you, the leader, to fix things. And you need to be able to do that directly in a neuroinclusive culture, not with subtle pointers and gentle asides. Name it, take the shame out of it and discuss it like adults. There's an excellent book called *Conflict Is Not Abuse* by Sarah Schulman,[2] which I read during a particularly difficult rupture, and it helped me. I absorbed the learning that I was allowed to make mistakes as a leader, but that I had a duty of care to try and repair. That said, the duty goes both ways. A neuroinclusive leader might try more than once, because we appreciate that people are traumatized, that they might need more processing time, but not to infinity. Your duty of care extends to the whole team, and they will suffer if you are stuck in a conflict loop that won't be resolved because the other party won't engage. Conflict feels like abuse when we are stuck in a parent / child ego state, but conflict is a normal aspect of trusting relationships and can be an instigator of needed growth and change.

☑ **DO** create your formal structures and artefacts for giving and receiving feedback safely in your community.

My example of the 'Eight "drama to calmer"' strategies works in my company because we have a solid HR team who live the values and enough well-trained managers who can facilitate. Even with a supportive infrastructure this is fallible. Not everyone wants their drama resolved, just as not everyone wants a solution. Some people will be passed the point of a solution and looking for an exit. The skill required in operating a structure like 8D2C is knowing which level suits the situation. You can't hang on to people who are ready to leave. Sometimes a situation needs to be resolved with an exit. This can be painful, but remember the story of the monkeys – if you leave a dynamic in place that isn't working, it spreads. You might need something more light touch, such as pulse surveys, but do something.

☒ **DON'T** let the process be abused.

I have mentioned my HR advisor, Gill Rudge, who has said to me many times: 'Nancy, your problem is that you are too forgiving and let people get away with poor performance.' Giving people the benefit of the doubt is admirable and the right baseline position, but as a leader you need to balance the needs of the many against the needs of the few. People who are not investing in working on their difficulties and giving others the benefit of the doubt can result in good people leaving you if you are seen to be a pushover. This is a form of interrelational injustice and it will demotivate others around the individual. Your feedback structure needs a clear escalation and exit strategy so that you know where to go next even if the other party won't play.

☑ **DO** celebrate elegant exits.

Support people who move on, even when you feel hurt and let down. If they want a clean break and distance, you can respect that by not talking too much about it in their absence, and holding them in a position of being grateful for what they contributed. This is sometimes a lot easier said than done, but remember that people are watching you – how you talk about ex-colleagues or members signals how you might talk about them. Tempting as it is to try and set the record straight, it is a clear source of psychological unsafety.

☒ **DON'T**, on the other hand, hold it all in, if you have felt hurt or are grieving.

This is where the close counsel of trusted allies comes in. You might need a sounding board or a little steam letting off space. That's okay – it is human and normal. But keep it professional, keep it small and maintain your dignity. Remember that your trigger to want to be trusted and understood by those around you and not villainized is a trauma response from ostracism; it isn't rational to expect everyone to think you are wonderful all the time – this is perfectionism rearing its ugly head. I have fallen foul of this many times and let more out than I should, or kept more in. These are the times I regret and ruminate on the most; they are the causes of many spillover ruptures or damage to my own well-being.

☑ **DO** keep investing in your own learning and institute double loop learning around feedback mechanisms at the individual and organizational level.

Corrective measures without preventative measures leads to firefighting, which leads to exhausted colleagues who will experience this as a lack of leadership competence. Things have to get better over time, even if they aren't perfect. The same feedback over and over is a clear warning that you either have lack of accountability, lack of competence or lack of good systems.

☒ **DON'T** neglect governance.

Good governance doesn't have to be the privilege of large companies – you can start right away. Even those in one-man-band advocacy leadership roles can implement safety structures and risk analysis. You, yourself, even on your own, are worthy of this consideration. How do you handle hate speech? What do you do with disclosures on your feeds / sites? Do you have a referral or escalation process for safeguarding? Very early in Genius Within's life we had a non-exec director who asked me one day how many risks were on my risk register. Cue Nancy quickly Googling 'risk register', devising a template and filling it in! I have mentioned how long-term, smouldering-under-the-surface issues have been identified with a risk register. Writing these things down reduces your cognitive load – dedicating time each month to reflect on the content reminds you to think about the prevailing winds and patterns that are affecting your leadership journey. You probably don't need an ISO accreditation or an incident reporting structure if you are a sole trader, but you do need to consider the risks to your role and have some space for medium- to long-term horizon scanning.

☑ **DO** take time to reflect on what's going well.

Where did it all go right? Implement my peer's suggestion of taking appreciative comments and storing them for future review. And review them! I've just done it. It's a lovely exercise and helps with your own healing journey as a marginalized leader. Share these to help ground your reputation and ask others for their positive comments.

☒ **DON'T** try and be all things to all people. You are enough. You do enough.

Most marginalized leaders fret and worry over their ability to the point of paralysis. It doesn't help! Delegate and bring in experts. Their competence doesn't make you less competent, it makes you wise. I shared some examples of leaders who I think do a great job of simultaneously owning their competence and knowing their limits. One of Madonna's greatest albums in my humble opinion was *Confessions on a Dance Floor*, produced by Paul Oakenfold, one of the greatest music producers of the era. This doesn't make the songs she wrote less brilliant; it makes her clever for collaborating with the person who could complement her skills.

CHAPTER 12

Doing the Work

Think about your organization or community's three levels of culture. What are the underpinning assumptions and operating beliefs? For example, in Genius Within we operate from the principle that diversity is a positive benefit. This is so fundamental that we rarely say it, but it is present.

What we have now	What I would like more of / less of

What are your espoused values? For example: if you also agree that diversity is positive, do you espouse values that are congruent with that in your daily practice? Do you role model inclusion and belonging in your work?

What we have now	What I would like more of / less of

What are the artefacts and hard coded practices that support this? At Genius Within, for example, we conduct an annual staff survey and compare the results by demographics to ensure representation and equity, as well as running an ethnicity pay gap analysis annually.

What we have now	What I would like more of / less of

Are you a Theory X or Theory Y person? How many of each are you currently working with? Consider the balance in your immediate circle. Are you supported by people who are intrinsically motivated, or are you having to provide the impetus for others to do more? I remember Fiona saying one day that she felt like she was pushing the car up the hill and not only were some people not helping, they were just sitting in the car and adding weight. Make some notes here:

. . . .

. . . .

. . . .

. . . .

Now think about the motivation factors that are needed for those operating from Theory X and Theory Y positions. What works for whom?

Theory X	Theory Y

Now think about the hygiene factors that matter for those operating from Theory X and Theory Y positions. What works for whom?

Theory X	Theory Y

Do you need to address pay?

Hours and scheduling?

Environmental conditions?

Administration?

Technology?

Psychological contract

Consider a time when you were surprised to find you had violated a psychological contract. What happened?

....
....

Did you recover? If so, what level of emotional and time investment was needed?

....
....
....

Did you recover? If not, what was the damage to you and your organization or community?

· ·

· ·

What could have been done to prevent the breach?

· ·

· ·

· ·

Now think of a time where you felt someone else violated a contract with you. What happened?

· ·

· ·

· ·

Did you recover? If so, what level of emotional and time investment was needed?

· ·

· ·

· ·

· ·

Did you recover? If not, what was the damage to you and your organization or community?

· ·

· ·

· ·

· ·

What could have been done to prevent the breach?

. . . .

. . . .

I have found over the years that honesty is a fundamental value for me in relationships. I prize honesty over most traits in business relationships. I understand why people lie – they are ashamed, fearful – but it triggers in me a sense of destabilization, reverting me back to a time where I didn't know what was true in my own life due to self-deception and hidden trauma. On the other hand, grumpiness does not bother me. If someone is having a bad day and they aren't friendly or polite, it doesn't affect me as long as they aren't trash talking colleagues or clients. I know that some of my colleagues feel the opposite and find it easy to forgive defensive lying or withholding the truth. Make some notes about what types of behaviour threaten the psychological contract for you.

Example	Your thoughts
Lying or withholding the truth	
Trash talk or grumpiness that creates a hostile environment	
Ethics – e.g., putting money priorities over people priorities	
Failing to take accountability for a mistake or assigned responsibilities	
Being unreliable around delivery of promises	
Duplicity – saying different things to different people based on what suits	

Clean feedback

Practise giving clean feedback. Notice if you are using words like 'clear' or judgements like 'brilliant' in your evidence section. These are not clean! They are inferences.

What worked well		
Evidence	Inference	Impact

What did not work well vs. what I would prefer					
Evidence	Inference	Impact	Evidence	Inference	Impact

Did you manage to give the benefit of the doubt? How would you feel if you received this feedback?

....

....

Review the feedback. Notice the impact sections. What does this tell you about your own values?

How do your values provide insight into your underpinning cultural assumptions? Do you, like me, have strong values related to timekeeping? Or perhaps direct communication? Or perhaps tact and sensitivity? Are these written down or explained to people when they join your community?

Spend some time reflecting on the unwritten rules in your company / community.

Drama to calmer

How is drama handled in your community? Write some out in the following table to create a timeline of the event.

Intention of action	Action / words and date	Interpretation of action

What difference does separating the intention from the interpretation make?

· ·

Can you hold the space that allows you to give the benefit of the doubt?

· ·

Can you accept that an action that was perceived negatively had a positive intention behind it?

· ·

· ·

Setting boundaries

Consider some occasions when you wish, in retrospect, that you had set clearer boundaries around negative behaviour or communication.

· ·

· ·

When did you intervene? When would you rather have intervened?

· ·

· ·

What were the contextual factors that hindered you? For example, the power dynamics in the relationship, your own emotional triggers, the location or time of the event and what else was happening.

· ·

· ·

Consider a time when you intervened at exactly the right moment and made the change you sought manifest.

· ·

· ·

What were the contextual factors that allowed you to do this? For example, the power dynamics in the relationship, your own emotional triggers, the location or time of the event and what else was happening.

· ·

· ·

Now give yourself some feedforward about what you have done well in intervening in drama, and list what you are proud of that you would like to repeat in the future:

· ·

· ·

Notice if you are more comfortable intervening when someone else is negatively affected versus when you personally are affected. Are you a better leader of interventions when acting protectively of others than of yourself?

· ·

· ·

Consider some ways we can hold our boundaries and level of comfort with enacting them.

Directly calling and naming what you are seeing / hearing (clean feedback):

Yes / No

Notes:

· ·

· ·

· ·

Withdrawing temporarily to think and process your own emotions:

Yes / No

Notes:

. . . .

. . . .

. . . .

If you are withdrawing, a 'holding email' to let the other person know that you aren't stonewalling them can be very helpful, depending on how much time you need. Are you comfortable with this?

Yes / No

Notes:

. . . .

. . . .

. . . .

Asking for a third party to review and mediate between people:

Yes / No

Notes:

. . . .

. . . .

. . . .

Setting improvement goals around performance or communication:

Yes / No

Notes:

. . . .

. . . .

. . . .

Ending a relationship:

Yes / No

Notes:

. . . .

. . . .

. . . .

Conflict versus abuse

Think about the book I described in Chapter 11, *Conflict Is Not Abuse* by Sarah Schulman. What does that bring up for you?

Score yourself in terms of how comfortable and safe you feel in a conflict (aka misunderstanding, mismatched expectations, rather than violence).

At work in general:

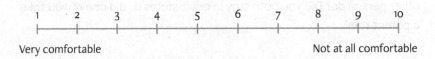

Very comfortable   Not at all comfortable

In your team:

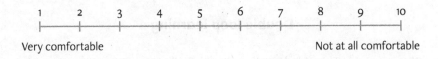

Very comfortable   Not at all comfortable

At home:

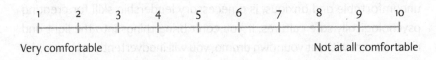

Very comfortable   Not at all comfortable

Are these the same or different? If different, where do the differences come from?

. . . .

. . . .

Can you think of a time you have fallen out with someone, made up and felt safe during the process? What happened?

. . . .

. . . .

What would / is in place to make you feel safe from rupture even when you are in conflict?

. . . .

. . . .

Can you think of a time when you felt unsafe but then the safety returned as you made up? What did you do to make this happen? What did the other person do? Did you both stay in adult states or did one of you take a parent role?

. . . .

. . . .

Double loop learning

The principle of double loop learning is similar to antifragility in that it encourages us to look more closely when there is a problem rather than to shy away. Looking closely at problems, even though they make us feel uncomfortable and anxious, is a necessary leadership skill for creating psychologically safe cultures. If you can't bring things into the light and resolve them without your own drama, you will inadvertently reinforce the message that some things are unspeakable. This leads to fear in resolving problems and a tendency to avoid them. It will ripple throughout your company or community. I have explained how we use techniques such as incident reporting and quality management at Genius Within. These provide frameworks for debriefing problems, mistakes, near-misses and customer service issues.

The key to implementing double loop learning is to separate corrective from preventative actions and make sure you are doing both. For example, when I had managers who were not able to meet the demands of their role related to financial reporting and analysis, which led to a crisis, I did two things.

Corrective: remodelled the finances myself and made a plan.
Preventative: provided ongoing training for managers in financial management.

Consider for yourself a few problems you have had to resolve and the corrective and preventative measures:

Problem	Corrective solution	Preventative solution

Keep track of these over a number of months and then review them for patterns, which will bring a deeper level of insight into the cultural norms and where more structural change might need to come from.

Governance

As a neurodivergent leader, even when you are a sole trader you need a level of governance around your practice to protect you and your community. Consider the following aspects of practice and how you might instigate oversight, ethics and support.

Governance example	A sole trader might...	A company or community leader might...	Actions...
Safeguarding	Experience direct messaging from people who are at risk of harming themselves or others as part of their online connections	Be alerted to the potential for harm to self or others in their community through the delivery of services	Corrective: referral to qualified person for direct support; supervision and reflective practice for the person who has received the disclosure Preventative: terms of engagement that explain that these disclosures might result in you needing to report a risk; taking next of kin details
Data and confidentiality breaches	Share details of confidential conversations, posts or direct messages outside the intended audience	Share confidential details held about customers or clients	Corrective: honest and immediate apology, self-reporting to data protection bodies, offering remuneration or pro bono service Preventative: training in confidentiality and data protection legislation; technology that restricts sharing of data
Financial oversight and management	Have large variations in earnings that are experienced as feast or famine	Have cash flow problems where customers are slow to pay or fail to plan for externally driven slow-downs	Corrective: temporarily cut spending or borrow money; increase reporting and monitoring Preventative: take a proportion of all sales (recommend 30%) and store in a separate account to build up reserves for tax bills and rainy days

| Risk management and business continuity | Be blindsided by changes in politics, economics, technology, market changes or competition that reduce influence or trading | Fail to predict changes in politics, economics, technology, market changes or competition that reduce influence or trading | Corrective: quick adaptation! For example, Genius Within coaching moved online within two weeks of the pandemic

Preventative action: maintain a risk register and 'worst-case scenario' planning and book time to review regularly; the pandemic was on our risk register from January 2020 and we had a dummy worst-case budget from February 2020 |

Your governance

Take a moment to look where your governance could do with some augmentation. This might feel like a load of extra admin, but it helps you feel calm, prepared and in control, and instils confidence for your colleagues or members.

Governance example	Risk to me	Corrective	Preventative
Safeguarding			
Confidentiality and data protection			
Financial planning and management			
Conflicts of interest			
Risk management and business continuity			
Decision-making oversight			
Quality control			

These are just examples. You might also want to consider:

- Whistleblowing, grievance and misconduct.
- Social impact responsibility.
- Environmental impact responsibility.
- Transparency and disclosure.
- Business ethics.
- Shareholder rights.
- Pay decisions and conflicts of interest.
- Financial oversight and checking of accuracy of reporting (auditing).

Make any additional notes here:

You're never too small a group to think about governance. And, as a leader, it's never not your job. Even if you feel that you aren't a senior enough leader to influence governance in your field or company, the people you lead will still expect this. So, the strongest learning point I have for you here is that governance is about accountability. You are accountable to the people you lead, and you may need to fight for them to instigate proper due process, fairness and transparency.

Do you currently feel powerful enough to effect good governance in your sphere of influence?

. . . .

. . . .

Do you have any allies you can co-opt to support with good governance?

. . . .

. . . .

Who are the people in your sphere who enact good governance that you could role model?

. . . .

. . . .

What are you doing a great job of right now in terms of good governance?

. . . .

. . . .

Where did it all go right?

Okay my dear neurodivergent or marginalized leader reader. Time to reflect on the joy. Notice if this is uncomfortable for you and, if so, persevere! You need to bring balance to your self-appraisal and internal validation to support your confidence.

Things I am most proud of in my organization:

1. . . . .

2. . . . .

3. . . . .

Best things about my culture:

1. ....

2. ....

3. ....

Points at which we made huge leaps forward:

1. ....

2. ....

3. ....

Our unique selling points (what we do better than others):

1. ....

2. ....

3. ....

Things I want to replicate going forward:

1. ....

2. ....

3. ....

Well done!

CHAPTER 13

Concluding Reflections

In writing this book I have forced myself to uncover yet another layer of defensiveness and vulnerability that characterizes the journey of late diagnosed neurodivergent people, but also the healing process in trauma recovery. The concept of post-traumatic growth has been applied to career development, exploring the narratives of people who overcame adversity to thrive.[1] I was once interviewed for a PhD by someone who was using post-traumatic growth to understand the process of neurodivergent entrepreneurs who had failed at school. I became angry with the interview; all I could think of was what might have been, the life I could have had if I had been provided with the safety, protection and adjustments I so desperately needed earlier on in my life. What was the point of all this pain? Healing is exhausting and I was interviewed right at the time that my chronic health condition was making itself apparent, reducing my resilience and resources for anything other than day-to-day survival.

Conversely, reflecting and self-scrutinizing to write this book has been cathartic and satisfying. I mentioned at the beginning that I barely recognize myself in the scrap of a teenager who was consumed by fear, but in charting this journey I can see clearly the justice sensitivity and rejection-sensitive dysphoria that was so crippling and has defined my work for decades. In seeking my own answers, I have hopefully contributed to opening a pathway for others. My journey into leadership involved deep personal healing. It was initially defined by self-awareness and self-reproach, horrified at the realization of what others thought about me, and determined to be better, striving to be perfect. I recognized the limitations of this approach and hope to save you the bother, or at least truncate it if you are already there.

Professor Almuth McDowall said to me 'a leopard doesn't change its spots, Nancy' when we were discussing the first draft of this book. She was reassuring me because my initial response to some of her feedback was anxiety and self-consciousness about aspects that were too glib, or vulnerabilities I shared that hadn't hit the mark. She was encouraging me to continue with the 'warts and all' sections and not hide them in case others judged me. I had embedded the perfectionist aim again – my dear colleague was reminding me that my journey became sustainable when I stopped trying to be a giraffe and delighted in being a leopard. I will never be a calm, consistent, careful leader, and I work best when I embrace the enthusiastic, problem-solving change agent that I am. My organization's journey improved when we had enough resources to maintain the right team with a balance of different natural styles, who respected each other's differences and weren't trying to make a leopard into a giraffe, or vice versa. I, and we, can still snap back to default roles such as rescuer, victim, bystander and persecutor. They are all around us and newcomers expect them; it takes us a while to absorb people into our culture, and their discomfort can sometimes seduce us back into old patterns. It takes a while to deprogramme ourselves from the expectations we absorb from society, and it is a life's work to forge a new pathway. I firmly believe that analysis, reflexivity, feedback and feedforward are the oil in the engine of a leader's career; we have to keep all the parts moving. It doesn't stop when we reach a certain age or stage. Those who stop working on themselves as leaders are open to rust and stagnation.

Post-traumatic growth occurs when people have the opportunity to reflect and make sense of their experiences with support systems and close allies who believe in their intrinsic worth. This is a part of the service that my company provides through coaching and workshops for several thousand people a year who have failed in education, failed to find work and who experience this as trauma. I cannot see how it would have been possible for me to create or maintain this service without my own experiences of social marginalization – and I cannot see how I can continue this work in isolation. In writing this book, I have hyperfocused on my own limitations as a leader, the areas where I am still vulnerable and defenceless, the areas where I am still defensive and closed off. It's still hard for me to accept my flaws, to celebrate my successes and to avoid the trap of seeking perfection. But true to the journey of post-traumatic growth, my reserves are regularly topped up by the shared leadership and mentoring of my dearest family, friends and allies.

As a case in point, as I am writing this final section, an email popped in from my leadership team colleague and Genius Within CEO, Jacqui Wallis. She wrote that during a reflective practice session with our esteemed business partner Royston Collins and our team coach, they realized that as a leadership team we had collectively invested 15.5 hours in double loop learning around a recent problem. She pointed out that we haven't spent more than a few minutes noting the positive outcomes achieved in the same timeframe. She proposed a workable plan for addressing this pattern and wanted to share their insights. And this is why the shared leadership of the team, with complementary cognitive profiles, works better than the sole heroic leader. Jacqui and Royston are naturally emotionally intelligent and sensitive to others. Their insights help buffer me when I am tired and unable to overcome my own emotional literacy challenges.

Ethical leadership is needed more than ever. The world is increasingly challenging, complex and conflicting. As neurodivergent (or otherwise marginalized) leaders, we bring creativity, ethics and problem solving to our communities and organizations. We are a part of the rich tapestry of human experience for a reason. Shared leadership, moral management and good governance are strong pillars within which a neurodivergent leader can safely develop confidence and competence to succeed. Many communities are in need of psychological safety; this won't happen without community leaders engaging in introspection and self-development. We won't engender inclusion without healing from exclusion. Sustainability for yourself and those around you is paramount for healing – you are a human being and not a human doing, and you cannot pour from an empty cup. Being a leader means making sure that what is essential is done, and not doing it all yourself. We cannot sustainably lead alone – finding, connecting and investing in the relationships we have with those who can share the work is the key to success for neurodivergent leaders.

Endnotes

Foreword

1   Smith, W.K. and Lewis, M.W. (2012) 'Leadership skills for managing paradoxes.' *Industrial and Organizational Psychology* 5, 2, 227–231. doi: 10.1111/j.1754-9434.2012.01435.x.

Introduction

1   Iwowo, V. (2015) 'Leadership in Africa: Rethinking development.' *Personnel Review* 44, 3, 408–429. doi: 10.1108/PR-07-2013-0128.
2   Ciancetta, L.M. and Roch, S.G. (2021) 'Backlash in performance feedback: Deepening the understanding of the role of gender in performance appraisal.' *Human Resource Management* 60, 4, 641–657. doi: 10.1002/hrm.22059.
3   Wall, S. (2006) 'An autoethnography on learning about autoethnography.' *International Journal of Qualitative Methods* 5, 2, 146–160. doi: 10.1177/160940690600500205, p.1.
4   Lewis, C.J. and Arday, J. (2023) 'We'll see things they'll never see: Sociological reflections on race, neurodiversity and higher education.' *The Sociological Review* 71, 6, 1299–1321. doi: 10.1177/00380261231184357, p.1.

Chapter 1: Leadership Theories

1   Roberson, Q. and Perry, J.L. (2022) 'Inclusive leadership in thought and action: A thematic analysis.' *Group & Organization Management* 47, 4, 755–778. doi: 10.1177/10596011211013161.
2   Yukl, G. and Gardner, W. (2019) *Leadership in Organizations*. Ninth edn. Pearson Education, Inc.
3   Schein, V.E. (1975) 'Relationships between sex role stereotypes and requisite management characteristics among female managers.' *Journal of Applied Psychology* 60, 3, 340–344. doi: 10.1037/h0076637.
4   Schein, V.E. and Davidson, M.J. (1993) 'Think manager, think male.' *Management Development Review* 6, 3. https://doi.org/10.1108/EUM0000000000738
5   Rippon, G. (2019) *Gendered Brain: The New Neuroscience that Shatters the Myth of the Female Brain*. The Bodley Head Ltd.

6   Colella, A., DeNisi, A.S. and Varma, A. (1998) 'The impact of ratee's disability on performance judgments and choice as partner: The role of disability–job fit stereotypes and interdependence of rewards.' *Journal of Applied Psychology 83*, 1, 102–111. doi: 10.1037/0021-9010.83.1.102.

7   Colella, A. and Varma, A. (2001) 'The impact of subordinate disability on leader–member exchange relationships.' *Academy of Management Journal 44*, 2, 304–315. doi: 10.5465/3069457.

8   Conger, J.A. and Kanungo, R.N. (1994) 'Charismatic leadership in organizations: Perceived behavioral attributes and their measurement.' *Journal of Organizational Behavior 15*, 5, 439–452. www.jstor.org/stable/2488215

9   Milton, D.E.M. (2012) 'On the ontological status of autism: The "double empathy problem".' *Disability & Society 27*, 6, 883–887. https://doi.org/10.1080/09687599. 2012.710008

10 Eva, N., Robin, M., Sendjaya, S., van Dierendonck, D. and Liden, R.C. (2019) 'Servant leadership: A systematic review and call for future research.' *The Leadership Quarterly 30*, 1, 111–132. doi: 10.1016/j.leaqua.2018.07.004.

11 Gardner, W.L., Cogliser, C.C., Davis, K.M. and Dickens, M.P. (2011) 'Authentic leadership: A review of the literature and research agenda.' *The Leadership Quarterly 22*, 6, 1120–1145. doi: 10.1016/j.leaqua.2011.09.007.

12 Liu, H. (2019) 'Just the servant: An intersectional critique of servant leadership.' *Journal of Business Ethics 156*, 4, 1099–1112. doi: 10.1007/s10551-017-3633-0.

13 Offermann, L.R. and Coats, M.R. (2018) 'Implicit theories of leadership: Stability and change over two decades.' *The Leadership Quarterly 29*, 4, 513–522. https:// doi.org/10.1016/j.leaqua.2017.12.003

14 Ngunjiri, F.W. and Hernandez, K.-A.C. (2017) 'Problematizing authentic leadership: A collaborative autoethnography of immigrant women of color leaders in higher education.' *Advances in Developing Human Resources 19*, 4, 393–406. doi: 10.1177/1523422317728735.

15 Pollak, D. (ed.) (2009) *Neurodiversity in Higher Education: Positive Responses to Specific Learning Differences.* Wiley-Blackwell.

16 Armstrong, T. (2010) *The Power of Neurodiversity: Unleashing the Advantages of Your Differently Wired Brain.* Da Capo Press.

17 Murdoch, S. (2007) *IQ: A Smart History of a Failed Idea.* Trade Paper Press.

18 Chapman, R. (2023) *Empire of Normality: Neurodiversity and Capitalism.* Pluto Press.

19 Wechsler, D. (2008) *Wechsler Adult Intelligence Scale – Fourth Edition.* Pearson.

20 Doyle, N. (2023) 'Universal design in psychometric testing.' *Assessment and Development Matters 15*, 2, 4–9. doi: 10.53841/bpsadm.2023.15.2.4.

21 Grant, D. (2009) 'The Psychological Assessment of Neurodiversity.' In D. Pollak (ed.) *Neurodiversity in Higher Education* (pp.33–62). Wiley-Blackwell.

22 Gardner, W.L., Cogliser, C.C., Davis, K.M. and Dickens, M.P. (2011) 'Authentic leadership: A review of the literature and research agenda.' *The Leadership Quarterly 22*, 6, 1120–1145. doi: 10.1016/j.leaqua.2011.09.007.

23 Taylor, H., Fernandes, B. and Wraight, S. (2021) 'The evolution of complementary cognition: Humans cooperatively adapt and evolve through a system of collective cognitive search.' *Cambridge Archaeological Journal 32*, 1, 1–17. doi: 10.1017/ s0959774321000329.

24 Antonakis, J., House, R.J. and Simonton, D.K. (2017) 'Can super smart leaders suffer from too much of a good thing? The curvilinear effect of intelligence on perceived leadership behavior.' *Journal of Applied Psychology 102*, 7, 1003–1021. doi: 10.1037/apl0000221.

25 Judge, T.A., Colbert, A.E. and Ilies, R. (2004) 'Intelligence and leadership: A quantitative review and test of theoretical propositions.' *Journal of Applied Psychology 89*, 3, 542–552. doi: 10.1037/0021-9010.89.3.542.

26 Kruger, J. and Dunning, D. (1999) 'Unskilled and unaware of it: How difficulties in recognizing one's own incompetence lead to inflated self-assessments.' *Journal of Personality and Social Psychology 77*, 6, 1121–1134. doi: 0022-3514/99.

27 Ciancetta, L.M. and Roch, S.G. (2021) 'Backlash in performance feedback: Deepening the understanding of the role of gender in performance appraisal.' *Human Resource Management 60*, 4, 641–657. doi: 10.1002/hrm.22059.

28 Cattell, H.E.P. (1996) 'The original big five: A historical perspective.' *European Review of Applied Psychology / Revue Européenne de Psychologie Appliquée 46*, 1, 5–14.

29 Judge, T.A., Bono, J.E., Ilies, R. and Gerhardt, M.W. (2002) 'Personality and leadership: A qualitative and quantitative review.' *Journal of Applied Psychology 87*, 4, 765–780. doi: 10.1037/0021-9010.87.4.765.

30 Judge, T.A., Bono, J.E., Ilies, R. and Gerhardt, M.W. (2002) 'Personality and leadership: A qualitative and quantitative review.' *Journal of Applied Psychology 87*, 4, 765–780. doi: 10.1037/0021-9010.87.4.765.

31 Thye, M.D., Bednarz, H.M., Herringshaw, A.J., Sartin, E.B. and Kana, R.K. (2018) 'The impact of atypical sensory processing on social impairments in autism spectrum disorder.' *Developmental Cognitive Neuroscience 29*, 151–167. doi: 10.1016/j.dcn.2017.04.010.

32 Engert, V. and Pruessner, J. (2009) 'Dopaminergic and noradrenergic contributions to functionality in ADHD: The role of methylphenidate.' *Current Neuropharmacology 6*, 4, 322–328. doi: 10.2174/157015908787386069.

33 van Steensel, F.J.A. and Heeman, E.J. (2017) 'Anxiety levels in children with autism spectrum disorder: A meta-analysis.' *Journal of Child and Family Studies 26*, 7, 1753–1767. doi: 10.1007/s10826-017-0687-7.

34 Guillén, L., Jacquart, P. and Hogg, M.A. (2023) 'To lead, or to follow? How self-uncertainty and the dark triad of personality influence leadership motivation.' *Personality and Social Psychology Bulletin 49*, 7, 1043–1057. doi: 10.1177/01461672221086771.

35 Pelletier, K.L. (2010) 'Leader toxicity: An empirical investigation of toxic behavior and rhetoric.' *Leadership 6*, 4, 373–389. doi: 10.1177/1742715010379308.

36 Graen, G.B. and Uhl-Bien, M. (1995) 'Relationship-based approach to leadership: Development of leader–member exchange (LMX) theory of leadership over 25 years: Applying a multi-level multi-domain perspective.' *The Leadership Quarterly 6*, 2, 219–247. doi: 10.1016/1048-9843(95)90036-5.

37 Rockstuhl, T., Dulebohn, J.H., Ang, S. and Shore, L.M. (2012) 'Leader–member exchange (LMX) and culture: A meta-analysis of correlates of LMX across 23 countries.' *Journal of Applied Psychology 97*, 6, 1097–1130. doi: 10.1037/a0029978.

38 Salovey, P. and Mayer, J.D. (1990) 'Emotional intelligence.' *Imagination, Cognition, and Personality 9*, 3, 185–211. https://doi.org/10.2190/DUGG-P24E-52WK-6CDG

39 Goleman, D. (1996) *Intelligence: Why It Can Matter More than IQ*. Bloomsbury Publishing.

40 Rajesh, J.I., Prikshat, V., Shum, P. and Suganthi, L. (2019) 'Follower emotional intelligence: A mediator between transformational leadership and follower outcomes.' *Personnel Review 48*, 5, 1239–1260. doi: 10.1108/PR-09-2017-0285.

41 Jyoti, J. and Kour, S. (2017) 'Factors affecting cultural intelligence and its impact on job performance: Role of cross-cultural adjustment, experience and perceived social support.' *Personnel Review 46*, 4, 767–791. doi: 10.1108/PR-12-2015-0313.

42 Kinnaird, E., Stewart, C. and Tchanturia, K. (2019) 'Investigating alexithymia in autism: A systematic review and meta-analysis.' *European Psychiatry 55*, 80–89. doi: 10.1016/j.eurpsy.2018.09.004.

43 Gottfredson, R. (2023) 'Emotional Intelligence 3.0: The next wave of leadership thought leadership.' *Emotional Intelligence Blog*, 17 July. https://ryangottfredson.com/blog/2023/07/17/emotional-intelligence-3-0-the-next-phase-of-ei-thought-and-development

44 Roberts, L.M., Mayo, A., Ely, R. and Thomas, D. (2018) 'Beating the odds: Leadership lessons from senior African-American women.' *Harvard Business Review 96*, 2, 126–131. www.hbs.edu/faculty/Pages/item.aspx?num=54215

45 McCluney, C.L., Durkee, M.I., Smith II, R.E., Robotham, K.J. and Lee, S.-S.L. (2021) 'To be, or not to be…Black: The effects of racial codeswitching on perceived professionalism in the workplace.' *Journal of Experimental Social Psychology 97*, 104–199. doi: 10.1016/j.jesp.2021.104199.

46 Richards, J.M. and Gross, J.J. (1999) 'Composure at any cost? The cognitive consequences of emotion suppression.' *Personality and Social Psychology Bulletin 25*, 8, 1033–1044. doi: 10.1177/01461672992511010.

47 Corbin, C.M. (2017) 'Terrorists are always Muslim but never white: At the intersection of critical race theory and propaganda.' *Fordham Law Review 86*, 2, 454–485. https://ir.lawnet.fordham.edu/flr/vol86/iss2/5

48 Shaw, S.C.K., Carravallah, L., Johnson, M., O'Sullivan, J., *et al.* (2023) 'Barriers to healthcare and a "triple empathy problem" may lead to adverse outcomes for autistic adults: A qualitative study.' *Autism*, 13623613231205629. doi: 10.1177/13623613231205629.

49 Brown, B. (2012) *Daring Greatly: How the Courage to Be Vulnerable Transforms the Way We Live, Love, Parent, and Lead*. Gotham Books, p.145.

50 Jones, B.F. and Olken, B.A. (2005) 'Do leaders matter? National leadership and growth since World War II.' *Quarterly Journal of Economics*, February. https://economics.mit.edu/sites/default/files/publications/DO%20LEADERS%20MATTER.pdf

51 Arendt, H. (2002) 'Selections from *The Human Condition*.' In D. Ingram (ed.) *The Political* (Chapter 1). Blackwell, p.49.

52 Dinh, J.E., Lord, R.G., Gardner, W.L., Meuser, J.D., Liden, R.C. and Hu, J. (2014) 'Leadership theory and research in the new millennium: Current theoretical trends and changing perspectives.' *The Leadership Quarterly 25*, 1, 36–62. doi: 10.1016/j.leaqua.2013.11.005.

53 Raelin, J. (2011) 'From leadership-as-practice to leaderful practice.' *Leadership 7*, 2, 195–211. doi: 10.1177/1742715010394808.

54 Brown, M.E. and Treviño, L.K. (2006) 'Ethical leadership: A review and future directions.' *The Leadership Quarterly 17*, 595–616, p.597. https://doi.org/10.1016/j.leaqua.2006.10.004

55 Bondü, R. and Esser, G. (2015) 'Justice and rejection sensitivity in children and adolescents with ADHD symptoms.' *European Child & Adolescent Psychiatry 24*, 2, 185–198. doi: 10.1007/s00787-014-0560-9.

56 Oakley, B., Knafo, A., Madhavan, G. and Sloan Wilson, D. (eds) (2012) *Pathological Altruism*. Oxford University Press.

57 Zhu, J., Liao, Z., Yam, K.C. and Johnson, R.E. (2018) 'Shared leadership: A state-of-the-art review and future research agenda.' *Journal of Organizational Behavior 39*, 7, 834–852. doi: 10.1002/job.2296.

58 Schmidt Harvey, V. and De Meuse, K.P. (2021) *The Age of Agility: Building Learning, Agile Leaders and Organizations*. Oxford University Press.

59 Argyris, C. (1977) 'Double loop learning in organizations.' *Harvard Business Review*, September–October, 115–126. https://hbr.org/1977/09/double-loop-learning-in-organizations

60 Senge, P.M. (1990) *The Fifth Discipline: The Art & Practice of the Learning Organization*. Doubleday / Currency.

61 Zhu, J., Liao, Z., Yam, K.C. and Johnson, R.E. (2018) 'Shared leadership: A state-of-the-art review and future research agenda.' *Journal of Organizational Behavior 39*, 7, 834–852. doi: 10.1002/job.2296.

62 Hogg, M.A. (2021) 'Uncertain self in a changing world: A foundation for radicalisation, populism, and autocratic leadership.' *European Review of Social Psychology 32*, 2, 235–268. doi: 10.1080/10463283.2020.1827628.

63 Kuada, J. (2010) 'Culture and leadership in Africa: A conceptual model and research agenda.' *African Journal of Economic and Management Studies 1*, 1, 9–24. doi: 10.1108/20400701011028130.

64 Iwowo, V. (2015) 'Leadership in Africa: Rethinking development.' *Personnel Review 44*, 3, 408–429. doi: 10.1108/PR-07-2013-0128.

65 Goodchild, M. (2021) 'Relational systems thinking: That's how change is going to come, from our Earth Mother.' *Journal of Awareness-Based Systems Change 1*, 1, 75–103. doi: 10.47061/jabsc.v1i1.577.

66 How Institute for Society, The (2020) *The State of Moral Leadership in Business*. https://thehowinstitute.org/moral-leadership-report-2020

Chapter 2: Becoming a Leader

1 Crook, T. and McDowall, A. (2023) 'Paradoxical career strengths and successes of ADHD adults: An evolving narrative.' *Journal of Work-Applied Management 16*, 1, 112–126. doi: 10.1108/JWAM-05-2023-0048.

2 Walker, C. (2014) *From Contempt to Curiosity: Creating the Conditions for Groups to Collaborate Using Clean Language and Systemic Modelling*. Clean Publishing.

Chapter 3: Advice

1   Egan, S.J., Hattaway, M. and Kane, R.T. (2014) 'The relationship between perfectionism and rumination in post traumatic stress disorder.' *Behavioural and Cognitive Psychotherapy 42*, 2, 211–223. doi: 10.1017/S1352465812001129.

2   Hill, J. and Oliver, J. (2019) *Acceptance and Commitment Coaching: Distinctive Features*. Routledge.

3   Cooperrider, D.L., Whitney, D. and Stavros, J.M. (2003) *Appreciative Inquiry Handbook: For Leaders of Change*. Berrett-Koehler Publishers.

Chapter 4: Doing the Work

1   Serrat, O. (2017) 'Understanding and Developing Emotional Intelligence.' In O. Serrat, *Knowledge Solutions* (pp.329–339). Springer.

Chapter 5: Work and Well-Being

1   HSE (Health and Safety Executive) (2016) 'Work related stress, anxiety and depression statistics in Great Britain 2016.' https://unionsafety.eu/ELibrary/media/elibrarymedia/HSEWorkRelatedStressAnxietyDepresssionStats.pdf

2   Anderson, C.R. (1976) 'Coping behaviors as intervening mechanisms in the inverted-U stress-performance relationship.' *Journal of Applied Psychology 61*, 1, 30–34. https://doi.org/10.1037/0021-9010.61.1.30

3   Logan, J. (2009) 'Dyslexic entrepreneurs: The incidence; their coping strategies and their business skills.' *Dyslexia 15*, 4, 328–346. https://doi.org/10.1002/dys.388; Nalavany, B.A., Logan, J.M. and Carawan, L.W. (2017) 'The relationship between emotional experience with dyslexia and work self-efficacy among adults with dyslexia.' *Dyslexia 24*, 1, 1–16. doi: 10.1002/dys.1575.

4   Jensen, J., Lindgren, M., Andersson, K., Ingvar, D.H. and Levander, S. (2000) 'Cognitive intervention in unemployed individuals with reading and writing disabilities.' *Applied Neuropsychology 7*, 4, 223–236. doi: 10.1207/S15324826AN0704_4.

5   CJJI (Criminal Justice Joint Inspection) (2021) *Neurodiversity in the Criminal Justice System: A Review of Evidence*. www.justiceinspectorates.gov.uk/cjji/wp-content/uploads/sites/2/2021/07/Neurodiversity-evidence-review-web-2021.pdf

6   Bakker, A.B. and Demerouti, E. (2016) 'Job demands-resources theory: Taking stock and looking forward.' *Journal of Occupational Health Psychology 22*, 3, 273–285. doi: 10.1037/ocp0000056.

7   Neufeld, J., Taylor, M.J., Remnélius, K.L., Isaksson, J., Lichtenstein, P. and Bölte, S. (2021) 'A co-twin-control study of altered sensory processing in autism.' *Autism 25*, 5, 1422–1432. doi: 10.1177/1362361321991255.

8   Oomen, D., Nijhof, A.D. and Wiersema, J.R. (2021) 'The psychological impact of the COVID-19 pandemic on adults with autism: A survey study across three countries.' *Molecular Autism 12*, 1, 1–22. doi: 10.1186/s13229-021-00424-y.

9   Ando, M., Takeda, T. and Kumagai, K. (2021) 'A qualitative study of impacts of the COVID-19 pandemic on lives in adults with attention deficit hyperactive disorder

in Japan.' *International Journal of Environmental Research and Public Health 18*, 4, 2090, 1–10. https://doi.org/10.3390/ijerph18042090

10 Wissell, S., Karimi, L., Serry, T., Furlong, L. and Hudson, J. (2022) '"You don't look dyslexic": Using the job demands-resource model of burnout to explore employment experiences of Australian adults with dyslexia.' *International Journal of Environmental Research and Public Health 19*, 17, 10719. doi: 10.3390/ijerph191710719.

11 Raymaker, D.M., Teo, A.R., Steckler, N.A., Lentz, B., *et al.* (2020) '"Having all of your internal resources exhausted beyond measure and being left with no clean-up crew": Defining autistic burnout.' *Autism in Adulthood 2*, 2, 132–143. doi: 10.1089/aut.2019.0079.

12 Bakker, A.B. and Demerouti, E. (2007) 'The job demands-resources model: State of the art.' *Journal of Managerial Psychology 22*, 3, 309–328. doi: 10.1108/02683940710733115.

13 Pemberton, A. and Kisamore, J. (2022) 'Assessing burnout in diversity and inclusion professionals.' *Equality, Diversity and Inclusion: An International Journal 42*, 2. doi: 10.1108/EDI-12-2020-0360.

14 Goldgruber, J. and Ahrens, D. (2009) 'Effectiveness of workplace health promotion and primary prevention interventions: A review.' *Journal of Public Health 18*, 1, 75–88. https://doi.org/10.1007/s10389-009-0282-5

15 Kinnaird, E., Stewart, C. and Tchanturia, K. (2019) 'Investigating alexithymia in autism: A systematic review and meta-analysis.' *European Psychiatry 55*, 80–89. doi: 10.1016/j.eurpsy.2018.09.004.

16 Wissell, S., Karimi, L., Serry, T., Furlong, L. and Hudson, J. (2022) '"You don't look dyslexic": Using the job demands-resource model of burnout to explore employment experiences of Australian adults with dyslexia.' *International Journal of Environmental Research and Public Health 19*, 17, 10719. doi: 10.3390/ijerph191710719.

17 Berne, E. (1964) *Games People Play: The Psychology of Human Relationships.* Grove Press, Inc.

18 Nyberg, A., Alfredsson, L., Theorell, T., Westerlund, H., Vahtera, J. and Kivimäki, M. (2009) 'Managerial leadership and ischaemic heart disease among employees: The Swedish WOLF study.' *Occupational and Environmental Medicine 66*, 1, 51–55. doi: 10.1136/oem.2008.039362.

19 Nolan, T. (2023) 'The No. 1 employee benefit that no one's talking about.' www.gallup.com/workplace/232955/no-employee-benefit-no-one-talking.aspx

20 Elzinga, D. (2023) 'The biggest lie in HR: People quit bosses not companies.' Culture Amp. www.cultureamp.com/blog/biggest-lie-people-quit-bosses

21 Christiansen, J. (2019) '8 things leaders do that make employees quit.' *Harvard Business Review*, 10 September. https://hbr.org/2019/09/8-things-leaders-do-that-make-employees-quit

22 Edmondson, A. (1999) 'Psychological safety and learning behavior in work teams.' *Administrative Science Quarterly 44*, 2, 350–383. doi: 10.2307/2666999, p.354.

23 Edmondson, A.C. and Lei, Z. (2014) 'Psychological safety: The history, renaissance, and future of an interpersonal construct.' *Annual Review of*

Organizational Psychology and Organizational Behavior 1, 1, 23–43. doi: 10.1146/annurev-orgpsych-031413-091305.

24 O'Donovan, R. and Mcauliffe, E. (2020) 'A systematic review of factors that enable psychological safety in healthcare teams.' *International Journal for Quality in Health Care 32*, 4, 240–250. doi: 10.1093/intqhc/mzaa025.

25 Pacheco, D.C., Arruda Moniz, A.I.D. de S. and Caldeira, S.N. (2015) 'Silence in organizations: A literature review.' *European Scientific Journal 11*, 10, p.296. https://eujournal.org/index.php/esj/article/view/6156

26 Pacheco, D.C., Arruda Moniz, A.I.D. de S. and Caldeira, S.N. (2015) 'Silence in organizations: A literature review.' *European Scientific Journal 11*, 10, p.295. https://eujournal.org/index.php/esj/article/view/6156

27 Taleb, N.N. (2012) *Antifragile: Things that Gain from Disorder*. Random House.

Chapter 6: The Reluctant Entrepreneur

1 Doyle, N. and McDowall, A. (2023) *Neurodiversity Coaching: Supporting Neurodivergent Talent and Career Potential*. Routledge.

2 van der Lippe, T., Treas, J. and Norbutas, L. (2018) 'Unemployment and the division of housework in Europe.' *Work, Employment and Society 32*, 4, 650–669. doi: 10.1177/0950017017690495.

3 Sandberg, S. (2015) *Lean In: Women, Work, and the Will to Lead*. W.H. Allen.

4 Schrenker, A. and Zucco, A. (2020) 'The gender pay gap begins to increase sharply at age of 30.' *DIW Weekly Report 10*, 10, 75–82. www.diw.de/documents/publikationen/73/diw_01.c.741919.de/dwr-20-10-1.pdf

5 Sandberg, S. and Grant, A. (2017) *Option B: Facing Adversity, Building Resilience, and Finding Joy*. Virgin Digital.

6 Kelly, C., Dansereau, L., Sebring, J., Aubrecht, K., *et al.* (2022) 'Intersectionality, health equity, and EDI: What's the difference for health researchers?' *International Journal for Equity in Health 21*, 1, 182. https://doi.org/10.1186/s12939-022-01795-1; Shaw, S.C.K., Carravallah, L., Johnson, M., O'Sullivan, J., *et al.* (2023) 'Barriers to healthcare and a "triple empathy problem" may lead to adverse outcomes for autistic adults: A qualitative study.' *Autism*, 13623613231205629. https://doi.org/10.1177/13623613231205629

7 Chapman, R. (2023) *Empire of Normality: Neurodiversity and Capitalism*. Pluto Press.

8 Nekvapil, K. (2023) *Power: A Woman's Guide to Living and Leading Without Apology*. Penguin Publishing Group.

9 Beard, M. (2017) *Woman & Power: A Manifesto*. Profile Books.

10 Walker, N. (2021) *Neuroqueer Heresies: Notes on the Neurodiversity Paradigm, Autistic Empowerment, and Postnormal Possibilities*. Autonomous Press.

Chapter 7: Advice

1 Kendall, M. (2020) *Hood Feminism: Notes from the Women White Feminists Forgot*. Bloomsbury Publishing.

Chapter 8: Doing the Work

1   Da Silva, C. (2018) 'Michelle Obama tells a secret: "I have been at every powerful table you can think of…they are not that smart." Newsweek, 17 December. www.newsweek.com/michelle-obama-tells-secret-i-have-been-every-powerful-table-you-can-think-1242695

Chapter 9: Creating a Sustainable Culture

1   Schein, E.H. (2016) Organizational Culture and Leadership, 5th Edition (The Jossey-Bass Business & Management Series). Jossey-Bass.

2   Kildahl, A.N., Helverschou, S.B., Rysstad, A.L., Wigaard, E., et al. (2021) 'Pathological demand avoidance in children and adolescents: A systematic review.' Autism 25, 8, 2162–2176. doi: 10.1177/13623613211034382.

3   Rousseau, D.M. (1989) 'Psychological and implied contracts in organizations.' Employee Responsibilities and Rights Journal 2, 2, 121–139. doi: 10.1007/BF01384942.

4   Taylor, F.W. (1911) The Principles of Scientific Management. Harper & Brothers.

5   Carson, C.M. (2005) 'A historical view of Douglas McGregor's Theory Y.' Management Decision 43, 3, 450–460. http://dx.doi.org/10.1108/00251740510589814

6   Herzberg, F. (1966) Work and the Nature of Man. World Publishing.

7   Wood, S., Leoni, S. and Ladley, D. (2023) 'Comparisons of the effects of individual and collective performance-related pay on performance: A review.' Human Resource Management Review 33, 4, 100982. doi: 10.1016/j.hrmr.2023.100982.

8   McDowall, A., Doyle, N. and Kiseleva, M. (2023) Neurodiversity at Work 2023: Demand, Supply and Gap Analysis. Neurodiversity in Business.

9   Adams, J.S. (2005) 'Equity Theory.' In J.B. Miner (ed.) Organizational Behaviour 1: Essential Theories of Motivation and Leadership (Chapter 11). Routledge.

10 Christiansen, J. (2019) '8 things leaders do that make employees quit.' Harvard Business Review, 10 September. https://hbr.org/2019/09/8-things-leaders-do-that-make-employees-quit

11 Greenberg, J. (1987) 'A taxonomy of organizational justice.' Academy of Management Review 12, 1, 9–22. https://doi.org/10.2307/257990

12 Bondü, R. and Esser, G. (2015) 'Justice and rejection sensitivity in children and adolescents with ADHD symptoms.' European Child & Adolescent Psychiatry 24, 2, 185–198. doi: 10.1007/s00787-014-0560-9.

13 Rousseau, D.M. (1989) 'Psychological and implied contracts in organizations.' Employee Responsibilities and Rights Journal 2, 2, 121–139. doi: 10.1007/BF01384942, p.123.

14 Kluger, A.N. and DeNisi, A.S. (1998) 'Feedback interventions: Toward the understanding of a double-edged sword.' Current Directions in Psychological Science 7, 3, 67–72. www.jstor.org/stable/20182507

15 Jellinek, M.S. (2010) 'Don't let ADHD crush children's self-esteem.' Psychiatry. www.mdedge.com/psychiatry/article/23971/pediatrics/dont-let-adhd-crush-childrens-self-esteem

16 Kluger, A.N. and Nir, D. (2010) 'The Feedforward Interview.' Human Resource Management Review 20, 3, 235–246. doi: 10.1016/j.hrmr.2009.08.002.

17 Bandura, A. (1997) *Self-Efficacy: The Exercise of Control*. W.H. Freeman and Company.

18 Walsh, B., Nixon, S., Walker, C. and Doyle, N. (2015) 'Using a clean feedback model to facilitate the learning process.' *Creative Education 6*, 10, 953–960. doi: 10.4236/ce.2015.610097.

19 Wilson, C. (2017) *The Work and Life of David Grove: Clean Language and Emergent Knowledge*. Troubador Publishing Ltd.

20 Sun, J., Zhuang, K., Li, H., Wei, D., Zhang, Q. and Qiu, J. (2018) 'Perceiving rejection by others: Relationship between rejection sensitivity and the spontaneous neuronal activity of the brain.' *Social Neuroscience 13*, 4, 429–438. https://doi.org/10.1080/17470919.2017.1340335

21 Bondü, R. and Esser, G. (2015) 'Justice and rejection sensitivity in children and adolescents with ADHD symptoms.' *European Child & Adolescent Psychiatry 24*, 2, 185–198. doi: 10.1007/s00787-014-0560-9.

22 Klein Tuente, S., Bogaerts, S. and Veling, W. (2019) 'Hostile attribution bias and aggression in adults – A systematic review.' *Aggression and Violent Behavior 46*, 66–81. doi: 10.1016/j.avb.2019.01.009.

23 Lewin, K. (1936) *Principles of Topographical Psychology*. McGraw-Hill Book Company.

24 Doyle, N. and McDowall, A. (2023) *Neurodiversity Coaching: Supporting Neurodivergent Talent and Career Potential*. Routledge.

25 Wrzesniewski, A. and Dutton, J.E. (2001) 'Crafting a job.' *The Academy of Management Review 26*, 2, 179–201. doi: 10.2307/259118.

26 Wang, H., Demerouti, E. and Bakker, A.B. (2016) 'Review of Job Crafting Research.' In S.K. Parker and U.K. Bindi (eds) *Proactivity at Work* (pp.77–104). Taylor & Francis.

27 Schumacher, R. (2013) 'Deconstructing the theory of comparative advantage.' *World Economic Review 2*, 1–83. http://wser.worldeconomicsassociation.org/papers/deconstructing-the-theory-of-comparative-advantage

28 Freeman, C. and Sotire, T. (2023) 'Economics and neurodiversity 3 – David Ricardo, comparative advantage, and specialisation.' Published 2023. Accessed 16 November, 2023. www.linkedin.com/pulse/economics-neurodiversity-4-karl-marx-alienation-charles-freeman-frsa-omvpe/?trackingId=h9UFK7YcQcK78WY9FJpn4g%3D%3D

29 Slay, H.S. and Smith, D.A. (2011) 'Professional identity construction: Using narrative to understand the negotiation of professional and stigmatized cultural identities.' *Human Relations 64*, 1, 85–107. doi: 10.1177/0018726710384290.

30 Colella, A., DeNisi, A.S. and Varma, A. (1998) 'The impact of ratee's disability on performance judgments and choice as partner: The role of disability-job fit stereotypes and interdependence of rewards.' *Journal of Applied Psychology 83*, 1, 102–111. doi: 10.1037/0021-9010.83.1.102.

31 Engel, J.M. (2018) 'Why does culture "eat strategy for breakfast"?' Forbes, 20 November. www.forbes.com/sites/forbescoachescouncil/2018/11/20/why-does-culture-eat-strategy-for-breakfast

32 Hamel, G. and Prahalad, C.K. (1996) *Competing for the Future*. Harvard Business School Press.

33 Seligman, M.E.P. (1972) 'Learned helplessness.' *Annual Review of Medicine 23*, 407–412. https://doi.org/10.1146/annurev.me.23.020172.002203

34 Seligman, M.E.P. (1972) 'Learned helplessness.' *Annual Review of Medicine 23*, 407–412. https://doi.org/10.1146/annurev.me.23.020172.002203

Chapter 10: The Genius Within Operating System

1 Way, M. (2013) *Clean Approaches for Coaches: How to Create the Conditions for Change Using Clean Language and Symbolic Modelling.* Clean Publishing.
2 Wilson, C. (2017) *The Work and Life of David Grove: Clean Language and Emergent Knowledge.* Troubador Publishing Ltd.
3 Dunbar, A. (2017) *Clean Coaching: The Insider Guide to Making Change Happen.* Routledge.
4 Tosey, P., Lawley, J. and Meese, R. (2014) 'Eliciting metaphor through clean language: An innovation in qualitative research.' *British Journal of Management 25*, 3, 629–646. https://doi.org/10.1111/1467-8551.12042
5 Doyle, N. and McDowall, A. (2023) *Neurodiversity Coaching: Supporting Neurodivergent Talent and Career Potential.* Routledge.
6 Argyris, C. (1977) 'Double loop learning in organizations.' *Harvard Business Review*, September–October, 115–126. https://hbr.org/1977/09/double-loop-learning-in-organizations
7 Rivera, L. (2022) *Workplace Neurodiversity Rising.* 3rd edn. Lyric Rivera – NeuroDivergent Consulting.
8 Roberson, Q.M. (2018) 'Diversity in the workplace: A review, synthesis, and future research agenda.' *Annual Review of Organizational Psychology and Organizational Behavior 6*, 1, 69–88. doi: 10.1146/annurev-orgpsych-012218-015243.

Chapter 11: Advice

1 Henley, A.J. and DiGennaro Reed, F.D. (2015) 'Should you order the feedback sandwich? Efficacy of feedback sequence and timing.' *Journal of Organizational Behavior Management 35*, 3–4, 321–335. doi: 10.1080/01608061.2015.1093057.
2 Schulman, S. (2016) *Conflict Is Not Abuse: Overstating Harm, Community Responsibility and the Duty of Repair.* Arsenal Pulp Press.

Chapter 13: Concluding Reflections

1 Maitlis, S. (2020) 'Posttraumatic growth at work.' *Annual Review of Organizational Psychology and Organizational Behavior 7*, 1, 395–419. doi: 10.1146/annurev-orgpsych-012119-044932.

Index